SATIRE

SATIRE
A Critical Reintroduction

DUSTIN GRIFFIN

THE UNIVERSITY PRESS OF KENTUCKY

Editorial and Sales Offices: Lexington, Kentucky 40508-4008

Library of Congress Cataloging-in-Publication Data

Griffin, Dustin H.
　　Satire : a critical reintroduction / Dustin Griffin.
　　　p.　　cm.
　　Includes bibliographical references and index.
　　ISBN 0-8131-1844-1; -0829-2 (acid-free paper)
　　1. Satire—History and criticism.　I. Title.
PN6149.S2G75　1993
809.7—dc20　　　　　　　　　　　　　　93-32688

*For Maynard Mack
and Christopher Ricks*

Contents

Acknowledgments

This book is the fruit of many years of thinking about satire. I owe thanks to my graduate and undergraduate students at New York University, especially those enrolled in my seminars on satire. Most of the first draft of the book was written when I held a fellowship from the John Simon Guggenheim Foundation. I am grateful to the Foundation for its support, and to New York University, which provided a salary supplement. I am also grateful to the staffs of the research libraries in which I worked: the New York Public Library, the Bobst Library at New York University, the Butler Library at Columbia University, the Huntington Library, and the British Library.

I also thank the several audiences before whom I presented early versions of various sections of this book: the Northeast American Society for Eighteenth-Century Studies meetings in Providence, Rhode Island and Worcester, Massachusetts; Hauppauge, New York, the Rutgers University English Department; the International Society for 18th-Century Studies; the Modern Language Association; and the Boston University English Department. Chapter 4, "Satiric Closure," appeared, in a rather different and shorter form, in *Genre* 18, no. 2 (Summer 1985): 173–89. Part of Chapter 6 is a condensation of material that first appeared as "Venting Spleen" in *Essays in Criticism* 40 (1990): 124–35. Both appear here by permission of the editors.

It is a pleasure to acknowledge publicly the colleagues who encouraged this project at an early stage—Paul Hunter, Earl Miner, Michael Seidel, and Patricia Spacks; those who responded generously and promptly to queries for information—Patricia Craddock, Michael Holquist, and James Young; and those who read drafts of chapters and provided valuable criticism—Carol Flynn, Charles Frey, Ernest Gilman, Gale Griffin, Charles Knight, Ruth Perry, and Frank Stack.

Finally, a word of thanks to the staff of the University Press of Kentucky, and especially to Pat Sterling.

The dedication records my gratitude to two teachers who set very high standards.

Introduction

This book is designed with several audiences in mind—the student relatively new to literary satire, the more experienced generalist, and the specialist. The student who needs an introduction to satire as a genre will find here a series of discussions focused on critical problems in satire. Although the book is not organized as a historical survey of the major satirists from Horace to the present, the student will find that I have turned repeatedly to the same dozen figures—Horace, Juvenal, Persius, Lucian, More, Rabelais, Donne, Dryden, Swift, Pope, Blake, Byron. Not surprisingly, since the great age of satire in English was roughly 1660 to 1800, I put major emphasis on the eighteenth century. For reasons of space, I exclude satire in the novel. I confine myself to literary satire from "high culture" and deliberately exclude nonliterary satire and satiric forms from popular culture (comic strips, newspaper columns, televised situation comedies, and so on).[1]

The more experienced reader will perhaps be moved to reconsider ideas about literary satire acquired from critics who wrote a generation ago. My discussion is prompted by a sense that the good general books are out of date, and that there is a curious disjunction between the best current critical writing about individual works of satire and the old theoretical consensus about the genre established in the early 1960s. According to that consensus, satire is a highly rhetorical and moral art. A work of satire is designed to attack vice or folly. To this end it uses wit or ridicule. Like polemical rhetoric, it seeks to persuade an audience that something or someone is reprehensible or ridiculous; unlike pure rhetoric, it engages in exaggeration and some sort of fiction. But satire does not forsake the "real world" entirely. Its victims come from that world, and it is this fact (together with a darker or sharper tone) that separates satire from pure comedy. Finally, satire usually proceeds by means of clear reference to some moral standards or purposes.

Such a consensus was established by a spate of books that appeared between 1957 (Northrop Frye's *Anatomy of Criticism*) and 1967 (Ronald Paulson, *The Fictions of Satire*). The work published during that decade—by Frye and Paulson, by Alvin Kernan, Robert C. Elliott, Edward Rosenheim, and Sheldon Sacks[2]—provided the terms by which most nonspecialist readers continue to read and judge satire. (The major elements of this theory—that satire is a moral form and a rhetorical art—were in fact clearly enunciated as long ago as John Dryden's 1693 "Discourse concerning the Original and Progress of Satire." The few general books on satire that have appeared since 1967 have—for the most part—left unchallenged the principles that were established thirty years ago.[3] Specialists conducted inconclusive debates in the mid-1960s in the short-lived *Satire Newsletter* under the headings "Norms in Satire" and "The Concept of the Persona in Satire."[4] But such controversy was not enough to displace the old consensus—it appears well represented in Robert C. Elliott's article "Satire" in the fifteenth edition of the *Encyclopaedia Britannica* (1984)[5]—or to prompt a new theoretical synthesis.[6]

Meanwhile, practical criticism of individual satirists has moved away from the certainties of 1960. Specialist critics have for some years emphasized the complexity and ambiguity of the best satire; it has become conventional to point to Pope's mixed motives and to the ways in which Swift vexes and embroils his reader. From the point of view of the best current criticism of satire, the old theoretical consensus is clearly inadequate. Editors of two collections of essays in the 1980s noted that their contributors seek "new definitions" of the form and "move it somewhat away from moral centrality."[7] But vigorous and probing criticism of individual texts has not led to a new theoretical consensus, and nonspecialists continue to rely on outdated assumptions.

The general critical climate has likewise changed considerably in the last thirty or thirty-five years. In 1960, New Critical assumptions were still in place and unchallenged. In the present theory-centered climate, traditional categories (on which most thinking about satire had depended) such as authorial intention, formal unity or coherence, referentiality, and even "author" are under interrogation. The New Historicism urges us to rethink the ways in which satire is embedded in history and in culture. Claims that all literature is based on "ideology" challenge us to think about the ways in which satire sustains or subverts the dominant social order. Interdisciplinary cultural analysis invites us to consider satire from socioeconomic and anthropological points of view: Do satirists tend to come from a particular social niche? What is the function of satiric aggression in a modern and "civilized" society?

This book attempts to build on the insights in the best contemporary practical criticism of satire and to respond to the challenges of recent literary theory. It also attempts to broaden the focus of most general books on satire (usually centered on "formal verse satire" from Horace to Pope) by reintegrating the loose "Menippean" traditions (from Lucian through the Renaissance to the eighteenth century). I do not claim, however, that all satire can be gathered under one generic heading. One result of broadening our recognition of satiric forms is to be reminded of satire's immense and perhaps incomprehensible variety: (in verse alone) formal satire, epistle, letter from the country, lampoon, epigram, session of the poets, advice to a painter—to say nothing of parodic forms. The (mostly prose) Menippean line is itself a miscellany, from fantastic voyage to dialogue of the dead and learned anatomy. Even the satire of a single writer (such as Horace) differs considerably from one work (say, the dialogues) to the next (say, the "Journey to Brundisium"). As Alastair Fowler notes in his "introduction to the theory of genres and modes," satire is "the most problematic mode to the taxonomist, since it appears never to have corresponded to any one kind." [8] This is of course only the beginning of the difficulty of comprehending satire within a single theoretical frame, since it can through parody invade *any* literary form: epic, pastoral, travel book, song, elegy, and so on. When satire takes over another literary structure, it tends not just to borrow it, as when a cuckoo finds another bird's nest for its eggs, but to subvert it or (in Michael Seidel's terms) to alter its "potential" [9] and (more like a body-snatcher) to direct its energies toward alien ends. Even when satire does not completely take over another form, it can infuse its spirit into comedy or tragedy or the novel so as to create a strange hybrid—"problem plays," for example, such as Shakespeare's *Measure for Measure* or *Troilus and Cressida*.[10] And if we consider satire as a mode or a procedure rather than a literary kind, then it can appear at any place, at any time. Can we find useful terms to cover all these literary phenomena at once?

In the last two hundred years satire in the Western tradition is most commonly found not as an independent form or as parody; it is found in the novel. But what happens when satire invades the novel is a subject so vast and unwieldy that I do not attempt to treat it here. It is perhaps sufficient to say now that despite what is commonly asserted, satire does not simplify narrative fiction. In traditional accounts, satire in fiction is said to be detectable in a certain flattening of character toward caricature, a stylizing of action toward the emblematic, a reductive sharpening of narrative tone toward ridicule, and what Mikhail Bakhtin would call "monological" discourse. The problem with such accounts is that the satire so identified is finally not very interesting, not very good. At most it induces easy laughter. A better account of the subject would show that satire typically complicates narrative fiction. If satire is not viewed simply as derisive reduction and rejection, if we broaden our conception—as I do in this book—to include inquiry and provocation, play and display, anything from Menippean fantasy to learned anatomizing, then we can find satire's mark not just presented in satiric set pieces (for example, the Veneerings' dinner table in Dickens) but woven into the fabric of several different varieties of the novel, from the narrative of probing moral intelligence (F.R. Leavis's "great tradition") to the playful and self-conscious antimimetic novels of John Barth and Vladimir Nabokov and the learned wit of Thomas Pynchon, or the encyclopedic or "farraginous chronicle" of James Joyce. The novel, more than any other literary form, has proved extremely hospitable to satire. Other literary forms—from song to epic—find themselves invaded and par-odically subverted by satire: the parasite overwhelms the host. What satire wants to do can generally be done within the generous confines of the novel without disturbing its economy (Evelyn Waugh's comic novels may be thought of as a limiting case, and in them "novel" may be swallowed up in "satire"). But to discover the various ways in which satire has found a home within the novel—as occasional visitor or as resident spirit—would require another book.[11]

Because satires are unruly, various, open to "whatever men do" (as Juvenal said), because satire comes in so many different forms, and because satire often seems a "mode" or a "procedure" rather than a single "genre," I do not offer a new comprehensive and unified "theory" that tries to account adequately for all of satire's features. What I offer is a set of critical perspectives, organized not around individual authors or periods but around critical problems. In some cases I reconsider the traditional topics of satiric theory—the role of the satirist as moralist, the nature of satiric rhetoric, the relationship of satire to the world of history, its alleged impact on political order. In some cases I look at satire from new angles—the special problems that satires seem to have in arriving at closure, the special pleasures that satire affords its readers and writers, the socioeconomic status of the satirist. Insofar as my perspectives converge, I argue in each case that

satire is problematic, open-ended, essayistic, ambiguous in its relationship to history, uncertain in its political effect, resistant to formal
closure, more inclined to ask questions than to provide answers, and
ambivalent about the pleasures it offers.

Specialists (those whom Swift called "Readers truly *learned*") will
I hope be engaged by my attempt to provide a critical conspectus of the
genre. In synthesizing a wide range of primary and secondary material, I seek to stimulate further rethinking and point the way toward
new theoretical exploration. More particular observations, in the
occasional close readings and in the notes, will perhaps uncover some
unobserved features of well-known works.

1

Theories of Satire
in Polemical Context

Most satiric theory, at least since the Renaissance, is polemical, rang-
ing itself against some previous practice or claim and attempting to
displace it. Typically the theorist establishes his model—Horace, say,
or Juvenal—and urges that all satire follow this pattern. More generally, satiric theory may be seen as a series of attempts to deny one or
both of two elements that have long clung to satire and challenged its
claims to morality and artistic unity—*satyr* (the half man-half beast,
suggesting that satire is lawless, wild, and threatening) and *lanx satura* (the "mixed" or "full platter," suggesting that satire is a formless
miscellany, and food for thought). Theorists have long sought to re-
press or domesticate the shaggy, obscene, and transgressive satyr that
ranges through satire's long history, lurking in dark corners, and to
make it into the model of a moral citizen. Or they have resisted satire's traditionally farraginous nature and insisted that every satire
must display thematic unity and formal clarity. When theorists happen also to be practitioners of satire (as in the case of Horace and
Dryden), they are likely to be propagandizing for their own particular way of writing satire. And not infrequently their theory fails to
account for their own practice. To recognize the unacknowledged
limitations of earlier theories helps us see more clearly that modern
theory has inherited the same limitations.

Classical Theory

Some of the earliest pronouncements about the nature of good satire
come from one of its first great practitioners, Horace. In several so-
called "programmatic satires" (1.4, 10; 2.1) Horace provides his own
implicit theory of satire: that the satirist, speaking out freely, seeks to

of Twain's pronouncements at the beginning of his novels

laugh men out of their follies. A long tradition of "Horatian" satire springs from these early pronouncements. So did the convention of announcing one's satiric program, typically by means of a verse satire toward the beginning of a satirist's "book."[1] But before we let Horace's words solidify into law, binding on all his successors, or let them swell into a "theory," we need to remember two aspects of Horace's situation as a writer. First, his satiric "program"—like all programmatic satires—is not so much a writer's preconceived manifesto as a response to attacks on his poems as malicious, libelous, or excessively bitter. Thus in defending his own satiric practice, he does not give a comprehensive account of what he called his *sermones* but focuses on the element of moral satire—the frank censure of abuses. Second, he was engaged in the complex process of honoring his satiric predecessor, Lucilius, declaring a continuity between their work and at the same time trying to distinguish himself carefully from the older poet.[2]

In defending himself Horace makes opportunistic use of his predecessors to make the best case for his own practice: Lucilius was outspoken before me; so were the writers of Old Comedy, who censured fools "multa cum libertate" (*Satire* 1:4.5). As classical scholars have pointed out, we should not assume that Horace's compressed account of satire's origins in Aristophanes and his fellow dramatists—"hinc omnis pendet Lucilius"—represents his considered view of the matter.[3] This "deliberate exaggeration"[4] is designed for local purposes—to defend an outspoken manner against attack. For this purpose Horace finds it convenient to emphasize his affinity with Lucilius.

But in other respects Horace wants to put some distance between himself and Lucilius, even where their practice is similar. Both poets, from our vantage, write in the *satura* tradition. Their satires admit a great variety of material and tones, as befits the "full platter" of mixed fruits and nuts after which it is named. But Horace, looking back at Lucilius, saw artlessness and even crudity (*Sat.* 1.10). Lucilius was a diamond in the rough, whose vigor needed to be smoothed and refined. Horace emphasized that his own work, by contrast, was polished and artful. Thus he at first determined to suppress the idea of his satire as *satura,* since for him the idea was discredited by its associations. In his first book Horace calls his work not *saturae* or *satirae* but *sermones,* "little talks" or "conversations" (another term derived in fact from Lucilius). It is only in his second book that Horace, having established his identity as an artful satirist, adopts the older term *satura.*[5] As William Anderson has noted, Horace (like his successors) represents his predecessor in such a way as to advance his own "satiric purposes."[6]

In fact, Horace's own practice is considerably different from that of Lucilius and Aristophanes. He is oblique rather than blunt, smiling and hinting rather than attacking directly. And the theory of moral satire that he advances misrepresents his own range of interests. One would not know from Horace's programmatic satires of his digressiveness, his chattiness, the ironic disparity between moral idea and practice, between spirit and material circumstance. From his "theoretical" pronouncements, one could not expect the famous "Journey to Brundisium" (*Sat.* 1.5), the meeting with "The Bore" (1.9), or Priapus's narrative of the witch Canidia (1.8). Sometimes, as Isaac Casaubon later said, Horace fails to follow his own rules for good poetry: "The very method that Horace wisely prescribed to others— that a poem should be *simplex* and *unum* [*Ars P.* 23]—he himself never or rarely kept to in his own satires. For whenever he sets out on some material, he soon deserts it, often piling up unadorned precepts. . . . And so most of the Horatian satires give us an exact idea of that very dish, so copious and fruit filled."[7] But the fault does not lie wholly in Horace himself. Later commentators and theorists have often misrepresented him and in particular neglected to remember his almost continuous irony, his facetiousness, his pretending not to be a poet, and his claim that his poems are mere trifles.

Satire, as Horace practices it, is considerably more diverse than laughter at folly. The Horatian *sermo* is "delicate" not only in its correctness (an artful improvement over the rough practice of Lucilius) and its gentle humor but in its extraordinary mobility of tone and nuance. Horace is not simply a stern moralist who speaks his mind with sincerity, like Persius. He slides noiselessly from plain speaking and ethical advice into ironically lofty and pompous verse (and sometimes into the mock-heroic), from there into sincere and artless emotion (as in the praise of friendship in 1.5), and thence into a highly allusive mode, quoting directly from his predecessors, often for ironic purposes.[8]

Horace's theoretical pronouncements about satire thus need to be read with great care, since they come down to us not as *theory* but as dramatic utterances, enmeshed in particular satiric poems at a time when the genre was still being shaped. What is more, the very terminology for the form was yet to be settled—*iambi, satyra, satura, sermo*—and its muddled ancestry retrospectively clarified. What, after all, was the practitioner-theorist in Horace's day to make of the rich variety of satiric forms, from the Greek satyr plays, Old Comedy, Stoic diatribe, and Archilochan iambics to the Latin Fescennine insults, New Comedy, and satirical "medleys" (miscellaneous in both versification and theme)? By distributing his satiric work over several forms—satires, epistles, and epodes—Horace himself only made the job of generic classification and definition more difficult.[9] Grammarians as early as the first century B.C. knew of satire's multiple forms. But as C.A. Van Rooy and others have shown, they disagreed about the lines of descent relating them. Did Lucilian invective descend from Old Comedy, from satyr plays, or from Archilochus? The point to insist on is that almost any reconstruction of satire's ancestry—even as early as the time of Varro—was a partisan interpretation and an implicit definition of the proper nature of satire.[10] It depended on what element the historian thought was most important in satire— its rambling variety, its defamatory invective, its free speaking, its ribald ridicule, or its moral function.[11]

This principle applies likewise to what is perhaps the most famous classical pronouncement about satire, Quintilian's claim—a century after Varro—that "satura tota nostra est." Some scholars argue that Quintilian was trumpeting the superiority of Roman to Greek satirists; others, that he means to speak of satire as a wholly Roman kind of poem, at least in its perfected form.[12] Classicists even today suspect that Quintilian, like other early Roman theorists and historians of literature, was engaged here in "patriotic labours," seeking to "construct an early history of Latin literature and derive the various literary genres from an Italian past, not Greek."[13] In any case, his claim (like many claims in the history of satire) simplifies a complicated history by focusing on one element—here the tradition and progressive refinement of formal verse satire from Lucilius through Horace, Persius, and Juvenal—to the exclusion of other satiric forms, particularly the Greek Menippean tradition and what might be called the unruly spirit of satyr.

The other theoretical *locus classicus* represents a similarly narrow focus. In the late fourth century the grammarian Diomedes defined satire as "a verse composition . . . defamatory and composed to carp at human vices" (maledicum et ad carpenda hominum vitia).[14] Furthermore, he has in mind only the tradition of Roman verse satire as written by Lucilius, Horace, and Persius (whom he names), omitting the Varronian or Menippean tradition altogether. Though he acknowledges satire's complex etymology, from satyrs or the *lanx satura* or the *lex satura*,[15] Diomedes defines the form in wholly moral terms. He says nothing of wit, humor, playfulness, exaggeration or fantasy or paradox, iconoclasm or the carnival spirit. It is ultimately writers like

Diomedes, reflecting what G.L. Hendrickson called the "moral obsession of literary criticism in later antiquity,"[16] who lead more or less directly to the emphasis on satire's moral function that dominates satiric theory from the Renaissance into the mid-twentieth century.

Elizabethan Theory

Sixteenth-century English writers on satire inherited several different traditions: a broad medieval tradition of "complaint"[17] that ranged in English alone from Langland and Chaucer to Barclay and Skelton; Lucianic dialogues, once prized for their sophistication but by the Reformation increasingly associated with scoffing atheism; a line of epistolary satire in Italy from Vingiguerra to Alamanni and Ariosto, based primarily on Horatian models. Oddly enough, with all this wealth of living tradition and despite the recovery of classical Roman formal satire, the dominant theory of satire among Renaissance writers was based on their notion of Greek satyr plays (of which they knew almost nothing), a theory that could account for very little of the satire with which they were familiar. Though they knew of the idea that satire derives its name from *satura* and ultimately from the *lanx satura*,[18] their theory in effect ignored or suppressed the notion of satire as miscellany.

For example, in his *Defence of Poetry* (1579) Thomas Lodge discovers the origin of satire in a form of early Greek drama, which "presented the lives of Satyers, so that they might wiselye, under the abuse of that name, discover the follies of many theyr folish fellow citesens."[19] George Puttenham's *Arte of English Poesie* (1589) reemphasizes that satire originates as drama and makes explicit the link between satyrs and satire: "The first and most bitter invective against vice and vicious men was the [dramatic] *Satyre*: which to th'intent their bitterness should breede none ill will, . . . they made wise as if the gods of the woods, whom they called *Satyres* or *Silvanes*, should appear and recite those verses of rebuke." In time there arose poets who, like the impersonated satyr-gods on the Greek stage, "taxe[d] the common abuses and vice of the people in rough and bitter speaches, and their invectives were called *Satyres*, and themselves *Satyricques*: such were *Lucilius*, *Iuvenall*, and *Persius* among the Latines, & with us he that wrote the booke called Piers Plowman."[20] As Kernan has shown, most of the practicing satirists in England from 1590 to 1620 thought a satire should be rude, derisive, harsh—written in the kind of language one might expect from a woodland satyr.

Such a theory may well have had its practical uses: it helped a generation of young English poets produce a satyrlike kind of satire in the 1590s. But *as theory* it is markedly deficient. It is based on misunderstandings about the nature of Greek satyrs (it was Roman artists who first portrayed them as the half man-half goat the Elizabethans imagined) and the nature of "Satyrique tragedy" (not bitter railing but comic parodies of mythical tales, like Euripides' *Cyclops*, "partly Serious, and partly Jocular," with happy endings).[21] It is based too, as the classical scholar Isaac Casaubon was soon to point out, on insufficient knowledge of the distinction between the Greek satyric tradition and the Roman *satira*. More important, the satyric theory is unable to account for the chatty or reflective-philosophical Horace. Elizabethan theorists have little to say about Horace. They much preferred Juvenal as their model; unlike Horace, he wrote nothing but satire (and was thus easier to categorize), and his rhetoric, to be sure, answers better to their theory. Even so, they were obliged to imagine a rancorous and savagely indignant Juvenal, not the highly skilled declamatory rhetorician. By the same token, the idea that a satirist should virtually fume and sputter in rage does little to explain those poems in which a satirist such as Joseph Hall constructs a kind of set piece "Against Lawyers" or "Against Doctors." True, Kernan is able to show that much but not all of the satire of Hall and John Marston seems to follow the theory of Lodge and Puttenham. It is possible that in their "Juvenalian" moods such satirists derived some encouragement from Renaissance discussions of the second-century rhetorician Hermogenes' "Ideas of Style," and especially from the "ideas" of asperity, vehemence, and vigor (all subcategories of Grandeur). One late sixteenth-century commentary on Hermogenes pointed to examples of asperity and vehemence in Persius.[22]

But Hall and Marston, though still too little discussed today, are finally secondary figures. The best of the Elizabethan satirists, by common consent, is John Donne, and the idea that the satirist is a sort of satyr founders when one takes up Donne's poems, whose rhetoric is derived more from Horace than from Juvenal. Donne's fawning courtiers (Satires 1 and 4) are Horatian, as is the satirist's presentation of himself as foolish victim. Donne furthermore rejects the satirist's angry rant. Though he "hates" the town, he says, foolish poets aren't worth hating. In his famous third satire, "kind pitty" chokes the satirist's "spleene." Donne's topic—the choice of true religion—is too serious for mere laughter or railing. Indeed, his declaration of hatred seems almost a perfunctory gesture. The life of Donne's satires is found not in

their intemperate disgust but in their drama and precise observation.[23]
It is Donne, among all the English imitators of Horace (including Jonson and Pope) who, in Reuben Brower's words, most resembles Horace
in "moral energy and rhythmic urgency."[24] Oddly enough, Kernan,
who among modern critics has most fully surveyed Elizabethan satiric
theory, has very little to say about Donne and nothing to say about Sir
Thomas Wyatt, another important English satirist (perhaps in his century second only to Donne in distinction) in the Horatian tradition.

Why a Horace-based theory of satire did not emerge in late
sixteenth-century and early seventeenth-century England is not clear.
It was not, as I've suggested, for lack of native satirists in the Horatian tradition. It was not for lack of knowledge of a strong Horatian
tradition in Italy, although Ariosto's satiries (published in 1534) were
not translated into English until 1608.[25] But Francesco Sansovino's
satiric anthology, with a prefatory *Discorso in materia della satira*
(1560), seems to have made little impact and was apparently never
translated. Perhaps the dominant Juvenalian theory prevented the
Horatian voice from being heard.

Even so, other equally partial theories of satire were current.
One stressed the satirist-as-physician, who dispenses a "medicinable
morall."[26] Another depicted the satirist as zealous Christian prophet.
Thomas Drant's 1566 edition of Horace included the Lamentations of
Jeremiah in the same volume. This inevitably involved interpreting
Horace as moral teacher and as proto-Christian, a familiar process in
the Renaissance whereby pagan writers were forcibly fitted into
Christian molds. Horace, says Drant's title page, is "Englyshed ac-
cordying to the prescription of saint Hierome."[27] Conversely, as John
Peter notes, the native Christian tradition of complaint was rein-
terpreted by those theorists who took their lead from newly printed
Roman satires. Medieval English satire was often seen not in its own
terms but as a lamentable deviation from standards set by the classical
pagan writers. For Drant, Horace is an inferior Jeremiah. For Puttenham, Langland (who wrote "the Satyr of Piers Ploughman") is "a
malcontent of that time," a sort of inferior Juvenal.[28]

Casaubon and Renaissance Theory

The central text in Renaissance theory of satire, from a modern point
of view, is Isaac Casaubon's *De Satyrica Graecorum Poesi et Ro-
manorum Satira* (1605). It is central to modern scholars because it
disentangled the Greek and the Roman satiric traditions, arguing

with massive learning that Roman satire was not in fact related to the Greek satyr. A distinguishing feature of Casaubon's treatise is his appreciation for various forms and styles of satire. Though he reveals a preference for Persius, who was "the first of all to enrich, correct, and change for the better Roman satire," Casaubon conveys a clear sense of the particular excellence of Horace and Juvenal as well. Thus Horace's satire is marked by "purity of statement," grace and "simplicity" of narrative, and "a certain inexplicable charm." Juvenal on the other hand displays a richness of invention, a copiousness of example, "the power of forming great conceptions," and "lofty and sublime speech." Because he "scarcely digressed from the thesis proposed at the beginning and certainly never left it entirely," Persius most effectively reproves vice and commends virtue.[29]

If Casaubon's work had been translated sooner or more widely, it might have had more a moderating influence on subsequent theorizing about satire and might have kept alive a more flexible and comprehensive sense of the genre.[30] But in fact his treatise was not able to banish the persistent notion that satire had something to do with satyrs; nor was he able to convince rival scholars and editors of his central thesis. As Dryden later noted, the Renaissance theory of satire that he inherited consisted not of a scholarly and critical consensus but a "long Dispute amongst the Modern Critiques" (4:28). On one side were Casaubon and his followers Nicolas Rigault and (late in the century) André Dacier. On the other were J.C. Scaliger and Daniel Heinsius, who challenged Casaubon, insisting that Greek and Roman satire formed a single tradition and reasserting the older view that satire was essentially a dramatic form, descended from satyr plays. More serious, perhaps, is that the participants in the dispute went on to champion one or another of the classical Roman satirists, each building a conception of what satire is and should be from the practice of his hero. Thus Scaliger, reacting to Casaubon's praise, had preferred Horace and attacked Persius for obscurity, ineptness, and ostentation.[31] Rigault, an editor of Juvenal and Persius, dismissed Horace as concerned with trivia, and Barten Holyday (another editor of Juvenal and Persius) argued that Juvenal's achievement in satire represented the "Perfection" of the form.[32] Heinsius, in turn, declared that Juvenal improperly attacked high crimes and "atrocities" inappropriate for satire—since we do not so much reprehend them as abominate them ("non vituperamus sed abominamur")—and made Horace (whose works he edited) the model for satire: satirists, he said, ought to excite laughter rather than horror and to employ a "low familiar way of speaking."[33] As Dryden noted, any critic who comments on a classical satirist "thinks himself oblig'd to prefer his Author to the other two" (4:49). Later critics, poets, and theorists, working from seventeenth-century editions of the Roman satirists, absorbed these preferences as they argued for the merits and the centrality of one kind of satire or other. So René Rapin in the 1690s champions Horace for his "Delicacy." Holding Juvenal to the same standard, he finds him wanting: "*Satyr* that takes off the Mask, and reprehends Vice too openly, is not very Delicate."[34] French critics in the seventeenth and eighteenth centuries on the whole preferred Horace to Juvenal. Dacier finds Persius and Juvenal considerably inferior to Horace: his *simplicité* is appropriate to satire; their affected *noblesse* and *majesté* are not.[35] Despite Weinbrot's recent argument that critics in the eighteenth century showed equal appreciation and understanding for the three major Roman satirists, all of whom are (in Addison's phrase) "Perfect Masters in their Several Ways,"[36] the partisan tradition remained strong, and continued to produce partial theory. Thus John Dennis writes in 1721 of the "Partizans of the *Roman* Satirists" and their "respective Favourite Authors."[37]

The most important and influential inheritor of Casaubon and the seventeenth-century commentators was Dryden. More than most critics, he retained Casaubon's appreciation for the variety of satire and the different excellences of the chief Roman satirists, and sought to assign to each "his proper due" (4:50). But in one respect a reading of Casaubon seems to have narrowed rather than broadened Dryden's view: the idea that a satire should be rigorously unified, attacking a single vice and commending the opposite virtue.

Dryden's Theory of Satire

Dryden's "Discourse concerning the Original and Progress of Satire" is the most prominent theoretical document in the great age of English satire. Published in 1693 as a critical preface to a translation of the complete satires of Juvenal and Persius, it has acquired a curious double reputation. On the one hand, it has been challenged as little more than a compilation of the work of Casaubon, Dacier, and other Renaissance editors and scholars, a critical and rhetorical hodgepodge, rambling, digressive, and inconsistent in Dryden's characteristic manner. On the other hand, it has had extraordinary influence on subsequent theoretical thinking about satire, both in the age immediately following Dryden and in the mid-twentieth century as well. Our reigning notion of satire as a moral art and as a carefully constructed and unified contrast between vice and virtue finds its fullest and most influential presentation in Dryden's essay. Dryden was himself drawing on ideas well established by Renaissance commentators, but it was his *version* of them that reached and shaped the thinking of a broad literary audience.

In either case, we tend to grant Dryden's "Discourse" an unusual kind of authority, especially because of his standing as a practicing satirist in his own day and in literary history. Whether we think of the "Discourse" as a mere summary of what oft was thought about satire or as the source of our moral theories, we tend to overlook the critical moment at which Dryden was writing, the larger literary context in which his theory needs to be placed and to which it served as a response. If we recall that context, Dryden's theory begins to look distinctly partial and polemical.

To begin with, we should remember that satiric theory was in considerable flux as Dryden wrote. As the California editors of his *Works* observe, despite Casaubon's massive scholarship there was confusion and disagreement in the late seventeenth century about several fundamental questions: was satire a form of drama, or poem? Were its origins in *satyr*, or *lanx satura*? Was the satirist an unbalanced and ferocious malcontent, or a man of good nature and high principle? Was satire ideally a rugged and rough-edged form, or should it display the same kind of polish and urbanity as the speech of witty gentlemen?[38] And as I have already noted, editors and theorists actively disputed the relative merits of Horace, Juvenal, and Persius and even their right to be considered true satirists.

Some of these controversies are of greater concern to Dryden than others. On the matter of origins, he sides with Casaubon, though without much heat and without adding any independent argument.[39] On the relative merits of Horace and Juvenal, as many critics have commented, Dryden is characteristically and delightfully ambivalent, finding much to praise in each, though he finally confesses a greater pleasure in Juvenal. As a translator, Dryden may be thought to have indicated his preference by his choice of Juvenal and Persius. Though he thought his version of one of Horace's odes to be his "Master-Piece in English" (3:291), he never attempted any of Horace's satires or epistles. The critical controversy to which Dryden made his most important contribution was not an old issue but a new one, still on the horizon in the early 1690s: the eighteenth-century argument over the dangers and usefulness of satire. When Dryden was writing, the battle lines had not yet been drawn. But within a generation many voices were declaring that satire was a lawless form that ought to be restrained, that it threatened innocent victims and endangered the state. Already by the later 1690s a reaction had begun to set in against some of the license of the Restoration and its witty writers. Sir Richard Blackmore's *Satyr against Wit* (1700) was an early salvo, attacking the excesses of witty satire with some of its own weapons. Blackmore's attack led to a series of later charges. In response, defenders of satire throughout the eighteenth century routinely had recourse to the kinds of arguments for satire's moral function that Dryden had earlier laid out—and often to the "Discourse" itself.

Dryden's "Discourse," then, was not simply an objective and reliable summary of late Renaissance or neoclassical theory; it joined a lively controversy and took a partisan position. Though Dryden devotes most of his attention to satire's Roman origin and its "progress" up through Juvenal, he is well aware of and implicitly reacting against modern satirists from Donne to the Earl of Dorset (to whom his essay is addressed). I say "implicitly" because Dryden is in fact rather reticent about modern practitioners. Reading his "Discourse" does not provide a clear picture of the extraordinary range and vitality of English satire in the seventeenth century, from the outburst in the 1590s through the paper war between Roundheads and Cavaliers that shadowed the Civil War at midcentury to the circulation of manuscripts by Charles's court wits: the "advice to a painter," the "sessions of the poets," and the other "poems on affairs of state" that kept up a kind of running commentary on political and literary matters for some forty years after the Restoration. Dryden (4:60) dismisses much of this work as a rank harvest of lampoon, without wit or decency.[40] Of the Restoration satirists that now seem important to us, Dryden says very little and thus tacitly minimizes their stature. He offers a handsome tribute to Samuel Butler for *Hudibras*, a poem (like *Paradise Lost*) "above" Dryden's censure[41] but paradoxically "below" the dignity that Dryden expects from "manly satire." Of Andrew Marvell and John Oldham he says nothing; of the Earl of Rochester he refers only to a single line (about Dorset) in order to quibble with it. Though Dryden as a historian was fond of constructing literary lineages and tracing his own poetic fathers, he finds no "family" of English satirists.[42] Of his predecessors in satire he briefly mentions only Spenser, Donne, and Butler and sees none of them as a master or a model.

The only model he in fact cites is Dorset, "the first of the Age" in satire, a poet who has even "excell'd the Ancients," especially in Horatian "fine raillery" (4:12, 70; see also 7, 26). Dryden's praise is usually dismissed as nauseous flattery and disingenuous modesty. But perhaps he is simply limiting himself to living writers. Apart from Dryden himself (and it would have been unseemly—though not uncharacteristic—to advance his own claims openly), there was no great satirist writing in English during the decade after 1684, by which time Butler, Marvell, Rochester, and Oldham had all died. In French there was of course Nicholas Boileau, in some ways a better model for satire, since he followed in the Roman and especially the Horatian tradition in a way that the English satirists (with the exception of Oldham) had not. In English there were only minor figures like Robert Gould, aging court poets like the Earl of Mulgrave, and a rabble of anonymous lampoonists.

Against this somewhat unruly tradition of English Restoration satire Dryden's "Discourse" can be seen as an attempt to lay down some rules, to impose order on the teeming variety of satiric forms, and to redirect energy into a Roman line. In this respect he was like Boileau, who in the contemporary *L'art poetique* (1674) wanted to purify French satire from the Scarronic burlesque tradition. Dryden specifically acknowledges that modern English satire falls into at least three kinds: the poems modeled on Horace and Juvenal (what we call formal verse satire); a Menippean or (as he calls it, following Casaubon) "Varronian" tradition whose modern examples include Edmund Spenser's *Mother Hubbard's Tale*, Butler's *Hudibras*, and his own narrative satires, *Absalom and Achitophel* and *MacFlecknoe*; and the lampoon or poem of personal attack produced by the "common Libelers" of the day. But Dryden dismisses the last as "for the most part unlawful" (4:59), and he shows no interest (despite his own poems) in promoting or even defining a Varronian tradition. Instead, he concentrates his theory (and thus the efforts of future satirists and theorists) on defining the nature of "true Satires" (4:9). In doing so, he recalls satire to its specifically Roman origins and in the process seeks to suppress its proliferation in native forms.

To recover those origins—as he defines them—Dryden has to construct a selective history of satire that puts the emphasis where he wants it, on satire as a form of "art." In Horace's account of origins, satire began as innocent rural merriment and declined into cruelty before it was restrained by law (*Epist.* 2.1.139-55). His myth is an Edenic story of innocence, fall, and recovery. Dryden's myth by contrast has no innocent Eden. His story tells only of "progress." As Dryden sketches its history, satire began in Rome and Greece (as it began in all nations) not as Art but as "Nature," "rude and barbarous, and unpolish'd, as all other Operations of the Soul are in their beginnings, before they are Cultivated with Art and Study" (4:38). Like man in a state of nature, satire was fallen or "deprav'd"; indeed, natural satire (the "defamation of others") began at the Fall, when Adam and Eve blamed each other. Such "satire" survives in his own days as "Invective." It was not until satire became an "Art," says Dryden, pursuing his agricultural/theological metaphor, that (like redeemed man) "it bore better Fruit."[43] (By contrast the Restoration lampoon is a "Harvest . . . spoil'd with rankness, . . . Fruits of the Earth in an unnatural Season" [4:60].)[44] And it is not until satire is considered as an art, as "a Species of Poetry" (4:28), that Dryden takes a real interest in it. This takes place, he says, not in Greece but in Rome. It is the "progress" of Roman satire from rural "Hedge notes" toward the refinement and higher polish of "Civil Conversation" that Dryden celebrates: "No art, or Science, is at once begun and perfected, but that it must pass through several Ages." Juvenal, who came after Lucilius and Horace, so he suggests, gave "the last perfection to the art of Roman satire" (4:73). But despite Roman improvements, satire would still seem to be in need of further reformation: thus Donne's rough meters need to be refined; thus (most important) the English satiric tradition displays natural vigor but little art. Dryden's task, and the strongest impulse behind the "Discourse" and the theory that informs it, is to provide a set of instructions for "how a Modern Satire shou'd be made" (4:78).[45] We need constantly to remember that Dryden's theory is the result not of disinterested observation but of acutely interested participation: he wants satire to change and deploys his theory to that end. Like his lesser contemporary John Dennis, Dryden too is committed to the "reformation" of modern poetry.

It may seem obvious to us that satire is a form of art, one of the classical genres, but the distinction between satire as "Art Compleated" (a kind of purposive discourse) and satire as "Nature without Art" (rough vigor and unruly energy) is a crucial one for Dryden (4:29),[46] far more important, for example, than the distinction between "Horatian" and "Juvenalian" satire. It perhaps seems odd that

Dryden should devote so much of a discourse on *satire* to the nature of *epic*, but we can see that to begin as he does with epic is a way of establishing the hierarchy of genres in which satire will fit; it suggests that the theorist should be prepared to treat satire with the same dignity and rigor with which he treats the other genres.[47] Dryden's model here is probably the contemporary discourse on the epic, of which René Le Bossu's *Traité du poème épique* (1675) is the prime example. Its formal citation of authorities, review of rules, survey of modern examples of the form, sequential consideration of the fable, characters, diction, and so on provide a model for Dryden's systematic study.[48] His plan has the additional advantage of associating satire—heretofore a somewhat suspect form because "low" and often libelous—directly with the highest and most respected of forms. Indeed, he goes so far as to argue that satire is a "species" of epic, sharing with epic several stylistic features (the "heroic" measure, "turns" of words and thought, a "majesty" and "sublimity" of expression), inspiring images of virtue, and a clear didactic function. Thus epic, according to Le Bossu, is "a Discourse invented by Art, to form the Manners by such Instructions as are disguis'd under the Allegories of some one important Action."[49] Satire, says Dryden, quoting Heinsius, is "a kind of Poetry . . . invented for the purging of our Minds" (4:77).

To discover the rules "for perfecting the Design of True Satire" (4:80), Dryden urges that we look not at contemporary practice but at the ancients. His "poetics" is to be based not on Donne and Butler, much less on the torrent of "state poems" in his own day, but on the classical triad of Horace, Persius, and Juvenal, "our best Masters" (4:79). His term "true Satire" implies that much satire of his own time is "false" and in need of reformation. Dryden returns to the "Masters" not simply as a scholar but as a practicing poet who would incite other poets to follow him, "that we may form our own [satires] in imitation of them" (4:79). Dryden's famous "rules" for satire (derived from the example of the Romans) are then offered quite prescriptively: satire "ought to treat of one Subject; to be confin'd to one particular Theme; or, at least, to one principally." A second instruction follows with undisguised didactic intent: "The Poet is bound, and that *ex Officio*, to give his Reader some one Precept of Moral Virtue; and to caution him against some one particular Vice or Folly" (4:80).

These rules are perhaps the most influential of all modern pronouncements about satire. Quoted more often, by both eighteenth-century and present-day theorists and critics, than any other statements, they lay the cornerstone for all subsequent theories of satire's artfulness and its moral purpose. What is remarkable about these rules is not just their constraining prescriptiveness (the poet "ought" or is "bound"), for much literary theory in Dryden's day was prescriptive, offering a set of rules (derived from original practice). It is rather that Dryden's authority is not Horace or Juvenal but Persius, and Persius as interpreted by an early seventeenth-century classical scholar. Dryden, closely and confessedly following Casaubon, says it is Persius "who found out, and introduc'd this Method of confining himself to one Subject" and Persius who, unlike Horace and Juvenal, "is never wanting to us in some profitable Doctrine, and in exposing the opposite Vices to it" (4:79-80). Casaubon before Dryden had said that Persius "scarcely digressed from the thesis proposed at the beginning and certainly never left it entirely," that "the soul" of his poetry was "the persecution of vice and exhortation to virtue."[50] Dryden goes beyond Casaubon and turns even Juvenal into a Persean moralist: "*Juvenal* Exhorts to particular Virtues, as they are oppos'd to the Vices against which he declaims" (4:63).

It is odd that Dryden should look to Persius as satire's master, for he was commonly thought (except by Casaubon) to be the least of the three Roman satirists.[51] Much of what we know about Dryden suggests that he would have felt little affinity with Persius. As the California editors note, we might expect that Dryden's skeptical temperament would find Persius's severe Stoicism unpalatable.[52] And Dryden's rhetorical practice corresponds more closely to Juvenal's witty declamation than to Persius's famous obscurity and crabbed style.[53] But Dryden in fact does not offer the moral philosophy or style of Persius's satires for imitation; he emphasizes only their thematic unity and bipolar moral plan. It is thus on a strikingly narrow foundation, a highly selective reading of Persius, that Dryden constructs his powerfully prescriptive theory. Why Dryden, in his campaign to reform and dignify the practice of satire, should have looked to Persius must remain a matter for our speculation. Perhaps Persius offered him the clearest opportunity to seize the high moral ground against satire's present (and future) critics. Perhaps Dryden was drawn by Casaubon's praise of Persius as himself a reformer of satre, "the first of all to enrich, correct, and change for the better Roman satire."[54]

The example of Boileau reminds us that for all Dryden's pleasure in Juvenal, and his insistence that satire follow the Persean bipolar moral mode, he wanted modern satirists to emulate the Horatian elegance and polish of his French contemporary.[55] Implicitly rejecting the rollicking Hudibrastic jog-trot model and the Juvenal-inspired ranting style of Oldham, Dryden wanted modern satire to aim at Horatian (and French) "fine raillery,"[56] a "sharp, well-manner'd way of laughing Folly out of Countenance" (4:81). It is a tall order: Juvenalian wit and "Majesty," Persean moral rigor, and Horatian finesse.

Dryden's theory of satire, I have tried to argue, needs to be situated in its fullest rhetorical context as an attempt to reshape contemporary thinking about satire,[57] to justify Dryden's own practice (especially in "fine raillery"), and to influence its reception. It remains to note, in summary fashion, that Dryden's theory is of limited value for present-day theorists seeking any comprehensive account of the genre and of limited value even for explaining the practice of satire in Dryden's own day.[58] Although it has been shown that Dryden's "Discourse" was widely known in the eighteenth century and that commentators on satire commonly quote it approvingly, his theory represents not so much what satire was and had been as what Dryden and his followers wanted it to be.

Consider first that Dryden makes no effort to apply his theory to satiric poems since Juvenal. Later critics of satire have done little more. Butler's burlesque narrative will not answer to Dryden's model of satire. It is hilariously unconfined to a single subject, and though vice and folly are everywhere to be seen, critics have found it very difficult to isolate any opposing "Precept of Moral Virtue." Dryden's own two mock-heroic poems have fared somewhat better. Even though Dryden considered them to be "Varronian" satires and perhaps governed by other (unspecified) rules, we can readily find in them a single subject and can identify a bipolar design, the good politicians and the bad, the good poets and the bad. But few critics would claim that to find such large-scale patterns is really to tell us very much about how those poems work. And by Dryden's rules, the satire of Rochester and Oldham (expect when they are imitating Horace or Juvenal) would have to be judged a failure, the former because it has no clear moral pattern, the latter because it is too lurid and declamatory.

More generally, one must call Dryden's theory limited because it is too narrowly based on formal verse satire. Though Dryden acknowledges a separate Varronian tradition, he devotes little attention to it and may not even expect that his rules will apply to it. When he later came to write a life of Lucian, he at first seemed to find little "positive" in this "Sceptic": "his business . . . was rather to pull

down every thing, than to set up anything." Later, however, even
Lucian is improbably transformed into a Persean satirist: "Our author's chief design was to dis-nest heaven of so many immoral and
debauch'd deities; his next, to expose the mock philosophers; and
his last, to give us examples of a good life in the persons of the
true."[59]

Most satire in the Restoration and the eighteenth century, to say
nothing of other periods, takes forms other than that of the moralized discourse patterned on Persius. If satire is, as Dryden claims
(following Heinsius), "a kind of Poetry, without a Series of Action,"
then such a theory can do little to account for satire that takes the
form of narrative. Lampoon, in Dryden's scheme, is likewise exiled
beyond the pale as a lawless and dangerous kind of poem. Dryden
will not consider as proper satire the Greek "Invectives against particular Sects and Persons," Horace's satirical odes written "against
his private enemies," or the "libels" that were a common feature of
Restoration literary life.

But theory that works by such acts of exclusion cannot inspire
confidence. Dryden's memorable image of the urbane satirist as
"Jack Ketch" (the notorious hangman) seeks to distinguish between
the fine strokes of the satirist and the "slovenly butchering" of the
lampoonist, but in the process it cannot explain what his own portrait of Shaftesbury in *Absalom and Achitophel* shares with the portrait of the same man in *The Medall*. To be fair to Dryden, we should
not overgeneralize his theory. If we remember that it is laid out in a
discourse prefatory to translations of Juvenal and Persius, we might
properly consider that Dryden may have intended his "rules" to apply only to formal verse satire.[60]

Surprisingly, however, Dryden's theory does not in fact fit one of
the crucial cases of formal verse satire. Horace has always stood as an
example of the rambling satirist, chatty, digressive, easily led from one
topic to another. Dryden admits as much when he notes that Horace's
defenders would argue that "Unity of Design" in satire "is not necessary; because the very word *Satura* signifies a Dish plentifully stor'd
with all variety of Fruits and Grains" (4:80). Dryden must argue, in
other words, that Persius and Juvenal, and Boileau after them, provide
examples of "true satire" but that Horace (who preceded them) wrote
before satire reached its perfected state. Though Horace knew the
importance of unity in drama, "he seems not to mind it much in his
Satires, many of them consisting of more Arguments than one; and
the second without dependance on the first" (4:79). Dryden here fol-

lows Casaubon, who had noted that Horace's satire was a veritable
lanx satura—"whatever matter he took up he soon deserted"—in
contrast to the sharp focus of Persius.[61] Nor does Horace fit Dryden's
second rule, that the satirist must recommend a single virtue and caution against a single vice. Perhaps because Dryden knows the weakness of his case, he makes no attempt to apply his rule to Horace,
limiting himself to Persius and Juvenal. But Casaubon had not hesi-
tated to observe that Horace "did [not] act as a sure teacher of virtue." Much less insistent on urging virtue than his fellow Romans,
Horace was furthermore inconsistent in his morality, now a Stoic,
now an Epicurean, now a follower of Aristippus.[62]

Dryden tacitly acknowledges that his notion of "true Satire"
must exclude much of Horace. As an editor of Juvenal and Persius,
he was not obliged to present a full defense of Horace as moralist.
But his theory, for all its weakness, led other editors and translators
to try to make Horace fit. Their efforts demonstrate both the influence of Dryden's "Discourse" and the impossibility of accommodating Horace, without violence, to a model of unified moral design.[63]

Horace, of course, has often been a difficult case for theorists of
satire, particularly when, like Dryden, they define satire as unified
moral discourse. What is more striking, and more significant, is that
Dryden's theory does not account fully for Persius and Juvenal. In his
prose headnotes (based largely on Casaubon) to the satires of both,
Dryden attempts to apply his theory of bipartite form. Though Randolph cites these headnotes as evidence of a commitment to show
theory borne out by practice, another reader might find that Dryden
repeatedly has to admit that the poems are not tightly unified. Thus,
for Juvenal's first satire Dryden notes: "Herein he confines himself to
no one Subject, but strikes indifferently at all Men in his way." For the
sixth, the famous satire on women, he finds "Lust" to be the "main
Body of the Tree" and the remaining female vices "but digression."[64]
Nor can Dryden imagine "what Moral" Juvenal "cou'd reasonably
draw" from his "bitter invective against the fair Sex." Perhaps, as he
notes in the "Discourse," there is a "latent Admonition to avoid Ill
Women." But Dryden finds little "Truth or Instruction" and wittily
observes that Juvenal "has run himself into his old declamatory way,
and almost forgotten that he was now setting up for a Moral Poet"
(4:80). In *Satire* 10, later imitated by Samuel Johnson as "The Vanity
of Human Wishes," Dryden finds Juvenal's subject to be "the *various*
wishes and desires of mankind" (my emphasis). Persius's six satires fit
the theory more closely, but even so, the fifth has "two distinct

Parts,"[65] and only the sixth carefully opposes a virtue ("the Virtue of Giving Well") and its corresponding vice ("the Defects of Giving or Spending"). Thus even Dryden's own notes sometimes concede a gap between "how a Modern Satire shou'd be made" and how the best models actually made them. On the title page of his translation Dryden in fact yields to the traditional view: his epigraph consists of the famous lines in which Juvenal says his satire is a farrago of whatever men do.[66]

The Eighteenth Century

Despite the abundance and variety of satire in the eighteenth century, there is little development of satiric *theory*. Most writers who present a rationale for satire are content with Dryden's formulations of Renaissance theory. Dryden's evenhanded comparisons among Horace, Juvenal, and Persius, his comments on the design of satire, and his discussion of the lampoon—a poem "for the most part Unlawful" but sometimes justified—were codified into typically Augustan binary formulas: Horace versus Juvenal, comic versus tragic satire, specific versus general satire, raillery versus chastisement, vice versus folly. (Despite Dryden's lead, eighteenth-century theorists paid little attention to the Menippean or Varronian satiric tradition.) John Dennis is characteristic: "*Horace* argues, insinuates, engages, rallies, smiles, *Juvenal* exlaims, apostrophizes, exaggerates, lashes, stabbs."[67] Joseph Trapp likewise elaborates the central distinction between Horace's comic and Juvenal's tragic satire: "The one is pleasant and facetious; the other angry and austere: the one smiles; the other storms: the Foibles of Mankind are the Object of the one; greater Crimes, of the other: the Former is always in the low Style; the latter generally in the Sublime."[68]

What is new perhaps is the defensive note: much satiric theory in the eighteenth century, as P.K. Elkin's title points out, is cast in the form of a "defence" of satire—against the increasing attacks on the satirist's morals and motives. Commentary on the nature of satire in the century might thus be said to be sharply polarized: on the one end, critics denounced satire as malevolent and destructive, an affront to the dignity of human nature and a threat to the commonwealth; on the other, critics and practitioners countered by insisting that satire was a highly moral art, motivated by the love of virtue and serving as a useful censor of public and private morals. Its hostile critics saw only spite, envy, pride, and sadistic delight. Its defenders could not see (or refused to see) any low motives or painful consequences; they saw only virtue and justice. Thrown on the defensive, they largely repressed or suppressed any notion that satire could be subversive or even disruptive of public order or private peace. And they were driven to insist not only that satire was a moral art but that it was clearly and explicitly didactic and moralizing: it told you what was good and what was bad and why.

An anonymous poem entitled *The Satirist* (1777), for example, finds that the satirist is a good man moved by love, "sense," and justice; he praises virtue and displays no wild or baseless rage or "foul detraction." The poem's heroic couplets have a forceful Johnsonian rhythn, but its notions about satire—asserted with some frequency—might have been drawn from Pope's idealized image of the moral satirist in his Horatian imitations of the 1730s. Why should a poet writing some forty years after Pope's *Epilogue to the Satires* feel obliged to state and restate a Popean defense of satire? Perhaps because in an age of "sensibility," satire came increasingly under suspicion and prompted the old defense. Perhaps too the insistent protest of the satirist's innocence suggests that the defenders themselves half realized that satire is not always an art of moral instruction. Dryden had noted in 1693 that the term *satire* "as it is us'd in all the Modern Languages" means a defamatory "Invective" (4:28). The common meaning survived: in his *Dictionary of the English Language* (1755) Johnson notes that "proper satire" (by which he meant "a poem censuring wickedness or folly") is "too frequently confounded" with lampoon. Despite prescriptive efforts (and note that Johnson implicitly tries to influence "proper" satiric practice through his definition), the old knowledge persisted: satire can be a dangerous and lawless weapon, as Pierre Bayle urged at great length in the "Dissertation Concerning Defamatory Libels" in his widely read *Historical and Critical Dictionary*.[69]

Moralists went to extraordinary lengths to counter such hostility. Even a satirist as different from Pope as Petronius is drawn under the same moral umbrella. Reacting against the traditional suspicion about Petronius's moral concerns, a translator in 1708 insisted that Petronius "wrote not by a *Spirit of Corruption*, but by the *disgust* of a *Court Philosopher*; who had been offended by the *Disorders* of the *Emperour* and his *Favourites*, whom he exposes to their own View in a most Satyrical manner."[70]

Defenders of satire were not content to argue that the satirist was prompted by a moral impulse or served to stimulate moral thinking.

They turned satire into an explicitly didactic art. It is striking that, in an age capable of intense and subtle moral reasoning, the moral defense of satire is presented in such crude terms, as if the satirist were offering elementary lessons in distinguishing good from evil, combating vice and regulating passion, to an audience of moral infants. Theorists devoted some attention to the *way* in which satire allegedly corrected its readers, but most were (by our lights, anyway) naive and optimistic about satire's power to "banish Vice and Folly."[71] "Horatians" tended to believe that the reader would listen to Horace and be laughed or cajoled into virtue. "Juvenalians" had a harder task, for one suspects that few parricides and adulterers will be moved to mend their ways by reading. The argument had to be that Juvenal aroused deeper powers of "moral disapprobation"[72] and inflamed the reader's ardor for virtue, or else that Juvenalian satire would punish the guilty with shame and even deter them from further evil.

And there were doubters. Edward Burnaby Greene in 1763 was "inclined to think that satire has rarely done any essential good." Horatian satire, he thought, served only to "exercise a wanton indiscriminate spirit of ridicule," and the Juvenalian kind "is either thrown aside as a downright scurrility, or only regarded from the exclusive merits of the diction." Thus, he concluded (in words that ought to be remembered by the moral apologists for satire), "the spirit of acrimony too much affrights, that of ridicule too much diverts."[73]

But "moral" art in the period did not always take the form of a bipolar labeling of virtue and vice. It might be "full of morality" or "moral reflections" without consisting simply of directive sententiae or explicit instructions. A theory of the indirect moral effect of satire might have been constructed on the practice of Horace, who (Dryden says), "tho' he hides his Sentences" and prefers to speak and preach "in jest," is nonetheless "perpetually Moral"; he "insinuates" virtue and induces his reader to think morally (4:57, 62-63). What looks like inert precept may in fact prompt reflection and inquiry. David Morris has recently reminded us that a poem like Pope's *Essay on Man*, once thought to be full of boring moral platitudes, might well be read in a different way if one considers its "aphoristic style" (a feature it shares with much eighteenth-century satire). Aphorisms, Morris quotes Francis Bacon as saying, "representing a knowledge broken, do invite men to enquire further."[74] The example of Swift reminds us that satire can be written "As with a moral View design'd" and yet not precipitate fixed moral precepts.[75]

For the most part, however, such readings do not emerge in the

comments on satire by eighteenth-century critics, who limit themselves to grosser didactic theories. One finds indications of dissent
from the standard Dryden-inspired views not in the full-scale "essay
on satire" (whether in verse or in prose) but in the occasional comments of the greatest satirists of the age—Pope and Swift. Pope is
candid enough to acknowledge that for all the satirist's high-minded
aims, he works with tools—the lash, the pointed pen, the flaying
knife—that inflict pain:

> What! arm'd for *Virtue* when I point the Pen,
> Brand the bold Front of shameless, guilty Men,
> Dash the proud Gamester in his gilded Car,
> Bare the mean Heart that lurks beneath a Star.[76]
>
> O sacred Weapon! left for Truth's defence,
> Sole Dread of Folly, Vice, and Insolence! . . .
> Reverent I touch thee! but with honest zeal;
> To rowze the Watchmen of the Publick Weal,
> To Virtue's Work provoke the tardy Hall,
> And goad the Prelate slumb'ring in his Stall.[77]

More than almost any other satire in the century, Pope's answers
to the moral theorist's model: it censures vice and praises virtue, and
commonly does so in the same poem. But Pope, though he often
claims the moralist's goal of correcting, amending, or perhaps just
deterring his victims' behavior, can also concede that at times the
satirist must speak regardless of the good effects in the world: "A
Knave's a Knave, to me, in ev'ry State, / Alike my scorn, if he succeed
or fail" ("Epistle to Dr. Arbuthnot," ll. 361-62). Even if the satirist
abandons hope of defeating the vicious, he will speak out simply to
please himself.

And Swift, though he plays with the conventional idea that the
satirist seeks to "reform" the world, seems concerned finally to
"vex" it: that is, to ruffle or disturb its smooth surfaces. No one can
doubt that *Gulliver's Travels* and *A Modest Proposal* are "moral"
satires. Yet it would take a confident critic to declare that we can
draw from Swift's work clear conclusions and moral directives: for
example, that we should all simply strive to be like Don Pedro, or
that the solution to Ireland's problems is to adopt the "other expedients" that Swift pretends to dismiss. It is easy to find excoriation of
vice and folly in Swift, and not very difficult to find the praise of
virtue. But Swift doesn't think the matter can be left there. It is now a
commonplace of satire criticism to note that Swift teases the reader

out of (or into) thought. Eighteenth-century satiric theory is not able to explain this process. Is Swift's work really the exception to the rule, or is it closer to the norm?

The Twentieth Century

Twentieth-century satiric theory has been largely built on Augustan foundations. When Mary Claire Randolph took up Dryden's definition of satire in the early 1940s, she presented a schematic diagram that influenced much mid-twentieth-century discussion: satire consists of a Part A in which the satirist lashes a vice, and a Part B in which he commends the opposite virtue. But as Randolph herself conceded, her account applies only to formal verse satire and not to the many other species of the genus satire. The bipolar pattern she discerned is often incomplete. The so-called "Part B" (she noted) is sometimes minimal or only implied.

Randolph in fact said little that Dryden and Casaubon had not said before her. She modestly offered nothing more than to "synthesize available information." The bipolar pattern, she carefully noted at the outset, is a simplifying reduction of an "intricate structure." What is more, she observed that formal verse satire readily "drifts and fades" into a myriad of affiliated forms. Particularly in the English tradition, always hostile to "regimented formalism," formal verse satire is in fact quite rare, though more common in French classicism from Régnier to Boileau. Even in eighteenth-century England it is the exception. As Randolph said, "Dryden himself wrote none; Swift, Gay, Addison, Steele, and Arbuthnot wrote none; only Edward Young and Alexander Pope, in company with a certain few of the lesser poets, wrote any formal verse satires that could properly be termed original." Translations and imitations of Horace and Juvenal were common, but (she concluded) "not one of the half dozen or so great English satires, it must be noted, is a formal verse satire."[78] Unfortunately, the caution with which Randoph presented her synthesis was not usually remembered or emulated by the commentators who came after her. Her bipolar model at the core of an otherwise unstable formal verse satire hardened into dogma and was casually applied to satire of all kinds. As a result, the narrow moral theory of satire, derived from Dryden and Casaubon, was confirmed.

Satiric theory after World War II developed at two major American universities, Yale and Chicago. Trained at Yale or teaching there in the 1950s, Maynard Mack, Martin Price, Alvin Kernan, Robert C.

Elliott, and Ronald Paulson collectively produced what might be called a rhetorical theory of satire. For them, satire is ideally understood as rhetorical art (as Price's title *Swift's Rhetorical Art* suggests). Satire is a kind of *laus et vituperatio*, praise and blame, cast in the form of a fictional war between good and evil. The satirist, not to be confused with the historical author, is a conventional figure who wears a mask appropriate to his rhetorical situation. Such a theory is a natural outgrowth and perhaps the inevitable consequence of the New Criticism, dominant at Yale during the same years, in that it takes as its object "the work of art"—satire in this view is above all a work of art—and tends to separate the work from the author who produced it, the world out of which it grew, and the audience toward which it was directed. This was a useful tactic at a time when a satirist like Pope still suffered from the hostility of Victorian criticism. More generally, a rhetorical theory of satire was designed to discredit the older biographical approach. And it served to strengthen the hand of the literary "critics" in their contest with the history-minded "scholars": satire, so the "Yale" critics argued, demanded a reader who was alert to the workings of wit and imagery more than a reader who knew the historical particulars concerning Thomas Shadwell, Colley Cibber, or Orator Henley.

The Yale critics provided a valuable corrective in their time and ensured that thenceforth satire would have to receive the same kind of careful and detailed critical attention that the most complex lyric poem had received from Cleanth Brooks and Robert Penn Warren. But a price was paid. New Critical satiric theory sharpened our sense of satiric art and convention, but it reduced our sense of satire's energies. Just as the New Critics came under increasing attack after about 1970, so this "rhetorical" view of satire has been challenged by those critics who want to resituate satire in history, to locate its origins in the interplay between the creative imagination of the satirist and his personal circumstances, and to focus on the character of the satirist's appeal to his reader.

The "Chicago" theorists of satire, whose main work was published in the 1960s, acknowledge that satire is rooted in history. Indeed, the characteristic feature of their theories—as exemplified in the work of Sheldon Sacks and Edward Rosenheim—is the claim that satire "consists of an attack by means of a manifest fiction upon discernible historical particulars."[79] They also challenged the rhetorical view by distinguishing between those satires that function as persuasive rhetoric and those that seek only to punish. Their work on satire needs to be seen as part of a larger attempt by Chicago critics to understand the principles that make for coherence within and distinctions among the literary genres. But by insisting on the generic identity and coherence of satire, Sacks and Rosenheim construct a schematic diagram that does not correspond to our intuitive sense of what actually goes on in satire. Because it is directed against identifiable particulars, satire in their view is a clear and unambiguous attack. And yet it is a commonplace that satire is often ambiguous, obscure, or double-edged. Because the fourth voyage of *Gulliver's Travels* appears not to attack historically identifiable particulars—except in a minor way—Rosenheim must call it not satire but "philosophic myth." Works such as Rochester's "Satyr against Mankind" must likewise be called something else. Because (in Sacks's view) satire is referential (directing our attention outside the work to our own world), we must understand Gulliver not as a "character" with an invented history and a developing experience but as a satiric device. And yet, granting that Swift makes opportunistic use of his Gulliver, it is difficult not to read the "Voyage to the Country of the Houyhnhnms" as in some sense a climactic event for Gulliver, the shattering and disabling discovery on the part of a man who has shed some of his illusions. Nor may we (if we follow Sacks) infer from satire anything about a satirist's own beliefs; we can determine only what it is that he attacks: pride in reason, the tyranny of English colonial policy, and so on. Here too the theorist's need to distinguish prose satire from other forms such as the "apologue" makes him discourage the inevitable attempt on the reader's part to seek out Swift's own beliefs in *Gulliver's Travels*. And his theory makes even less sense of Pope's late verse satires, which prominently advertise their "positives."

The critic-theorists in the 1950s and 1960s had enough confidence and comprehensive vision to make large claims about satire as a genre, as their very titles suggest. Thus Mack wrote about "The Muse of Satire" (though his essay in fact dealt solely with Pope's satire); Kernan about "The Plot of Satire" with examples drawn from the seventeenth through the twentieth centuries; Paulson about "The Fictions of Satire"; Elliott about "The Plot of Satire"; and Gilbert Highet (at Columbia) about "The Anatomy of Satire." Perhaps the largest claims in this century for satire as a genre came from Northrop Frye, the first modern theorist in the field. His discussion of satire in *Anatomy of Criticism* (1957) was anticipated in his early essay "The Nature of Satire."[80] But Frye's analysis, though immensely suggestive, seems to have had little influence on other theorists, perhaps because it was too abstract and overarticulated—he finds six different "phases" of satire.

Since the 1960s there has been something of a retreat from large-scale theoretical claims about "the nature of satire." Most commentators have abandoned the attempt to account for the genre as a whole or even for a wide range of satiric works from several centuries. They have instead focused—as Claude Rawson, perhaps the most influential of recent critics, has done—on the satire of a single writer.[81] The characteristic book on satire in the last twenty years is a discussion of some features of Pope's satiric poems or Swift's prose satires, or a study of lesser-known satirists such as John Marston, Joseph Hall, John Donne, the Earl of Rochester, Charles Churchill, or Lord Byron. Other students of satire have taken a frankly historical perspective and surveyed classical satiric theory (Van Rooy), the standard defenses of satire in the eighteenth century (Elkin), the various traditions of verse satire available to a writer such as Pope,[82] or the translations and imitations of Roman satire in seventeenth- and eighteenth-century England.[83] In the meantime classical scholars, working for the most part independently of their colleagues in English departments, have continued to produce studies of Roman satire[84] or of single satirists[85] and valuable but narrowly focused commentaries.[86] For many years classicists lagged behind their literary colleagues in critical sophistication, but recently they have begun to look beyond their Roman borders and naive biographical readings. By the same token, students of post-Roman satire can learn a great deal from the subtle reconstruction of the Roman rhetorical world of classicists such as William Anderson and Niall Rudd, and from such delicate readings of Horace—not as moral teacher of eternal truths but as one skeptical "about the actual possibilities of moral achievement"—as those of Edward Fraenkel, Gordon Williams, and Frank Stack.[87]

Overshadowed by the formal verse satirists, the long Menippean tradition in satire has attracted very little critical attention. Menippean writers—Lucian, Apuleius, Petronius, More, Erasmus, Rabelais, Burton, Fontenelle, and others—have always been studied for their individual achievement and have sometimes been seen as precursors of Swift. But few attempts have been made to integrate their tradition with that of formal verse satire or even to account for the special features of the Menippean genre. Dryden, though he inherited a critical tradition descending from Varro and a diverse body of *satyre Menippée* in the Renaissance, can only define Menippean or Varronian satire as (in form) a "mixture of several sorts of Verses,"

sometimes mixed with prose, and (in content) a mixture of "Philosophy" and "Pleasantries" (4:47). Dryden conveys no strong conviction
that Erasmus and Spenser have much in common with Lucian and
Petronius.

The variousness of Menippean satire—its motley nature and the
variety of its exemplars—has probably prevented modern critics
from defining the nature of the form any more precisely. For Kernan,
Menippean satire includes "any satiric work obviously written in the
third person, or where the attack is mentioned under cover of a fable" (Cankered Muse, p. 13). But this says little more than that Menippean satire includes all satires that aren't first-person diatribes.
Eugene Kirk, in a copiously annotated catalogue of Menippean satire, identifies some "family resemblances," but his procedure is simply and narrowly inductive; he gathers common features but finds
no common principle. Even Kirk laments that it is difficult to see
continuity between classical and post-1500 examples of the form.[88]

Northrop Frye, who has done most in this century to popularize
the notion of Menippean satire, identifies a generic principle, but (as
part of his program of mapping all of literture in a single coherent
system) his procedure has the defects of the overly deductive. It locates
Menippean satire—renamed "anatomy"—in relation to neighboring
genres: the novel, the confession, and the romance. The anatomy, he
says, is extroverted and intellectual as opposed to introverted and
personal. Frye's idea is that the Menippean satirist "relies on the free
play of intellectual fancy" in order to present "a vision of the world in
terms of an intellectual pattern."[89] This description remains somewhat cryptic, and though he tosses out titles, Frye does not take the
time to work through detailed analysis. His scheme is dazzling but has
not proved critically useful. It can be and has been applied to a great
variety of fictions, from Geoffrey Chaucer's tales to Herman Melville's Confidence Man, but the theory itself has remained sketchy and
resolutely ahistorical.

A third attempt to define Menippean satire is that of Mikhail
Bakhtin. First published in 1929, his Problems of Dostoevsky's Poetics—not well known in the West until the 1980s—offers a systematic
analysis of what he calls "the Menippea." For Bakhtin, the leading
features of "the Menippea" are its bold use of fantastic adventure;
inserted genres and styles producing a multistyled and multivoiced
discourse; a presiding spirit of "carnival" in which ridicule is "fused
with rejoicing" and orthodoxies of all kinds are freely challenged;
and a "philosophical end."[90] I will return to Bakhtin, but I say now

that his theory—for all its attractiveness—has its limits for students of satire. To rename the form "the Menippea" is to split it off from "satire." Indeed, Bakhtin is explicitly concerned to define Menippea as "ambivalent" and satire as purely "negative." His Marxism disposes him to idealize the "folk" and all folkish ways. He does not see the element of erudition that Frye finds central or the tradition of "learned wit" that links Erasmus, Rabelais, Burton, Swift, and Sterne. For him "the Menippea" grows out of the marketplace, not the study.

Indeed, it almost seems as if Frye and Bakhtin are describing different forms. Perhaps we need to acknowledge that the Menippean family has several branches: a tradition of fantastic narrative, from Lucian to *Gulliver's Travels* and beyond; a parallel tradition of wild and parodic display of learning, from Erasmus through Robert Burton to *A Tale of a Tub*; and a tradition of dialogue and symposium from Plato and Lucian to Fontenelle and Blake. Bakhtin may prove to be a more fruitful theorist than Frye, but he does little to help us see the resemblances between, say, Rabelais and Juvenal, or Lucian and Pope.

The Menippean tradition has continued to attract attention from critics and theorists in recent years, but their tendency has been to focus not on what Menippean works share with other satire but on what is distinctive about them. Michael Seidel's *Satiric Inheritance: Rabelais to Sterne* (1979) is an apparent exception. Acknowledging a debt to Frye, he develops the idea that a "satiric action" typically involves decline, degeneration, loss of potential or of "inheritance"; and he takes his examples from both prose (Rabelais, Cervantes, Swift, Sterne) and poetry (Butler, Marvell, Dryden, Pope). But Seidel is primarily interested in satiric narrative, and his theoretical claims point not toward a general theory of satire but to a general theory of narrative. He forces fresh thought about narrative satire and provides acute and striking readings of individual texts but does not tell us what the narrative *Dunciad* shares with the nonnarrative "Satire against Mankind."

Frank Palmeri's *Satire in Narrative: Petronius, Swift, Gibbon, Melville, and Pynchon* (1990) is in turn indebted to Seidel for the focus on narrative, and to Bakhtin for the idea that Menippean narrative satire typically displays "dialogical parody." According to Palmeri, prose satire deploys "levelling strategies," reducing high to low, spirit to body, but withholding assent from either, in a spirit of "tolerance of heterogeneous languages and forms of understanding."[91] "Parodic, dialogical satire" embraces neither orthodoxy nor heterodoxy but distances itself from both. What lies behind Palmeri is not so much Bakhtin's idea of "the Menippea," in which ortho-doxies are challenged and subverted from below, as his idea of the "dialogical," in which different voices or points of view enter into unresolved dialogue. But in practice, Palmeri finds that narrative sat-ire tends to be "subversive." By contrast, he continues to assume that most verse satire is "monological," "conservative," even "reaction-ary"; he thus preserves a distinction between the Menippean tradi-tion and the rest of satire.

John Snyder's discussion of Menippean prose satire in *Prospects of Power: Tragedy, Satire, and the Theory of Genre* (1991) likewise aims to break new ground but remains within old paradigms. As Snyder conceives it, "ordinary satire" itself remains primarily a "straight and narrow critique" (113) with "targets" (121) at which it aims by means of reason and rhetoric. He recognizes that Men-ippean satire—his examples are from Petronius, Cervantes, Butler, Twain, and Hasek—"excels in sustaining complex ironies" (139), but in doing so the Menippean writer typically shifts from satire into some other genre: tragedy, romance, or the realistic novel.[92]

My argument, in contrast, is that when Menippean writers sus-tain "complex ironies," they are writing satire; and when they en-gage in "dialogical parody," they are doing what verse satirists do. To read Menippean works alongside those of Horace, Donne, or Pope is to see poetic satire, even formal verse satire, in new light. The moral design is but one of several elements. Neither tradition, in Bakhtin's terms, is "monological."

2

The Rhetoric of Satire:
Inquiry and Provocation

Conventional satiric theory—by which I mean the consensus of
those theorists who published their work around 1960—holds that
the satirist operates in a world of clear standards and boundaries. As
Kernan puts it, the satirist "sees the world as a battlefield between a
definite, clearly understood good, which he represents, and an equally clear-cut evil. No ambiguities, no doubts about himself, no sense
of mystery troubles him, and he retains always his monolithic certainty" (*Cankered Muse*, pp. 21-22). To be fair, Kernan here describes not the author of satire but the author posing as "satirist."
And yet the author behind the satirist is still armed with moral certainty. The best satire, Kernan argues later, is unified "by a firm,
definite understanding of the moral issues involved," by the "clear
and consistent" moral point of view that, so he says, characterizes
the work of Juvenal (pp. 88, 89).

The satirist, in this view, is quite certain of his own moral position; he also assumes such certainty in his readers. As John Bullitt put
it, "Satire can become a vital form of literature only when there is a
fairly widespread agreement about what man ought to be. The satirist
needs the convictions that fixed intellectual ideas or norms can give
him, and the assurance that he will receive understanding from his
readers. . . . Satire is best able to develop from a basis of general
agreement on moral and intellectual standards."[1] Other modern theorists have endorsed this view. Frye says that satire's moral norms are
"relatively clear," that satire "assumes standards against which the
grotesque and absurd are measured." It thrives on certainty: "Whenever a reader is not sure what the author's attitude is or what his own
is supposed to be," says Frye, "we have irony with relatively little
satire" (*Anatomy of Criticism*, p. 223). Compare Maynard Mack:

satire "asserts the validity and necessity of norms, systematic values and meanings that are contained by recognizable codes" ("Muse of Satire," p. 840). The business of the satirist is to insist on the sharp differences between vice and virtue, between good and bad, between what man *is* and what he *ought to be*. To make those differences especially clear, the satirist has to exaggerate or simplify, to paint with a bold brush: "complexity as such," says Ernest Tuveson, is not his business.[2] A satire is single-minded and clearly focused on its target. In a work organized as a satire, according to Sheldon Sacks, every formal decision is ideally designed to sharpen the ridicule on the object of the satire (*Fiction*, p. 7). Or, as Paulson puts it, "there is always a strong sense of efficiency in satire: nothing is done without a purpose" (*Fictions of Satire*, p. 4).

A generation later, these confident assurances about the way satire works seem almost quaint.[3] If the satirist's job is to assure us, in no uncertain terms, that the established norms about good and bad, right and wrong, are solidly in place, one wonders how satire ever attracted any mature readers or retained their interest. It would not be surprising if readers, instructed to look for clearly stated moral messages and clear-cut distinctions between vice and virtue, found even a satirist like Horace "pedestrian, obvious, and boring" (Williams, *Tradition and Originality*, p. 607). Should we not take another look at the way satiric rhetoric works?

Granted, some satires do in fact seem relatively simple in their conception and their execution. Borrowing Rosenheim's term, we may call them "punitive" satires, designed to heap abuse on a target (often an enemy or a rival). Some lampoons work this way. Perhaps even *MacFlecknoe* works this way. But how long would such a poem hold our attention if it were really reducible to its vector of attack and its "norms" or moral-literary standards? Why bother to read *The Dunciad* if all we "learn" is that Cibber et al. are bad writers? Why read *Absalom and Achitophel* to learn that the Duke of Monmouth is dangerous? Furthermore, we intuitively acknowledge, by our practical criticism on great satire, that the best examples of the genre—*Gulliver's Travels, The Praise of Folly, The Dunciad*—do not work by reaffirming traditional moral certainties or by transferring the satirist's own assurance to the reader. When satire seems devoted, like George Lyttelton's *Dialogues of the Dead* (1746), to solidifying, consolidating, confirming eternal verities or contemporary standards, we dismiss it as safely conventional.[4]

In order to identify the inadequacy in conventional theory, we can break that theory down into several assumptions: (1) that the bipolar praise-and-blame pattern is the formal core of a satire; (2) that the thematic center is some moral standard against which deviations are measured; (3) that the satirist appeals to, and thereby confirms and assumes we share, some traditionally sanctioned values; and (4) that the satirist works like the preacher-rhetorician to persuade his audience to virtue.

Now it is true that one can find a bipolar moral pattern in many (though not all) satires. One thinks of Belinda versus Clarissa in *The Rape of the Lock*, Sporus versus the "manly" Pope in the *Epistle to Arbuthnot*, or Gulliver versus the King of Lilliput. But how *significant* is such a pattern? As Johnson said, he who thinks rationally thinks morally. And in moral discourse some kinds of opposed pairs are almost inevitable. It is not possible to think of a virtue without implicitly identifying a vice, if only as the absence of the virtue. Novelists, dramatists, and poets not engaged in satire find opposed pairs useful in presenting character or in clarifying a moral issue: witness Tom and Blifil, Edgar and Edmund, Satan and Abdiel. It does not follow, however, that a particular moral antithesis contains the sum of a satire's moral wisdom. The bipolar pattern may be simply *one* of the many devices that a satirist employs. We should think of it as the satirist's point of departure rather than the destination. True, Pope and Sporus are presented as opposites, but in some suggestive ways they are strikingly similar. Pope the satirist stands up as a hero against the world of Walpole. But the satirist is also revealed to be a naive fool. Yes, Dryden presents David as true godlike king (as opposed to the false king, Monmouth), but the satire really engages us insofar as we are asked to hold in mind two conflicting thoughts: David's "mildness" saves the day, but David's mildness is also a sign of weakness and indulgence.

The notion that clear moral standards are at the center of satire is likewise open to challenge. The moral "ideas" in satire are often so elementary—one should avoid pride, avoid excess, control passion, use reason—as to be a kind of irreducible moral minimum for sentient beings, the sort of "loose variety of Stoicism" that Kernan finds in Juvenal, the moral clichés of every age, and thus not thematically significant.[5] (The irony of course is that the satirists themselves often violate these very standards—in their righteous pride and their rage.) Again, do simple moral ideas perhaps constitute the raw materials for the satirist, the place to begin rather than to end?[6] What we behold in satire is not a neatly articulated homiletic discourse but the

drama of an inflamed sensibility, or a cool and detached mind playfully exploring a moral topic. The reader's interest is not in redis-
covering that greed is a bad thing or that deceit is to be avoided[7] but
in working through (with the satirist's help) the implications of a
given moral position (how far do you have to go in the public defense
of virtue?), the contradictions between one virtue (justice) and another (forgiveness), or the odd similarities between a vice (brazenness) and a virtue (steadfastness against censure).

Is satire in fact based on shared cultural values? Does it work by
confirming contemporary moral standards? If so, we would have to
concede that most of the great satires have failed. *Gulliver's Travels*
and *A Tale of a Tub* aroused sharply opposed reactions among Swift's
contemporaries, who couldn't agree about his moral underpinnings.
Modern critics have been no more able to arrive at consensus interpretation. We still notoriously disagree about Swift's targets and his
attitudes, and we are beginning to be less sure about the apparent
straightforwardness of the satire in Dryden and Pope.

Finally, does the satirist write with the faith that his rhetoric will
persuade his readers to love virtue and avoid vice? Pagan moralists and
Christian preachers for millennia have perhaps operated on this optimistic assumption, but their arguments(unlike those of the satirist) are
implicitly bolstered by a philosophical system or the threat of divine
punishment. Some commentators on satire shared this optimism. Walter Harte, in his poetic *Essay on Satire* (1730), confidently asserted that
"*Stoicks* learn their Foibles" from watching a comedy by Aristophanes. In a *Discourse concerning Ridicule and Irony* (1729) Anthony
Collins went so far as to declare that "intelligent People" who read *The
Praise of Folly* will "remove out of their Minds all Bigotry contracted
by Ignorance and an evil Education, all Peevishness, Hatred, and Ill-
Nature towards one another, on account of different Sentiments in
Religion." But increasing numbers of contemporaries were skeptical:
perhaps satire only causes the fools to smile and the wicked to carry on
as before.[8] Even worse, as Dryden noted, "A perpetual Grinn, like that
of *Horace*, does rather anger than amend a Man" (4:70). By the end of
the eighteenth century William Cowper thought that satire might possibly "correct a foible" or "displace a patch" but could do little more:
"What vice has it subdued? Whose heart reclaim'd / By rigour, or
whom laugh'd into reform?"[9] And the greatest English satirists of the
age—Pope and Swift—expressed considerable doubt on this matter.
Pope acknowledged that some scribblers were literally "shameless"—
you couldn't penetrate their dullness or impudence. His interlocutor in

the *Epilogue to the Satires* expresses Pope's suspicion that you only anger the fools and don't mend your foes (1:54-55). And Swift in dark moments thought satire a kind of magical protective mirror in which beholders may see "every body's Face but their Own." It is not surprising to discover that modern empirical research has been unable to document that satire has any persuasive power.[10]

Quite apart from these objections to the conventional theory of satire's moral rhetoric, we should resist reducing the satirist to the kind of single-mindedness and tunnel vision that we expect to find in no other writer (in our practical criticism—as opposed to our theory—we of course acknowledge that satirists, like everybody else, are ambivalent and aware of complexity). Even if we wish to call the satirist a rhetorician, we need not think of satiric rhetoric simply as the communication of previously codified moral knowledge or the persuasion of a reader toward a particular course of action. I want to suggest in this chapter and the next that rhetoric can be, and historically has been, conceived of in quite different terms and that we may arrive at a fuller understanding of the way satire works if we think of a rhetoric of inquiry, a rhetoric of provocation, a rhetoric of display, a rhetoric of play.

Satire as Inquiry

In the conventional view, the satirist not only begins with a clearly articulated intention but executes that intention by means of a fiction precisely designed to accomplish its predetermined purpose.[11] Stated baldly in this way, such an approach makes the satirist seem an unusually calculating and controlling artist. It does not require deconstructive doubts about authorial intention and control to make us suspect that few satirists have in fact proceeded in this cut-and-dried fashion.

How much satire even *begins* with a clearly formulated plan of attack? Some satires, both classical and modern, it is true, take as their model the apparently closed form of the sermon or the legal brief.[12] But many satires are not constructed on the basis of such settled conclusions, with the satirist presenting a predetermined argument. Rather they are designed to be more open-ended (or at least to appear to be so): the satirist writes in order to discover, to explore, to survey, to attempt to clarify. Remember that many of the traditional features of satiric discourse suggest that the satirist does not really know where he is going. Lucilius called his satires *sermones*, "little chats," casual or informal conversations in which one topic naturally leads to another. As one late eighteenth-century commentator said of Horace's *sermones*, the poet "throws out his opinions on manners, morality, and literature, in the free and familiar stile of conversation."[13] Horace's habit, said another, was "not marking his Transitions from Thought to Thought, but giving them as they lay in his Mind."[14] Sometimes (especially in Horace) the conversation becomes two-sided: satirists in both the formal verse and Menippean traditions have often adopted the dialogue as a form. Indeed, dialogue and debate have been prominent features of satire from its pre-Horatian beginnings in Aristophanes, Ennius, Lucilius, and Varro.[15]

In some cases, to be sure, the dialogue consists only of the satirist and his straight man, as in Cowper's *Table-Talk* (1782). This is perhaps dialogue in name only. But it is not uncommon in Horace, Pope, the Lucianic dialogues of the dead, or Denis Diderot's celebrated *Neveu de Rameau*,[16] for the dialogue or conversation to reach a stalemate in which an issue is by no means resolved. Juvenal calls his satire a farrago, invoking the old idea that satire contains a platter full of mixed fruits, a miscellany. As a Renaissance commentator put it, the word *satyra* originally signified "any kind of miscellaneous writing, which we now term *Essayes*."[17] "Essay" strongly suggested to the Renaissance mind its French meaning of "tryout," "tentative effort," especially of a frankly personal sort (like Montaigne's *Essais*). Pope's frequent use of the term "essay" in the titles of his satiric poems—both the fully satiric *Moral Essays* and the didactic-satiric *Essay on Criticism* and *Essay on Man*—suggests that he still thought of satire as an essayistic genre. When satire becomes a more systematic survey, it is sometimes called an "anatomy" (as in the case of Donne's *Anatomy of the World*). The term preserves its medical meaning of dissection as a means of discovery, and as Burton's encyclopedic *Anatomy of Melancholy* shows, the anatomist—when he takes a close look—might well discover almost anything. Burton's Menippean anatomy (he refers often to Lucian's Menippus) reminds us that the tradition of Menippean satire—with its mixture of prose and verse, its digressions, its mingling of forms, its openness to anything new—preserves the original spirit of satire as farrago. And it preserves too the inquiring impulse behind Lucian's imaginary travels and dialogues: as Lucian says in *The Fisherman*, he has spent years seeking the True Lady Philosophy and finding only pretenders. That spirit and impulse are characteristic of the whole range of satiric forms, and we have perhaps overlooked or forgotten it by concentrating on those relatively few formal verse satires that aim at a higher degree of unity and closure.

Many of the terms we use to describe the formal properties of satiric discourse—*lanx satura, sermo,* farrago, dialogue, essay, anatomy—suggest that the form lends itself to open-ended inquiry rather than to steady progress toward conclusion, either predetermined or (as in scientific discourse) predicted. But commentators, by and large, have not proceeded to provide a theoretical frame. One exception is Bakhtin, whose work on the Menippean tradition points toward just such a theory of inquiry. In Bakhtin's view, a Menippean satire represents "the adventures of an *idea* or a *truth* in the world." Unlike Northrop Frye, Bakhtin sees not just the presentation of a vision of the world in terms of an "intellectual pattern" but the testing of that pattern. The Menippean satirist, he says, uses fantasy to create "extraordinary situations for the provoking and testing of a philosophical idea." "The menippea" does not embody a truth (even a conjectural truth); it tests it: "The menippea is a genre of 'ultimate questions'," questions asked but not definitively answered (Bakhtin, *Problems of Dostoevsky's Poetics*, pp. 114-15.). In Swift, for example, we might say (applying Bakhtin) that *A Tale of a Tub* explores and tests the idea that the world consists not of spirit but of matter; *Gulliver's Travels* provokes and tests the idea of a "rational animal," asking how such an animal would really behave.

We can also build on Bakhtin's claim that "the menippea" is characteristically dialogic or polyphonic rather than monologic, that it speaks with more than one voice. Sometimes the polyphony is literal, not only in dialogues but also in Swift's use of "Wotton" and "Bentley" as contributors of footnotes; sometimes it is figurative, as in the destabilization of the authority of the narrator's voice. We are actively encouraged *not* to trust (or to take literally) the speaker in Lucian's *True History* or in Swift's satires. If the satiric "truth" is not located in a reliable narrator, we as readers must seek it out.

Some weaker theoretical support for the notion that satire is often a form of inquiry comes from the rhetoricians. Modern rhetorical theories of satire focus narrowly on rhetoric as persuasion through the use of such devices as the rhetorician's ethos: a satirist who can convince the audience that he is a *vir bonus* has increased the chances that it will accept his attack on evil. But rhetoric has not always been conceived as persuasion. In scholarly disputation, rhetoric is a means for detecting error: the truth (or the heresy) will emerge only through rhetorical contest in which arguments and counterarguments are offered to challenge and discredit an opponent. *The Praise of Folly* is a mock-encomium constructed as a formal oration, a piece of epideictic rhetoric designed to engage and refute a reader's objections. Rochester's "Satyr against Mankind" is presented as a kind of disputation.[18]

More important evidence in support of an argument for a satiric rhetoric of inquiry is the change during the seventeenth century in the way rhetoric was conceived. In his massive study of logic and rhetoric in England from 1500 into the nineteenth century, W.S. Howell argues that there was a gradual rejection of the older rhetoric under pressure of modern epistemology and natural science. Howell distinguishes between an older rhetoric of "communication of what we already know" and a new rhetoric of "inquiry." The older was concerned with the transfer of knowledge, the newer with the discovery of it. Thus invention, under the old model, was the "process of establishing contact with the known, so that the storehouse of ancient wisdom would yield its treasures upon demand, and would bring the old truth to bear upon the new situation." Under the new model, invention means not just the refinding but "the process of discovering what [has] been hitherto unknown."[19] This is essentially Bakhtin's distinction between a "monologic" work, which "pretends to *possess* a *ready-made* truth," and a "dialogical" one, which involves "searching for truth" in the process of "dialogic interaction" (*Problems of Dostoevsky's Poetics*, p. 110).

Howell is concerned with treatises on rhetoric; he does not consider the uses to which rhetoric is put by satirists or other writers. But it is well known that traditional logic and rhetoric long formed the backbone of formal education in Europe and that as late as the 1680s the schoolboy Swift was being instructed by means of disputation. Still, it is not clear that we can assume a direct link between rhetorical theory and the practice of satire. And the newer rhetoric of inquiry was designed not simply to ask questons (like Bakhtin's menippea) but to answer them, to arrive at a conclusion. Moreover, the shift toward a rhetoric of inquiry in the seventeenth century cannot explain how satirists before that date—Donne, for example—might have conducted satiric inquiries. But it is reasonable to suspect a correlation between the change in rhetoric and the flourishing of satire in late seventeenth-century France and eighteenth-century England. At the very least, a rhetoric of inquiry would have encouraged those tendencies toward inquiry that have been part of satire from its beginnings.

The practice of satirists from Roman times suggests that they were often concerned to explore a moral issue rather than to settle it. Consider how many of Horace's *sermones*—or casual conversations—are cast as dialogues, particularly in his second book: *Satire* 2.1, is an exchange between Horace and Trebatius; 2.3, Horace and Damasippus; 2.4, Horace and Catius; 2.5, Ulysses and Tiresias; 2.7, Horace and Davus; 2.8, Horace and Fundanus. The first of these, an imagined conversation between Horace and a famous lawyer, concerns the risks the satirist incurs by speaking freely. Though the dialogue comes to an ostensible conclusion—since Horace's poems are *bona carmina* (good verses) rather than *mala carmina* (bad verses or libelous verses), he is safe from reprisal—the wit evades and does not answer the real question: is the satirist's freedom compromised by his fear of the state? To imagine that judges will always find the satirist blameless (*ipse integer*) and the objects of satire deserving of abuse (*opprobriis dignum*) is to beg the question. Perhaps it is only the protection of powerful friends—including above all Caesar himself, who intervenes as judge—that saves the satirist.

In other satires Horace proceeds by constructing a strongly moralized discourse but then "brackets" it by placing it in the mouth of an interlocutor. Instead of himself declaring the virtues of the simple life (*vivere parvo*) or demonstrating that the world is full of madmen who think themselves sane, Horace assigns the tasks to Ofellus and Damasippus. "These are not my words" (*nec meus hic sermo est*), Horace begins (*Sat.* 2.2) and maintains his distance from the plain philosopher, whose "wisdom" consists of moral commonplaces. The effect of the distancing device is to ask us not simply to accept the truth of Ofellus's words but to reconsider them in the context of the larger and more complicated moral (and political) world that Horace himself inhabits. Simplicity is a traditional Roman ideal (with recurrent appeal), but is every wise man ready to give up everything for a diet of bread and salt? Ofellus, like Horace, has apparently had his farm confiscated and its title assigned to one of Caesar's soldiers. He has thus made a virtue of necessity. His stoic response is to inure himself to misfortune (*adversis rebus*). This stirs our admiration, even if we (like Horace) are lucky enough to have been given a little Sabine farm where we can (if we choose) practice the principles of Ofellus in suitably moderated (or should we say compromised?) form. From Horace's point of view there is perhaps something a little too simple about Ofellus; but from Ofellus's angle (and he gets the last words) perhaps Horace's worldly success entails a sacrifice of moral purity. Read in this way, the poem uses Ofellus not to present a moral but to set a moral problem—a problem that is not neatly resolved.

Even when Horace is not engaged in dialogue with another voice, we can see his satires as an instance of what Shaftesbury later called "inward Colloquy." Shaftesbury uses the term to describe his own poetic practice, founded (he claims) on the example of Horace: thus in *Satire* 1.4 Horace debates a moral issue "with himself" (*ego mecum*), and in *Epistle* 2.2 he asks himself questions. Shaftesbury called this "self-examining Practice" the "Method of Soliloquy."[20]

Such a reading of Horace—and it might be extended to his other satires—yields a moralist but not a moralizer. It is characteristic of Horace to treat with some irony any spokesman who holds firmly to any narrow moral position. This accords well with the Horace of recent classicist criticism. Thus, William Anderson finds in Horace not "doctrinal pronouncements" but "ethical inquiries." Horace's intent as a moralist, he suggests, is that of Socrates, not to preach but to induce reflection. "The Socratic inquirer [uses] ordinary conversation to compel men to think about vital ethical questions" such as those asked in Epistle 1.18: Is virtue the product of nature or education? How do you remain friends with yourself? Particularly in Book 2, the "truth" is not presented to us; it "awaits our investigation" (*Essays on Roman Satire*, pp. 36, 42). That investigation, so Reuben Brower reminds us, is the real essence of Horatian "philosophy": for Horace, as Brower says, philosophy is "a part of a mature and civilized life, not a system or a doctrine, but the act of asking the important questions." The point is not in "finding the answers" but in "realizing at least partially [one's] capacity as a reflective animal."[21] What is more, such a view allows us to bring together two sides of Horace's traditional reputation that are usually imagined as antithetical: the stout dispenser of moral wisdom, and the temporizing court poet. Horace is not *simply* a moral philosopher (though commonly praised for being one) and not *simply* a kind of client of the court (though sometimes attacked as one). Moral principles are set into a context of life as it must be lived, where what we ought to do is conditioned and even limited by what we can afford to do and what we are permitted to do.

Juvenal is less inclined than Horace to moral inquiry. His typical manner is to declaim from a fixed moral position. But on some occasions he too uses satire to explore a moral problem—how should a just man react to a world of vice and evil?—or to question a truism. Thus *Satire* 13 implicitly challenges the comforting cliché that the wicked suffer from a guilty conscience. Juvenal begins with resolute reassurance to his addressee: "All deeds that set evil examples result in unpleasantness / For the doer himself." But this moral consolation is immediately abandoned, as Juvenal turns against the betrayed plaintiff. Treachery, he says, is so common that you should not be surprised: "One's indignation / Should never get overheated." He goes on cynically to urge resignation to a world of chiselers, embezzlers, and thieves. As recent critics have argued, Juvenal proceeds in a largely ironic spirit, deploying traditional moral topics in a mock-solemn manner, and probes the need for revenge. He finally returns to the theme of guilty conscience with which he began and luridly imagines the pains and fears that invade the wicked even when they sleep. Is Juvenal serious here, as Courtney thinks (*A Commentary on the Satires of Juvenal*, pp. 533-36), or still ironic? In any case he abandons his theme for the shrewd admission that criminals are soon "back to the same old tricks." But not to worry: sooner or later they'll get caught. You can take pleasure in "the bitter sentence / Your enemy's serving" and you'll agree that the gods aren't deaf. By the end Juvenal has considerably muddied the moral waters. Is it divine justice or human justice that rules? Does conscience in fact punish? Is it our sense of justice or our taste for vengeance ("insulting over vice," as Dryden called it) that is gratified?

The effect of the best Renaissance satire, if we look beyond the special case of the 1590s, is likewise not to reaffirm conventional moral wisdom but to conduct an open-ended moral inquiry. Consider three examples, one from the Menippean or Lucianic tradition and two from the tradition of formal verse satire: Thomas More's *Utopia* and Donne's third and fourth satires. In the case of More I need not argue for a *new* reading; the current critical consensus tacitly ignores conventional satiric theory and recognizes that *Utopia* is not simply an endorsement of the Utopian society or a condemnation of it. More created a uniform, self-contained, and perfectly regulated society against which we can measure modern Europe. Like Ofellus, his Hythloday (who has traveled to Utopia) offers a critique of the way of the world and a theoretical alternative to it. In several respects the Utopians' world seems ideal, but some of their customs appear designed to give any reader pause: a community of goods, an economy without money, capital penalties for consulting on public business outside the senate or assembly, warfare coldly conducted by means of expendable mercenaries. "More," the counselor and diplomat, finds the visionary Hythloday a little absurd, though he also finds some Utopian ways—which he carefully does not specify—worth imitating. Hythloday's "scholastic philosophy" is perhaps less effective in the world than that which "More" recommends: a kind of accommodation, accepting a part in the "drama in hand," attempting to "influence policy indirectly."[22] But "More" specifically notes that Hythloday isn't simply a naïf: he is "highly experienced in the ways of the world." And Hythloday is allowed to make the point that those who accommodate their principles to the way men live will have to throw out the teachings of Plato and of Christ himself. The implicit debate between the two points of view ends not with resolution but with differences clearly articulated. Readers do not enlist behind Hythloday's banner, or "More's" but are now endowed (or burdened) with a sense of disparity between the world they live in and a world organized along pure Christian principles. The purpose of the satire is not to force the reader to make a choice but, as Douglas Duncan puts it, "to enforce awareness of difficulty, . . . coaxing rigid minds out of their reliance on scholastic formulae, and persuading them to welcome complexity in a spirit of witty and liberal inquiry."[23]

When read in the context of a tradition of moral inquiry, Donne's fourth satire, "On the Court," is not simply an attack on the world of the court. The poem offers us a satirist who reports on the spectacle of pride and vain display he has beheld at court. Borrowing its situation from Horace's *Satire* 1.9, Donne has his satirist meet one of those "things" that dwell at court, one who flatters, gossips, and finally begs a crown. Presenting himself comically as discomfited victim, the satirist finally escapes and flees to the safety of his home. But the poem does not (as in Horace) end there. The satirist returns to court to behold another scene of folly. (Howard Erskine-Hill, the poem's best recent interpreter, notes that it is not clear whether the satirist actually returns to court or only revisits it in a Dantean "trance."[24] But the particularity of " 'Tis ten o-clock and past" [175] suggests to me that the satirist is physically present.) His apparently motiveless return—"I had no suit there; no new suit to show" [7])—turns our attention more firmly to the satirist himself and implicitly sets the poem's moral problem: Why does an honest and sensible man willingly descend into a den of corruption and flattery?

The poem offers no clear answer (the satirist himself does not seem to know), but it encourages our speculations. Clearly, a court (or any comparable seat of power and bounty) exerts some attraction. But it also sends a man of principle fleeing in indignation. To judge by his rededication to "mistress Truth" (163) and his summary judgment of "the sins of this place" (239), the satirist may find that going to court is a means of maintaining his moral bearings or reaffirming his standards and confirming the crucial difference between "them" and "me." To speak out is thus not only to serve Truth but to serve the satirist's own needs. (Donne implicitly supplies such a "personal" motive for any high-minded satirist.) But why does the satirist need to reaffirm his moral standards? Does he suspect some weakness? Donne perhaps suggests as much, for the satirist displays, from the beginning of the poem, a curious sense of "sin": "Well; I may now receive, and die; my sin / Indeed is great" (1-2). What is this "sin of going" (12)? A foolish wish to see?[25] A venial folly comically exaggerated into a sin so that it may be comically punished with God's "wrath's furious rod" (50)? (Pope comically presents himself, in similar fashion, as tortured victim in the *Epistle to Arbuthnot*.) Or is the reiteration of "sin" (cf. 138 and 161) a sign that the satirist suspects that he bears some affinity with the vice and folly he beholds?[26] To be at court makes him feel guilty: he feels himself "becoming traitor" (131); he shakes "like a spied spy" (237); he flees from the court as from a gaol (230). To some extent the poem hints at the dangers of the Renaissance court, where papists like Donne were under suspicion and subject to entrapment and arrest.[27] But it may hint more broadly at a kind of complicity with evil of which satirists have long been suspected. "We make *Satyrs*," Donne later wrote, "and we looke that the world should call that wit; when God knowes that this is in great part, self-guiltinesse."[28]

It is a little odd that theories of Renaissance satire have not been designed to accommodate Donne, by consensus the best of the English satirists in the 1590s. His third satire, "On Religion," perhaps the best of Renaissance verse satires in English, aims not to enforce the claims of a particular path or a particular church but likewise to urge the reader toward rigorous inquiry:

> On a huge hill,
> Cragged, and steep, Truth stands, and hee that will
> Reach her, about must, and about must goe;
> And what th'hills suddennes resists, winne so;
> Yet strive so, that before age, deaths twilight,
> Thy Soule rest, for none can work in that night. [79-84]

As one critic puts it, Donne's purpose is to "describe the state of mind that is necessary if the search is to have any chance for success." That state of mind is one of "uncertainty," fear, and courage to "seek the true religion" even though there is "no certain path."[29]

For the most part Donne rejects simple laughter or the satirist's

"spleene." His satirical portraits are not designed—like Swift's allegory in *A Tale of a Tub*—to expose the failings of one church or
other; they expose instead the weakness of the reasons men usually
offer for choosing a church (because it was the true church a thousand years ago, because it is plain, because it is the local faith) or for
not choosing one (because it is impossible to know the true one,
because they are all equally good). What the poem urges is a wise
doubt: "doubt wisely; in strange way / To stand inquiring right, is
not to stray; / To sleepe, or runne wrong, is" (77-79). But doubt for
Donne is not an end in itself, and he firmly rejects any Pyrrhonist
suspension of belief. The point, in the end, is to make a good choice.
Herein Donne differs from the skeptical Lucianic tradition and reminds us that, for all their commitment to inquiry, to the free play of
irony and the skeptical intellect, most satirists are at the same time
roused by a sense of urgency about moral ugliness or its idiocy, by
the sense that something must be done or at least said. It is the nagging pressure of a world of fools (or worse)—even if one doesn't
quite know what to do about it—that keeps satire from being a
bloodless moral exercise. When we move to the eighteenth century, it
is not difficult to find examples in which satire seems designed primarily to carry on an open-ended moral inquiry in the context of
some offensive or ridiculous conduct. As if in disregard of modern
theorists,[30] critics now regularly argue that great Augustan satire—
Gulliver's Travels,[31] *Rasselas*,[32] *Candide*[33]—leaves a reader with
more questions than answers. But, as in Donne, satiric inquiry is not
conducted as a detached Pyrrhonistic exercise in skepticism in which
one simply withholds assent. In Swift's satire, because as moral beings we must choose and act, uncertainty is a painful burden. In the
terms from the "Digression on Madness" in *A Tale of a Tub*, should
we prefer "Curiosity" or "Credulity"? The former is a "pretended
Philosophy which enters into the Depths of Things, and then comes
back gravely with Informations and Discoveries, that in the inside
they are good for nothing." It corresponds to that urge in the satirist
to unmask, to anatomize, to expose the unpalatable truth, or (with
Strephon) to penetrate the lady's dressing room and discover the
dirty secrets of the hoary deep. The latter, "Credulity," is "a more
peaceful Possession of the Mind" and is content to "converse about
the Surface." It corresponds to that need in us to avert our eyes, to
avoid dwelling on civilization's dirty secrets (lest such obsession disable us), to accept less than the ideal, and if necessary to stuff our
noses with "Rue, Lavender, or Tobacco-Leaves" (like Gulliver) to

block out the smell. Characteristically, Swift does not settle the debate but requires that we weigh both the gains and the costs of either "Credulity" or "Curiosity." You can not have it both ways; choose either one and you lose.

The inquiry into the merits (and dangers) of curiosity and credulity in the *Tale* is one instance of a recurrent inquiry (not just occasional misgivings) throughout Swift's work into the nature of satire itself, its morals and its efficacy. The *Tale*, in the midst of its own satire, wonders whether satire can be anything more than a bandying game in which everyone carries a racket about him to strike the ball from himself into the rest of the company, or (worse) the perverse gratification of our perverse need to be lashed. Other examples are readily found. The early "Meditation upon a Broom-stick" (1703), primarily a parody of Robert Boyle's moralizing "Meditations," works also as a satiric meditation on satire. It encourages us to ask whether the satirist is not a kind of broom, "destined to make other Things clean, and be nasty itself." Like the reforming satirist, the broomstick "sets up to be a universal Reformer and Correcter of Abuses; a Remover of Grievances." He sets about to "rake into every Slut's Corner of Nature, bringing hidden Corruptions to the Light." But to what effect? He "raiseth a mighty Dust where there was none before; sharing deeply all the while in the very same Pollutions he pretends to sweep away."[35]

In the late poem "To a Lady Who Desired the Author to Write Some Verses Upon Her in the Heroic Style" (1733), Swift makes of an occasion that lends itself to the satirist's conventional refusal—I cannot write heroic verse because I must write as a satirist—an occasion instead for asking searching questions about what a satirist can expect to accomplish. On the one hand, Swift presents himself as a man of raillery whose style is to laugh at folly. Though he claims to avoid "storming" (242), "hate" (152), and "spite" (154), he in fact does not conceal his "rage" (178) and his "passion" (192). He writes (so he claims) in Horace's belief that "Ridicule has greater power / To reform the world, than sour" (211-12). But "reform the world" should tip us off—especially if we remember *Gulliver's Travels*— that Swift overstates in order to scrutinize a hopeful cliché. He allows doubts about the satirist's power into the poem. "All the vices of a court / Do but serve to make me sport" (155-56). "Make me sport" seems to mean "make sport *for* me"—that is, serve as material for my satire and thus (as a secondary meaning) "make me laugh." If we remember that a common seventeenth-century meaning of "sport" is amorous dalliance,[36] we may even suspect that the satirist derives a kind of erotic pleasure from the scene. But in the end he seems impotent: does the "court" in fact "make sport *of* me," as a court jester is simultaneously wit and butt, or (more darkly) as the backsliding Jews "make sport of [God's] prophets" (1 Esdras 1:51)? In the back of Swift's mind may stand the ambiguous figure of Samson, both powerless and potent. Bound and led before the Philistines, in the great arena he "made them sport" and meditated his revenge (Judges 16:25).

In a telling passage, perhaps with Horace in mind,[37] Swift compares his little outriding vessel with the misguided ship of state:

> Safe within my little wherry,
> All their madness makes me merry:
> Like the watermen of Thames,
> I row by, and call them names.
> Like the ever-laughing sage,
> In a jest I spend my rage.
> (Though it must be understood,
> I would hang them if I could.) [173-80]

Removed from the madness, the satirist, like Horace in retreat, is "safe" from general disaster. But at what price? Though Swift directs us to a respectable antecedent, Democritus, the "ever-laughing sage," a less obvious allusion to Milton makes the "rage" seem harmless, quickly "spent" or discharged, used up. In *Paradise Lost* Belial imagines that in any further resistance to God, "the almighty victor" would "spend all his rage, / And that must end us" (2.144-45). By contrast, Swift's own rage ends nothing and displays not the potent victor but the impotent railer who would wreak real destruction "if he could."[38]

Pope is often cited as the clearest example of a satirist whose work can be explained by conventional moral-rhetorical theory. There is no doubt that he distinguishes between good and bad writers, between foolish and sensible women, between the generous person and the spendthrift, and assumes that we can recognize the difference. But perhaps we should see such moral distinctions as the ground rather than the figure of Pope's satire. Against that clearly articulated moral landscape he frequently poses puzzling cases: man is "the Glory, Jest, and *Riddle* of the World." Woman is "at best a Contradiction still," a "hard thing" to hit, a "true No-meaning puzzle." Belinda in *The Rape of the Lock*, vain and flirtatious, is at the same time a kind of awesome goddess. Clarissa is the woman of sense who speaks "the moral of the poem," but her motives, as many critics have suggested, are open to question; her principles are little more than reasoned opportunism.

Even when his subject is political vice, and he leaves no doubt in his reader's mind about the contrast between Walpole's henchmen and Virtue's friends, Pope nonetheless raises questions about the effectiveness of moral outrage. In the *Epilogue to the Satires* (1738), the satirist concludes "Dialogue I" with a heroic gesture—"Yet may this Verse (if such a Verse remain) / Show there was one who held it in disdain." But as some critics have suggested, the hero is perhaps half a fool, for what real difference can one man's disdain make? The poem serves to raise Horace's (and Sir Thomas More's) implicit inquiry: To what extent should we be prepared to make an accommodation with a less-than-ideal world (as Pope did in his own life) in order to have some pleasure in it and perhaps some influence on it, and to what extent should we stand apart in righteous isolation? When in the imitation of Horace's *Satire* 2.1 Pope asks his lawyer friend, Fortescue, what response he will receive if he writes "grave epistles" rather than "lawless satires," the answer suggests that the satirist may win his freedom at the cost of an audience. In Horace's Latin, Caesar intervenes as judge to save the day. Pope undercuts the satirist even more: the judges will laugh "and you're dismissed." Pope's pun points simultaneously at the satirist's triumph and his irrelevance. The charges against you are dismissed, but *you* are dismissed too—that is, nobody pays any attention to harmless moral "epistles." [39]

Pope's satires on bad writers likewise raise as many issues as they appear to settle conclusively. I have suggested elsewhere the crosscurrents in the *Dunciad*, some of the elements that make the poem more than simply an attack on dull writers. [40] Emrys Jones has argued that "what Pope as a deliberate satirist rejects as dully lifeless his imagination communicates as obscurely energetic." He tends to find Pope's conscious satire complicated by some nonsatirical "other point of view." [41] My point is that since critics now regularly find evidence in the greatest satire of a fascination with folly, imaginative excitement or ambivalence, we need to reexamine our narrow notions of satire. It is not that satire is *accompanied by* nonsatiric fascination; the satirist *as satirist* is both repelled and attracted by the world of folly.

Byron's satire has conventionally been described as a departure from Augustan practice, a bold venture into a new world where there are no longer any absolute moral standards by which to judge evil and folly. But in the light of the long tradition of satiric inquiry,

Byron may in fact have simply followed classical practice. Like other satirists before him, Byron could describe *Don Juan* as "a satire on abuses of the present state of Society," written with "a moral end."[42] But critics rightly find no authoritative satiric spokesman, "no clear norms, only relative judgments and unresolved ironies." Just as satirists from Horace to Pope conduct open-ended inquiries, so Byron presents what has been called an "unresolved debate on Stoicism," and an "unresolvable dialectic" between the romantic Juan and the cynical, worldly narrator.[43] Or as he put it at the end of the fragmentary Canto 17, "I leave the thing a problem, like all things."

Satire as Provocation

If the rhetoric of inquiry is "positive," an exploratory attempt to arrive at truth, the rhetoric of provocation is "negative," a critique of false understanding. In each case the satirist raises questions; in provocation, the question is designed to expose or demolish a foolish certainty. Here too current satirical theorists do not allow for the effects that practical critics have commonly observed, especially in the satire of Swift. It is now something of a commonplace that Swift attacks his reader's complacency, seeks to disorient or unsettle. But Swift is often regarded as exceptional. I would argue just the opposite—that Swift is the paradigmatic satirist. After surveying Augustan assumptions that satire reforms or corrects, P.K. Elkin argues that in modern eyes satire is "a catalytic agent rather than an arm of the law or an instrument of correction: its function is less to judge people for their follies and vices than to challenge their attitudes and opinions, to taunt and provoke them into doubt, and perhaps into disbelief" (*Augustan Defence of Satire*, p. 201). What is needed is broader recognition, on the base that Elkin provides, of the way in which great satire—and not just Swift's— often works to "taunt and provoke."

One obvious way in which satire provokes its reader is in its calculated "difficulty." Satire has traditionally been considered a form that cultivates obscurity, using elliptical syntax, cryptic or abrupt allusiveness, brevity, and roughness of rhythm. Renaissance translators, with the shaggy satyrs in mind, aimed at harshness of manner and even an obscurity of sense, especially in translations of Persius. But their excesses brought reactions from Dryden and others that Latin satire was not obscure to its original readers and, further, that there is no particular virtue in an obscurity that serves only to "puzzle the understanding" (*Works*, 4:54). Augustan translators strove to make Juvenal comprehensible without a vast apparatus of notes, and in their original satires they aimed at a fluent clarity that distinguishes their works from Donne's and those of the other Elizabethans. But <u>Swift, particularly in *Tale of a Tub*, works in an older tradition that requires the concentrated attention of its readers and challenges or exercises their wits.</u>

A more important kind of provocation than obscurity in satire often takes the form of paradox, an ancient rhetorical form and a favorite device of daring and witty writers from the early Renaissance through the seventeenth century and beyond.[44] The term has now lost some of its rhetorical and satirical potency. For us a paradox is an apparently self-contradictory statement that may or may not prove to be well founded. But as late as Johnson it carried within it the notion of a challenge to "received opinion," as para-dox challenges ortho-dox.[45] The challenge is not merely destructive: in John Dunton's words, a paradox serves to "rouze and awaken the Reason of Men asleep, into a *Thinking and Philosophical Temper*."[46] Paradox thus might serve as an opportunity for the display of rhetorical ingenuity, for advancing an unorthodox opinion or (more often) exposing vulgar errors, or for stimulating a thinking temper.

Some of the best-known satire in English makes use of paradox for just such purposes. Rochester's *Satire against Reason and Mankind*—the title itself is impudently paradoxical—asserts the paradox that it is better to be an animal than a man. It is largely directed against conventional praise of "blest, glorious man" and the dignity of human nature from philosopher and preacher alike. The poem unsettles not by convincing us of its truth but by relentlessly pressing us to abandon any easy faith in human "wisdom" and human "nature."[47] *Gulliver's Travels* derives much of its disturbing power from a similar paradox: it would be better (Gulliver asks us to believe) to be a Houyhnhnm—calm, always reasonable, all passion well contained— than a human being, even if it meant giving up most of modern Western culture. We may dismiss Gulliver as a madman, but we cannot dismiss his indictment, or wholly dismiss his dream of escaping from the tyrannical demands of the human body, its unruly appetites, and its restless imagination. Much of Swift's other satire works by means of paradox too. *A Modest Proposal* is only the most obvious case of a shockingly heterodox opinion designed to shatter the comfortable belief of administrators and reformers, merchants and projectors, English and Irish, that proper measures are surely being taken to solve the "problem" of Irish poverty. In other works, from *Tale of a Tub* to the "Dressing Room" poems, Swift makes artful defenses of the paradoxical idea that it is better not to look too deeply, as a way of exploding the cliché (especially beloved of satirists) that one must always strip away specious surfaces to get at the truth. On his showing, too much contemplation of "the truth" can disable the seeker. Bernard de Mandeville's contemporary *Fable of the Bees* (1714) exposes the Swiftian paradox that the "Public Benefits" of a thriving modern society are built upon a base of "Private Vices." It promptly succeeded in disturbing the calm of Shaftesburyan moral complacency.

But it is not just Augustan satire that takes the form of provocative paradox, provocative either because it seems absurd or because it challenges received opinion. We can briefly look at a series of examples from Lucian to Blake to note that paradox informs both formal verse and Menippean satire, from late antiquity through the Humanist revival, neoclassical France, and post-Augustan England.

Lucian is perhaps the best example in the long Western tradition of a satirist who sets out, in Paulson's words, "to discomfit his reader, shake up his cherished values, and disrupt his orthodoxy."[48] He wrote in Greek at a time (second century A.D.) when the great heritage of Greek myth and religion had ossified into forms that commanded little more than formal observance from the traditionally devout and aroused skepticism in the rest.[49] His "very End" in writing, according to one eighteenth-century view, was "to unmasque Characters, to disrobe counterfeit Virtue, and attack common Opinions and Pre-possessions."[50] Far enough removed from the great classical past of Golden Age Greece, Lucian could even look back at Homer with some detached amusement. He did not hesitate to "degrade the Hero's of Antiquity" in his witty parodic revisions of the old epic stories.

Lucian's ability to provoke a response in the orthodox is suggested by the persistent ambiguity of his reputation. On the one hand he exposed the ridiculous "Jugglers and Impostors" of a discredited paganism.[51] He was admired as a great wit—the "Father of true Humour,"[52] and even promoted to the ranks of the moralists.[53] But there remained a nagging sense that Lucian was dangerous. As a Renaissance commentator put it, Lucian was "one of the Pyrrhonists; who affirm nothing, but leave all doubtful issues unresolved."[54] Pyrrhonism could be tolerated so long as it limited itself to philosophy, but in Lucian it extended to scoffing and blasphemy, even atheism. Any satirist who made such fun of pagan religion might well be undermining the foundations of religion itself. Rapin's description of Lucian catches well the ambivalence in his admirers: "The Author is a pleasant *Buf-foon*, who makes Sport with the most serious Matters, and insolently plays upon whatever is great in the World: He is on all Occasions infinitely Witty; but this, I confess, is a kind of Foolish Character."[55] An unregulated spirit of ridicule arouses concern, not just for decorum—"*Lucian* laughs too loud, is often licentious, and sometimes course [*sic*] in his Raillery"[56]—but for the safety of whatever one holds dear. Even his genial skepticism is suspect, not so much a principled Pyrrhonism as a cynical opportunism. Dryden wrote that Lucian "doubted of every thing; weighed all opinions, and adhered to none of them; only used them as they served his occasion for the present dialogue, and perhaps rejected them in the next."[57] (By contrast, there is a "Spirit of Sincerity" in all that the severe moralist, Persius, says: "You may easily discern" says Dryden, "that he is in earnest and is perswaded of that Truth which he inculcates" [4:57].) One senses a kind of commonsense rationalism in Lucian's debunking, but his work remains an unusually pure example of satire detached from principles. It is worthwhile to remember how much he has been admired and imitated by a line of great European satirists—More, Erasmus, Rabelais, Jonson, Burton, Fontenelle, Swift, Voltaire, and Fielding—who embodied the Lucianic spirit in their ridicule of the complacent and the orthodox.

Juvenal is a provocative and paradoxical satirist in quite a different sense. In Anderson's influential reading, each of Juvenal's first five satires is organized around a central paradox. Anderson's best example is *Satire 3*—"Rome is no longer Rome." That is to say, the virtues that always characterized the idea of Rome are no longer to be found there, and with Umbricius leaving, the last true Roman has departed. Juvenal finds paradox useful, Anderson argues, because of its "capacity for indignation," its power to sustain emotional fervor and to organize a series of ringing denunciations into a single theme. We can add too that the paradox enables Juvenal to strike at the heart of false Roman pride, based as it is on the "received opinion" of the imperial city's greatness. *Satire 2* asserts that in Rome's decline, low-born satire is "the truly tragic genre"; *Satire 5*, that "a tolerant guest like Trebius is really a slave" (Anderson, *Essays on Roman Satire*, p. 251). Even *Satire 6* fits the pattern: Roman women are no longer women, for they have lost their womanhood.

Erasmus belongs in the Lucianic rather than the Juvenalian tradition, but for all his admiration of his model he turns the Lucianic tradition to much less skeptical ends. As Douglas Duncan has recently argued, Erasmus is no Pyrrhonist. His ultimate concern is not to withhold assent from dubious propositions, much less to turn all to ridicule. As a committed Christian moralist, Erasmus (like Donne) prepares the reader to make choices and to take actions that are no less necessary than they are difficult. Duncan finds in the satire of Erasmus and his contemporary, More, a seriocomic "art of teasing," a "process of educative testing, variously playful or hostile, whereby the moral intelligence of the public was to be trained by being subjected to attempts to undermine or confuse it." The Lucianic genres of the fantastic voyage (in the case of More) and the paradoxical encomium and the dialogue (in the case of Erasmus) provoke their audiences by challenging their received opinions (about folly, for example) and bombarding them with powerful arguments. But the ultimate purpose, as Duncan argues, is to "foster the critical spirit." The *Colloquies* of Erasmus "raise more questions than they answer, rarely if ever leave the feeling that a subject has been settled, and constantly undermine any kind of simplistic or dogmatic certainty."[58] Paradox serves not so much to demolish old pieties as to exercise readers' wits, much as scholastic disputation was designed to enable disputants to construct powerful arguments and to identify weakness or fallacy in their opponents. Later admirers of the *Praise of Folly*, who saw only ridicule of the abuses in the Roman church or of folly itself, deflected the real force of Erasmus's satire by shifting the burden to other readers' shoulders.[59] By the same token, modern admirers who find in Erasmus a radically skeptical spirit forget the educative mission of the Renaissance Humanists. Inquiry for its own sake has no value, as it perhaps does in Swift, a more skeptical churchman. Erasmus seeks not to leave his reader in suspended judgment, in a state of musing doubt and irresolution, but (like Donne) to urge him toward a better choosing.[60]

A number of Fontenelle's *Dialogues of the Dead* (1683) center explicitly on the challenge to conventional judgments. In the tradition of witty and candid dialogue between speakers who no longer have any motive to withhold or evade, they are, as a recent editor describes them, "comprehensively ironic," "sophisticated conversations on morals and manners, which, ending in unconventional 'turns,' would unsettle received opinions, promote skepticism, and entertain the enlightened."[61] Fontenelle's titles remind us that he wrote at a time when satirists as well as skeptical moralists questioned the value of reason: "That People will deceive themselves as much as they have Occasion for"; "That Reason is chagrin, and not always useful"; "Whether one can be happy by Reason."[62] The dialogue "On Prejudices," between Strato and Raphael Urbino, asks impudently whether we should be guided by reason or prejudice. Raphael argues for retaining the prejudices of "custom" and "understanding." Strato argues—conventionally and naively—that men should follow reason and "rid themselves of all Prejudices." Raphael concedes a little ground but concludes that "together with that small Share of Reason which Men possess, they must have their *Quantum* of Prejudices too, as usual. Prejudices are the Supplement of Reason" (pp. 122-23). Fontenelle's English translator, John Hughes, comments that the dialogue serves to "expose the Imperfections of Human Reason, and the fantastical Condition of Life, both which make *Prejudices*, in a manner, necessary" (p. xxxvii). In a related dialogue, Seneca argues that reason "has the sole Right to govern Mankind," but Marot gets the last word when he says that men in the world in fact do not value reason (p. 99). In the typical dialogue Fontenelle seeks to undermine conventional opinion, especially when it is held with complacence or blithe assurance. We routinely believe that men should live the life of reason and should free themselves from all deception, but Artemisia and Raymond Lully come to see that it is perhaps better to be deceived in thinking we can attain some end—she to maintain conjugal fidelity, he to find the philosopher's stone—else we would never aspire.[63] The witty rebuke to human pride and the ironic acknowledgment of weakness recall Fontenelle's great contemporary, the *moraliste* La Rochefoucauld, whose provocative *Maximes* scandalized the orthodox and attracted the attention of satirists such as Swift.[64]

Lyttelton's *Dialogues of the Dead* were published in 1760 (and had gone through a fourth edition by 1765); Lucian's works, which had been published in a collaborative translation in 1710-11 (with a "Life" by Dryden) were again translated into English in 1780. The dates are suggestive, because within ten years Blake had written the mock-symposium *An Island in the Moon* (1784)[65] and was at work on his *Marriage of Heaven and Hell* (published in 1793), a Lucianic satire that drew on the conventions of the fantastic voyage and the dialogue of the dead.[66] Although Blakeans have seen the *Marriage* as prophetic satire, they have by and large done little more than label it a "Menippean satire."[67] They have not recognized that the satire works largely by means of provocative paradox and have furthermore mistaken Blake's wit for revisionist seriousness.

The *Marriage*, commonly read as an attack on priest-ridden conventional Christianity and its "Bible of Hell," is seen as the herald of Blake's own later prophetic poems, in which a new religious "system" is created. To be sure, Blake's satire is directed against the "System" of "Priesthood" that abstracts the world of the "sensible" and represses desire. But his means to this end is not to substitute his own principles of "sensual enjoyment." Rather he contrives a set of provocative "Proverbs of Hell" that challenge the received wisdom, secular and spiritual, of conventional (and in Blake's view rigidified) Christianity. And he offers a "contrary" to the traditional (Miltonic) account of Satan's fall. Some readers (especially Miltonists) have hastily assumed that we should take the words in the poem as representing Blake's own views, especially in the famous remark that Milton was "of the Devil's party without knowing it." But Blake clearly assigns the remark to "the Voice of the Devil," who after all is presented as a partisan witness, one of the two opposing "contraries" or "parties" in the contention between Heaven and Hell. "Without contraries," as Blake says, "there is no progression." But Blake does not expect us to take one of the two contraries as the new gospel. The Devil gives an account of the restraint of Desire by the usurper Reason (or Messiah, in Milton's account). Yet Blake does not endorse any simplistic rejection of Reason. As he says earlier, "Reason and Energy . . . are necessary to Human existence." The function of the Devil's account is not to supplant Milton's but to challenge the complacency of conventional religion.

In like fashion, the "Proverbs of Hell" are deliberately provocative. Often quoted out of context to suggest that they embody Blake's revisionism ("Exuberance is Beauty"; "One thought fills immensity"; "The tigers of wrath are wiser than the horses of instruction"), they are in fact a mixed bag. Some are designed to unsettle conventional morality: "The road of excess leads to the palace of wisdom"; "Drive your cart and your plough over the bones of the dead." But a few are quite consonant with Christian meekness: "The most sublime act is to set another before you"; "The thankful receiver bears a plentiful harvest." Many are original variants of traditional (and rather tame) proverbial wisdom: "The busy bee has no time for sorrow"; "The best wine is the oldest, the best water is the newest." Some are gnomic or emblematic: "The cistern contains: the fountain overflows." Some are satiric, like La Rochefoucauld's maxims: "Prudence is a rich, ugly old maid courted by Incapacity." Taken as a group, they do not present a "new religion," nor do they endorse an ethic of "energy" or sexual fulfillment. Instead, they keep the reader off balance with their combination of unexceptional truisms and shocking inversions of conventional morality. Even their apparent disorder (Bloom calls it a "curious disarrangement") [68] prevents the reader from reducing them to a code.

This quality has been recognized by Blake critics. Bloom notes that the proverbs "break down orthodox categories of thought and morality." [69] Lawrence Lipking puts it more sharply: the proverbs "sting and taunt the complacent mind." [70] But both make Blake seem too intense or solemn. If we look at *The Marriage of Heaven and Hell* as a Menippean or Lucianic satire, we should expect some levity and wit. [71] The work is much funnier than most commentators have acknowledged. Blake's "Memorable Fancies," in which he dines with Isaiah and Ezekiel and walks "among the fires of Hell," might seem the reports of a madman or a visionary, or merely a parody of Swedenborg's "Memorable Relations." But if we remember the Lucianic visits to the underworld, Blake's "Fancies" are dryly witty variations on an old satiric theme. Blake reports in a deadpan tone, underplaying the strangeness of his fantastic voyage, that he talks with his "friend the angel," or that he "leap'd into the void between Saturn and the fixed stars." His interlocutor waxes wroth and outdoes any merely Miltonic angel: Raphael in *Paradise Lost*, 8.619, turns "rosy red"; Blake's angel becomes "almost blue, but mastering himself he grew yellow, and at last white, pink, and smiling"—as Blake must have been when he imagined the scene. Sometimes Blake sounds oddly like Swift in *A Tale of a Tub*, not only in his maggoty-headed digressive manner or his anatomy of mental and religious perversion and tyranny but in his wild metaphorical inventiveness and the unsettling combination of confidential intimacy and high-handedness with which he affronts the reader. In Blake's final "Note"—a kind of satiric envoi— he reports in matter-of-fact manner that an angel consumed in fire, transformed into Elijah, and now turned into a Devil "is my particular friend: we often read the Bible together in its infernal or diabolical sense which the world shall have if they behave well." Blake here apes the cozy tone of the morally superior parent but suddenly drops the coziness: "I have also: The Bible of Hell: which the world shall have whether they will or no." This is the voice not of a visionary but of a teasing author like Swift's impersonated Hack, who promises to deliver dark mysteries and alternately flatters his reader and drags him by the nose.

It is commonly recognized that Blake is a satirist, but satire is not just a matter of attack on what Bloom calls "intellectual error and spiritual deception." The satire in Blake's *Marriage* lies primarily in its continuous irony (a quality Bloom recognizes but does not see as satiric). If we consider the rhetoric of provocation and paradox, then Blake stands in a long line of satirists—from Lucian through Eras-

mus, Fontenelle, Swift, and others—whose satire works not by drawing a clear line between "Good" and "Evil" but by teasing readers
with the play of "contraries." His work is designed, so he wrote to a
friend, not to make matters "too Explicit." A calculated obscurity is
better for Blake's purposes, since it "rouzes the faculties to act."[72]

Satirists can provoke by challenging received opinion; they can
also provoke by holding up to scrutiny our idealized images of ourselves—forcing us to admit that such images are forever out of reach,
unavailable to us, or even the last things we would really want to
attain. This is often the function of the "positives" in major satire
from Juvenal to Swift. Juvenal characteristically calls up a virtuous
Republican past when men were courageous and civic-minded and
women were chaste. Against such a world and its standards, Rome
under Nero and Domitian is the sinkhole of the Mediterranean. But
Juvenal and his readers know all too well that the Roman Republic is
long past; neither its political structures nor its cultural fabric will ever
be restored. To remember the past is not to be guided by it or to hope
to bring it back but to rub Roman noses in a dirty imperial present
from which they cannot escape. The inaccessibility of the virtuous
past is clear, and not just because the clock cannot be turned back.
Even Juvenal's method of remembering that past is usually uncritical
nostalgia.[73] As Courtney remarks, Juvenal does not base his comparisons between present and past on "sustained, rational analysis"; instead, what he does is "express and appeal to an attitude of mind
rooted in certain prejudices" (A Commentary on the Satires of Juvenal, p. 30). He arouses prejudices and old cultural memories but gives
them no outlet. Even the satirist himself is trapped in a world where
ancestral virtue is dangerous. Lucilius may have spoken out in his day,
but after firing himself up with the Lucilian example at the end of
Satire 1, Juvenal consciously and ironically turns cautious: nowadays
it is risky to point the finger at anybody with influence, so the heroic
satirist will have to content himself with attacking those who are safely dead and buried.

Horace in his sermones avoids the Juvenalian note of righteous
anger, but in the later Epodes, still satiric in character, he sounds a
dire warning to a divided Rome and pretends to offer a solution that
works, only to leave the reader (as in Juvenal) imprisoned in the
present. The sixteenth epode laments the ruins wrought by civil war,
brought on by an "impious generation, of stock accurst" (impia per-
demus devoti sanguinis aetas).[74] The only way to escape the utter
destruction of the city is for the entire state (omnis civitas) to flee,

take ship, and seek the Fortunate Fields and the Islands of the Blest. There the earth will bear unbidden, and as in the Golden Age we will live righteous and innocent. Horace dallies with the dram of escape but leaves us with no doubt that it is only a dream. The poem concludes with a reminder that we live not in a golden age but in an age hardened by bronze and then iron. Any flight (*fuga*, the poem's last word) can only be in imagination.

Swift's satire works in similar fashion. The "positives" do not serve as hortatory models or as blueprints for social engineers; instead, they teasingly hold up an ideal that cannot be attained. The *Argument . . . [against] the Abolishing of Christianity* (1710) distinguishes between a nominal and a true Christianity, between the demeaning compromises practiced in accommodation with the world and the original spirit of the apostles. The satire leads us at first to measure a degraded, institutionalized faith against a pure origin. But it then turns on us, mocking any notion that we might be able, or might wish, to return to the faith of our forefathers: nobody wants to abolish our merely nominal faith if "the Bank and *East-India* Stock may fall, at least, One *per Cent*." This is merely the final flick of the smiling satirist's whip. The real sting comes earlier, when Swift disposes of any naive belief that we can reinfuse the present world with true religion. When we first read these words, we take them to be ironic. When we return to them, we find them only too "straight":

> To offer at the Restoring of that [i.e., "*real* Christianity"], would indeed be a wild Project; it would be to dig up Foundations; to destroy at one Blow *all* the Wit, and *half* the Learning of the Kingdom; to break the entire Frame and Constitution of Things; to ruin Trade, extinguish Arts and Sciences with the Professors of them; in short, to turn our Courts, Exchanges and Shops into Desarts: and would be full as absurd as the Proposal of *Horace*, where he advises the *Romans*, all in a Body, to leave their City, and seek a new Seat in some remote Part of the World, by Way of Cure for the Corruption of their Manners.

In his later satire Swift teases his gentle reader with other dreams of possibility. In Lilliput, Gulliver finds a utopian legal system where fraud is a greater crime than theft and ingratitude is a capital crime. But that system is then displaced: "In relating these and the following Laws, I would only be understood to mean the original Institutions, and not the most scandalous Corruptions into which these People are fallen by the degenerate Nature of Man" (chap. 6). Such laws are displaced too by their very excess: ingratitude a *capital* crime? The

effect of this double displacement is not to make the Lilliputian original available as a human possibility but to challenge European legal
systems—exposing their inequities, procedural snarls, and protection
of the powerful—without offering any real alternative.[75] Swift follows
a similarly provocative satiric path in describing education in Lilliput
and the government of Brobdingnag, where writing a commentary on
a law is punished by death and (despite enlightened principles) the
country has been plagued by civil war as recently as two generations
earlier.

   Gulliver's Travels concludes with one final attempted escape—
from the human condition itself. Gulliver's last voyage brings a vision
of a world governed by reason, where desire is easily moderated, appetites are easily satisfied, language has no word for a "lie," and the
inhabitants are "the perfection of nature." One can resolve the debate
about the Houyhnhnms—are they cold and inhuman, or are they
Swift's ideal?—by claiming that both sides are right: the Houyhnhnms at once embody our own highest conception of ourselves and
yet are forever beyond the human reach. Almost everything that characterizes Houhyhnhnm life corresponds to the oldest and deepest
standards of Swift's Christian culture: a life of simplicity, universal
brotherhood, calm preparation for death, even (if we remember the
primitive Christians) community of property. The most painful satiric
point is that the Houyhnhnms serve as the face we are looking for in
the mirror. We think of ourselves as rational animals, predisposed to
virtue (especially if we believe in a moral sense), capable of keeping
our wants and our passions in check. But when we look in the mirror
we see only a human face, or a Yahoo. What Swift has done is to
embody our highest image of ourselves and show us that we are not it.
All the more effective, then, to put that image in the body of an imaginary horse. A gulf forever comes between human nature and the
Houyhnhnms. As John Traugott has noted, the point about human
nature is that by definition you can't change it. You cannot go back to
that mythical moment when two Yahoos appeared on the shores of
Houyhnhnmland and began to degenerate.[76] The ultimate provocation—what Swift calls vexing the world—is to make readers look in
the mirror and see that they are not and can never be what they claim
to be. Satire cannot mend them; it can only hope to make them *see*.
Swift is here less idiosyncratic than characteristic of major satirists. As
Elkin rightly says, the classics of the form, which "deal with basic
features of human nature and society," "can never bring about any
inprovement, simply because neither human nature nor society is ca-

pable of fundamental change." What satire can do is to make people "at least *see* the world's enormities and absurdities." [77] But the task is a formidable one, given the fatal human tendency to avert our eyes from whatever is disagreeable to contemplate. As Byron wrote, "All gentle readers have the gift / Of closing 'gainst the light their orbs of vision" (*Don Juan* 6.88.4-5). All his satire could hope to do is "to show things really as they are, / Not as they ought to be" (12.40.1-2). This is what his readers will call "immoral." Byron's act of telling the uncomfortable truth is in fact the real "moral end" of his satires: "Till we see what's what in fact, we're far / From much improvement with that virtuous plough / Which skims the surface, leaving scarce a scar / Upon the black loam manured by Vice" (12.40.4-7).

Byron in fact probably had no more real expectation than Swift did that satire can ever "mend" the world. Byron's end was more modest: to remind his English readers that "You are *not* a moral people" (11.87.7). The "ought to be" that satire sometimes presents may be purely imaginary. Swift's Houyhnhnmland is a utopia, and utopias are by definition to be found "nowhere." For some writers, utopian visions can provide a "pattern set up in the heavens" which, like Plato's *Republic*, can serve to guide those in the world below. Satirists typically make darker use of utopias, often by exaggerating them or making them seem "merely ideal," not so much to serve as a star for earthly mariners as to enforce a sense of the great distance between earth and heaven. Houyhnhnmland is also a kind of Edenic myth. And though Western culture has long cherished the dream that it is possible to return to Eden or to rebuild a paradise,[78] satirists are typically suspicious of all Edenic or Golden Age myths. Bishop Hall's satire "On the Decline from the Golden Age" (3.1) is an ironic set piece on a traditional topic. Hall smiles as he praises primitive delights. Dryden in *Absalom and Achitophel* laughs at the notion of earlier "pious times," before the modern world of politics and institutionalized religion. Such an imaginary era is just a libertine fantasy created for the purpose of excusing David's philandering. Likewise the "Sen'es of new time" proclaimed at the end of the poem is no Virgilian golden age restored. If David has been restored "once more," his recovery is not definitive: he may have to be restored again, and again, for his people, as we recall, "once in twenty Years, . . . / By natural Instinct . . . change their Lord" (*Works*, 4:12,36). Pope so far subverts the idea that we have declined from a golden age—an age that might be used to measure our fall and direct our recovery—that he makes Chaos the great original of the mind in *The Dunciad*.[79] Man's native mental state is not clarity but sluggishness; the poem records not a fall but an ironic restoration of an "anarchy," the original Kingdom of Dulness. Gulliver discovers in the land of the magicians that even the classical world of Greece and Rome was corrupt. By robbing us of an image of pristine order, satirists leave us with the inescapable burden of the present.

Unstable Irony

Thus far I have argued that satirists characteristically regard their targets with an attitude more complex than simple rejection, and further that we misrepresent satire if we assume that the satirist sets out to arrive at a predetermined endpoint—convincing the reader that X or Y is vicious or foolish. We need to supplement the old rhetoric of persuasion with a rhetoric of inquiry and provocation: not just conventional assertions (Cibber is an immoral man and a bad poet) but questions (why do we find Cibber both offensive and beguiling? is "dulness" really threatening, or is it finally harmless and self-defeating?). The notion of a rhetoric of inquiry and provocation assumes that satirists—though they may not have answers to all their questions—exercise an overall control over the process of exploration, leading us to raise questions we must then ponder. Sometimes, however, we may suspect that satire gets out of hand, that the satirist has raised so many questions as to lose control of the inquiry. It can be difficult for readers to judge whether the satirist is leading them along, or is only pretending to have lost the way (in order to confuse the readers), or has in fact lost the way (and wishes to share that confusion with the readers—or to conceal it). This can be a matter of divided feelings on the satirist's part. Does Pope fully acknowledge and thus contain his fascination with the dunces, or does he unconsciously reveal ambivalence? Does Swift deliberately subvert Martin, the spokesman for his own Anglican church in *Tale of a Tub*? Or it can be the consequence of intimacy, as the satirist conceives a kind of fondness for the victim. Dryden conceded that "it has been the common fault of all satirists, to make vice too aimiable, while they expose it."[80]

In other cases, we may sense that satire, once set in motion, acquires a momentum of its own. Once Swift decides that in the clothes philosophy Man is a "*Microcoat*," where the "soul was the outward, and the Body the inward Cloathing," the very rules of the game invite ironic reversals and satiric strokes. The brilliant passage on

conscience—it is "a *Pair of Breeches*, which, tho' a Cover for Lewd-
ness as well as Nastiness, is easily slipt down for the Service of
both"—seems not so much part of Swift's larger purpose (laying out
the clothes philosophy) as the lucky stroke prompted by the idea that
inner is outer. The satire almost writes itself.[81] Rawson has noted the
"tear-away energies of the fiction world" that Swift creates and the
"strange, unpredictable autonomy of Swift's irony, which sometimes
forgets its positive standards and even momentarily ignores its official enemies."[82] We sometimes suspect that the satirist-as-moralist is
supplanted or overtaken by the satirist-as-artist. More simply, the
satirist may simply be unable to resist a joke—as when Swift takes a
gratuitous slap in *Gulliver's Travels* at the slanting handwriting of
"the ladies in England."[83] Dryden seems to have been aware of a
strong and not completely controlled satiric streak in himself; he
attributes to satire a kind of autonomy and even willfulness: "Satire
will have room, where e're I write" (*Works*, 4:464)

These reflections may serve to introduce the larger problem of
satiric irony and the satirist's control of it. In traditional theory, the
satirist makes use of irony as a weapon, and that irony is, in Wayne
Booth's terms, "stable," so that we can arrive at a single fixed meaning. But is this so? Does satiric irony not in fact often display insta-
bility? In his *Rhetoric of Irony* (1974) Booth argues, against the
grain of much modern commentary, that the use of irony does not
plunge us into a sea of doubt and indeterminacy. There is, he insists,
"an astonishing residue of unquestioned agreement" in our inter-
pretations of irony (133). He seeks to recover an area he calls "stable
irony," in which readers are called upon to reconstruct an author's
true meaning—and claims that they are able to do so. Not all irony
is satiric, but when it is, Booth argues, it is typically "stable." We
determine, through a procedure that Booth breaks down into four
steps, that the satirist does not mean *x* (what he appears to say), but
in fact means *y*. Booth provides a useful corrective to the unex-
amined belief that all irony is unstable, evasive, tending ultimately
toward what Hegel and Kierkegaard called "infinite absolute nega-
tivity."[84] But there is reason to believe that he has simplified the
problem of understanding satiric irony. More often than he acknowledges, I would argue, satiric irony is in his terms "unstable," so that
we are unable to reconstruct the author's meaning with confidence.

To begin with, irony should be understood not simply as a binary
switch, either "on" or "off," but more like a rheostat, a rhetorical
dimmer switch that allows for a continuous range of effects between

"I almost mean what I say" and "I mean the opposite of what I say." Booth is probably right to argue that we are usually able to determine *whether or not* an author is being ironic. The difficulty arises, or course, when we try to determine the *degree* of irony: To what degree has the entire surface meaning been subverted? Does any part of it survive intact? In Horace's famous *Epode* 2 ("Beatus ille qui procul negotiis"), how much of our sense of the pleasures of country life survives when we discover that Horace has put the praise of rural simplicity in the mouth of the usurer Alfius, who gets out of the financial markets—only to reinvest? We reduce the poem if we focus on the famous "beatus ille . . ." and not equally on the ironic coda. But we also reduce it if we see the poem as primarily the revelation of hypocrisy. Presumably Horace does not mean us to repudiate the praise of rural life as mere cliché and self-deception, as a *fully* ironic reading would suggest; presumably he wants us to acknowledge that the rural idyll has become a kind of generic dream that many city dwellers indulge and never act upon. But it is difficult to decide how far the irony extends: is the dream mere pastoral prettifying, or are we finally unwilling (or unable) to give up the pleasures and pains of the city? Do the dreamers even know?

Irony is more problematic in some satiric forms than in others. The ironic praise in mock-encomium such as *The Praise of Folly* can rarely be *simply* inverted in order to arrive at true meaning. Mock-epic does not operate in a mechanical way, holding modern folly up to an unquestioned epic standard. It sets up a triangulated interplay between classical original, modern analogy (whether trivial as in *The Rape of the Lock* or crude as in *MacFlecknoe*), and what Pope calls a "new world," a fantastic Alice-in-Wonderland scene as far removed from the real Hampton Court or Grub Street as it is from Homeric Greece.[85] Each world makes a kind of claim on us—as good, true, or beautiful—and calls the others into question. Particularly when a satirist seems to speak to us through an assumed mask, it is difficult to apply any set of rules like Booth's to determine when and to what extent the author "agrees with" the apparent speaker—whether that speaker is Moll Flanders, the "modern" writer in *Tale of a Tub*, Lemuel Gulliver, or the Modest Proposer. Booth in fact sees *A Modest Proposal* as a particularly clear example of stable irony, where we have no doubt about how to interpret. He concedes that the tract displays a "shifting surface" and notes that we feel under "intense pressure" as we hear now an angry but rational voice and then a "mad, almost cheerfully 'rational' voice." But in his view the proposer is nonetheless exposed, and when we come to the apparently rejected "other Expedients," we know we have discovered Swift's real proposal for solving Ireland's economic problems, "absolute Swift, without a touch of irony."[86]

But reading Swift we should perhaps hesitate to say that we ever discover anything "absolute." If we take into account that in the years before he published *A Modest Proposal* Swift had worn himself out with unheeded practical advice (such as his *Proposal for the Universal Use of Irish Manufacture*); if we know that Swift (hardly a sentimental or modern liberal) was not opposed to hard measures for Irish beggars (see his *Proposal for Giving Badges to the Beggars*); and if we remember that in his letters he often looked on the Irish poor with both compassion and contempt, then we may be forced into a reading quite different from Booth's.[87] If the existing conditions in Ireland are in fact "morally worse" than cannibalism (as Booth concedes), then perhaps the speaker is *not* ironic after all. Perhaps he gives voice to Swift's anger and despair. In such a world Swift thinks the unthinkable: maybe it *is* better to kill them young. The "other Expedients," in this reading, do not represent "absolute Swift." Instead, they represent an impossibility: "what you must do—of course, I know you won't do it."

Booth's rhetoric of irony does not admit such satiric complexity. More often than he allows, satirists make use of the sort of unstable irony that (in his terms) lets us know what the satirist "deplores" but not what he endorses, and finally gives us "no secure ground to stand on" (248). In his rhetoric, furthermore, there is inadequate room for ambivalence or for the simultaneous assertion of opposite opinions. It is telling that Booth does not attempt to comment on *A Tale of a Tub*, though he does briefly note its "manifold reversals from irony to straight invective through many shades in between" (49).[88] Much satire, I have argued, involves what Booth calls unstable irony: though we assume an author in control of the irony, we cannot reconstruct that author's precise meaning with any confidence. In some cases we have reason to think that even satirists cannot contain the irony they have let loose.

One traditional problem for the satirist, even when not being ironical, is to limit the extent or implications of the attack. When the satirist attacks fanatical preachers in *Tale of a Tub*, some readers will think he attacks the clergy. If the Reformation is introduced into a ridiculous allegory, some readers think it is "burlesquing *Religion*," as William Wotton complained: "He that diverts himself too much at the Expense of the *Roman Catholics* and the *Protestant Dissent-ers*, may lose his own Religion e're he is aware of it, at least the Power of it in his Heart."[89] When Juvenal attacks lascivious women, even sympathetic readers such as Dryden think he ungallantly at-tacks the entire sex. Satirists have commonly defended themselves against these complaints, and we have usually assumed that they have been unjustly accused. But the recurrence of the complaints is perhaps more than a sign of the traditional hostility to satire. Is it always easy to distinguish the cautionary example, singled out of the herd for its abuses of the norm, from the representative particular? As Frye puts it, "Once a hypocrite who sounds exactly like a good man is sufficiently blackened, the good man himself may begin to seem a little dingier than he was."[90] Satirists who do not take care to make their intentions explicit or to provide—as Pope often does—contrasting examples of virtue perhaps cannot blame their readers for assuming that the satire extends beyond the specified target to include a wider range of similar figures.

Sometimes the intended attack is qualified in another way: in-stead of spreading, it turns into a more benign amusement. The sati-rist discovers that his preexisting animus—against the Puritans, say, or a literary rival, or a rabble of dunces—is modified by other emo-tional or aesthetic responses. Samuel Butler, as has been suggested, comes to take some pleasure in his Hudibras. A nineteenth-century editor imagined that Butler begins with "a little spite" at Hudibras "as the representative of his class" but later displays a "lurking fond-ness" for his hero and by the end has "fairly laughed himself into good humour" with him.[91] Dryden, so we have plenty of evidence to believe, held his rival Shadwell in some contempt, but critics have long recognized something "genial" in his portrait of Shadwell in *MacFlecknoe*. Perhaps as Shadwell is converted into "Sh—," Dryden begins to think of him aesthetically and can imagine the delights of his absurdist "realms of nonsense." And Pope, as Emrys Jones sug-gests, makes his dunces seem like boisterous children in whom we can take a perverse pleasure.[92] Pope is not the only satirist who be-comes fascinated with the folly or evil he sets out to decry, fascinated to imagine and explore it, not simply to deplore it.[93] Though we usually presume satire to be premeditated and univocal in its judg-ments, it is rather like other genres—Robert Browning's dramatic monologues or Samuel Richardson's novel *Clarissa*—in that the "vil-lain" proves to be fascinating.

Finally, irony itself is not a wholly manageable power. Booth limits himself to "intended ironies," setting aside "unconscious ironies," and assumes that even unstable ironies—whether overt or covert, local or infinite—are under the control of their users. But some theorists, looking back to Kierkegaard, would argue that irony is inherently ungovernable. It takes the form of an evasion, a refusal to commit, a negation rather than an assertion.[94] Thus we may find it virtually impossible to know where irony stops. The ironist may find it impossible to draw a line that says "there, but no further." Irony tends toward an infinite regress. Booth himself acknowledges that the "ironic temper" can "dissolve everything, in an infinite chain of solvents."[95] and Robert Elliott has noted that "major satire" often spreads unchecked: "Let the conscious intent of the artist be what it will, the local attack cannot be contained: the ironic language eats its way in implication through the most powerful-seeming structures."[96]

Can we go on to speculate that unless it is closely harnessed, the energy released in satire tends to run away with the satirist? Does satire have a kind of dynamic of its own? Does it in some sense write itself ("Fools rush into my Head, and so I write"), invite the satirist to provide more and more examples of folly or to allow the implications to spread wider and wider? Satire encourages the satirist to look "squint-eyed" at the world (as Marston suggests),[97] to exaggerate or to exceed the limits of "absolute truth." "'Tis the Genius of Satire," says a traslator of Fontenelle's *Dialogues*, "often to say things for which there is some Occasion given, and yet which cannot be admitted for absolute Truths."[98] Indeed, one suspects that many satirists privately agreed with Rochester, who confessed without shame that he "mixed Lies with Truth" in his satires: "The lies in these Libels came often in as Ornaments that could not be spared without spoiling the beauty of the *Poem*."[99] To some extent, such squinting and lying are the result of deliberate choice; but as the satire gains momentum, one suspects that the satire draws the satirist on, soliciting a libelous imagination to make claims and charges not part of any premeditated plan. As Frye wrote of the satiric treatment of the human body in *Gulliver's Travels*, Swift "is simply following where his satiric genius leads him." Readers are usually ready to follow, "without raising any questions about his 'purpose.'"[100]

Sometimes one may suspect the satirist of consciously giving in to the attractions of irony in order to let the satiric inquiry go where it will. Perhaps the inquiry is all, the end in itself. In such limiting cases, the process of inquiry is truly open-ended; its exploration has no territory to map, no particular complacency to disturb. The danger is that the satirist will fall into a mindless cynicism where everything is subject to satire, or the kind of "free-thinking" that Swift would have called no thinking at all. Of the major satirists, perhaps Lucian and Butler come closest to this indiscriminate mockery. For them nothing is sacred, and everything is subject to ridicule. But as Pope reminds us, a satirist usually hesitates to bid farewell to all "Distinctions." Satire that "sowze[s] on all the Kind" (*Epilogue to the Satires* 2.15.64-65) is paradoxically harmless. The satire that attacks everybody touches nobody. And the satirist who laughs too widely may be, like Lucian, dismissed as a buffoon.

3

The Rhetoric of Satire:
Display and Play

If satire is inquiry and provocation, it shares a boundary not (as we usually hear) with polemical rhetoric but with philosophical (and especially ethical) writing. But by focusing on the way satire explores a moral problem or presses against our complacency, we run the risk of overemphasizing its moral intensity—to the exclusion of some other important elements. Here I want to sugget that we also need to think of much satire as a kind of rhetorical performance or rhetorical contest: as display, and as play.

Satiric Display

As rhetorical performance, satire is designed to win the admiration and applause of a reading audience not for the ardor or acuteness of its moral concern but for the brilliant wit and force of the satirist as rhetorician. Traditionally, satire is thought of as persuasive rhetoric. But Frye, noting that rhetoric is not devoted solely to persuasion, distinguishes between "ornamental speech" and "persuasive speech." "Ornamental rhetoric acts on its hearers statically, leading them to admire its own beauty or wit; persuasive rhetoric tries to lead them kinetically toward a course of action. One articulates emotion; the other manipulates it" (*Anatomy of Criticism*, p. 245). More often than we have acknowledged, satire makes use of "ornamental rhetoric."

From its earliest days satire was associated with public performance. Aristophanes competed for the prize awarded annually to the best comic dramatist (and has his chorus—as in *The Clouds*—refer to the "crown" he seeks from his judges).[1] Menippus, the eponymous founder of Menippean satire, was a Cynic orator. Lucian and Juvenal began their careers as rhetorical performers, and readers from the Renaissance to the present day have thought of Juvenal's satire as witty oratorical declamation. Satire retained its close associations with oratory and with public disputation in the highly rhetorical culture of the Renaissance. And satirists as late as Byron self-consciously displayed their rhetorical skills along with their satirical mastery. Hostile commentators have often suspected, with eighteenth-century critic Edward Burnaby Greene, that satire is designed rather "to shew the wit of the satirist, than the means of the delinquent's reformation." [2]

All traditional rhetoric looks back to Aristotle's distinctions among (1) deliberative or legislative rhetoric, designed to persuade an audience about what should be done; (2) forensic or judicial rhetoric, intended to persuade an audience (or a jury) about the guilt or innocence of the accused; and (3) epideictic or demonstrative rhetoric (from *epideixeis*, "demonstrations"), or what a modern translator calls "the ceremonial rhetoric of display," [3] which takes the form of praise or blame. The audience for epideictic rhetoric is not a deliberative or legal body; it is not called upon to take any action or to make a decision but serves only as "spectator" (Greek *theoros*), and its function (as at any dramatic spectacle) is "to decide on the orator's skill" (1358b). As Kenneth Burke notes, this rhetoric of display was designed to win the audience's praise not for the subject discussed but for the oratory itself. Praise and blame in Aristotle's day had a clear public function; the ceremonial orator might deliver a funeral oration, a tribute to or a diatribe against some public figure, or an address to stir up patriotic feeling. But from the beginning, as Burke says, the epideictic rhetorician was freed from "ulterior motive" and concerned "to give delight in the exercise of eloquence as such." And the more difficult his task—for example, praising the apparently unworthy— the greater the delight and the praise. Several centuries later, "Silver Age" rhetoric was even more focused on performance and display, perhaps in part for the historical reason that under the Roman Empire vigorous public debate on political and legal matters was curtailed; and "public rhetoric, with only the forms of persuasion left, came eventually, as in school exercises, to deal with arbitrarily chosen subjects, which were then developed with all the resources of amplification, displayed for their own sake." [4] It is in this rhetorical climate, I suggest, that we need to locate satire. Once the training ground for citizenship, rhetoric was by the first century A.D. a source of public entertainment, an opportunity for the display of ingenuity, and a means to advancement—if not as a legislator, then as a lecturer.

I do not mean to suggest that after the first century epideictic rhetoric served only as entertainment,[5] or that in making use of epideictic rhetoric satirists do not seek to bring discredit on their subject (the enemy). It would be idle to deny that Dryden wanted to make Shadwell look bad. And of course, Pope in the *Dunciad* wanted to praise Swift and to dispraise the dunces. But such praise and blame are in a sense only the satirists' stock-in-trade. The question to ask is: how good are they at their work? I am arguing that satirists implicitly (and sometimes explicitly) ask that we observe and appreciate their *skill*. It is to be suspected too that satirists judge themselves by such a standard. Anybody can call names, but it requires skill to make a malefactor die sweetly.

Lucian spent a successful career in the second century A.D. as a traveling orator before turning to the written pieces we now read—the narratives (the *True History; Lucius, the Ass*), the *Vitarum Auctio* (or "Philosophies for sale"), and the satirical dialogues of the gods and the dead. Although some commentators distinguish the writings that belong to Lucian's lecturing career from the satirical work, it has been argued not only that his best satires retain considerable traces of the rhetorician but that they were conceived and presented as "platform pieces" for a rhetorically sophisticated audience.[6] As Christopher Robinson suggests, Lucian's materials—both his stock characters and his themes—derive from the commonplaces of Cynic diatribe and rhetorical exercises. Though virtually no evidence survives about the conditions of his presentations, Robinson infers an audience familiar with Lucian's "sources" in Greek literature and diatribe, and thus able to recognize his allusions, pastiches, and parodies; they would be more interested in a speaker's command of rhetoric than in what he had to say. The orator's purpose is to "amuse, to dazzle, and to tease the audience by keeping them alert for stylistic and thematic allusions to well-known works" (*Lucian*, p. 26). The reader of the *True History*—a fantastic voyage—finds repeated allusions to the voyages of Odysseus. *Charon* contains parodies and pastiches of the journeys to the underworld in both Homeric epics, and so on.

The rhetorical element in Lucian has not always been apparent. Over the centuries he was remembered sometimes as a pagan moralist and sometimes as a merely derisive scoffer. But practitioners of the mock-encomium must have savored the self-incriminating display of rhetoric in "The Professor of Public Speaking," a forerunner of the praise of bad writing in Dryden and Pope. And the use of allusion to classical and modern epic—a prominent feature of satire in the seventeenth and eighteenth centuries—may well owe more than we have realized to Lucian's playful allusiveness. In our day critics such as Ronald Paulson have fully acknowledged Lucian the rhetorician: "More than any of the other great ancient satirists, Lucian is the rhetorician first, the moralist second, and his surprises and constant striving for effect sometimes suggest that the effect is achieved for its own sake."[7] They have also recognized that ever since Lucian (and Varro before him) the traditional Menippean satire has been marked by what Frye calls "the display of erudition" (*Anatomy of Criticism*, p. 311). The Menippean satirist from Rabelais and Burton to Swift and Sterne does not simply collect shining bits of obscure learning; he mock-pompously shows them off. Scholarship becomes spectacle.

Juvenal too was trained in the rhetorical schools, and his satire displays, even more than Lucian's, the traces of that training. As Johnson put it, "The peculiarity of Juvenal is a mixture of gaiety and stateliness, of pointed sentences, and declamatory grandeur."[8] By *declamatory*, Johnson meant "Relating to the practice of declaiming; pertaining to declamation; treated in the manner of a rhetorician" (*Dictionary*)—the rhetorician who in the classical schools would have been trained to make formal set speeches on assigned themes. By *sentences*, Johnson meant the maxims or moral axioms that were part of the rhetorician's stock and are a prominent feature of Juvenal's satires. Casaubon confirmed the point: "Without doubt [Juvenal] went from the schooling of the rhetoricians and the declamatory exercises to the writing of satire. Whence are those sharp expressions and . . . *sententiae*."[9]

For most commentators since Casaubon there is such difference between the declaiming orator or rhetorician on the one hand, and the moralist or philosopher on the other—the old dispute between philosophy and rhetoric—that Juvenal's sincerity is questioned. One persistent critical tradition holds that Juvenal is more interested in dazzling an audience with striking effects than in presenting a thoughtful moral judgment. Casaubon thinks Juvenal lacks "philosophical committment" and appears in his satires "like an orator rather than a philosopher."[10] Rigault thinks Juvenal's talent is "for declamation rather than satire."[11] Rapin contrasts Juvenal's "violent manner of Declamation," his "strong Expressions, *Energetick* Terms, and great flashes of *Eloquence*," with Horace's delicacy and naturalness. Juvenal may "dazzle the weaker Sort of Apprehensions" with his "common Places of *Morality*," but to subtler ears it is not "true Zeal" but "a Spirit of

Vanity and Ostentation." [12] That is, Juvenal is more concerned to display his wit and rhetorical skill than to persuade an audience to accept his satiric judgments. Boileau belongs to the same critical tradition: Juvenal, he says, having been trained in the rhetorical schools, pushed his hyperbole to excess ("Juvenal, élevé dans les cris de l'Ecole, / Poussa jusqu'a l'excès sa mordante hyperbole"). [13]

This was not the only critical tradition. As Weinbrot has shown, Juvenal had his defenders in the seventeenth and eighteenth centuries, defenders who praised him as a fearless satirist (*Alexander Pope*). Shadwell, for example, denied that Juvenal is "too severe and bitter, and that his *Satyrs* are more fit for *Declamation* than *Poems*." To him, Juvenal shows "the *Wisdom* and *Dignity* of *true Roman Satyr*." [14] Broadly speaking, then, one might regard Juvenal with approval as a sincere and angry moralist, or with some reservations as a witty orator. This double tradition continued into the twentieth century, with Gilbert Highet representing the former position and E.V. Marmorale the latter. [15] And it is still found now. Though Juvenal's stature among students of satire and especially English satire has never been higher, H.A. Mason in an influential essay has asked, "Is Juvenal a Classic?" [16]

But a third position is possible. Mason challenges the view that Juvenal is an "indignant prophet." Juvenal, he claims, "lacks any consistent standpoint or moral coherence." His style is declamatory, hyperbolic. The "chief ingredient" in his wit is "the belittling remark in the style of epic grandeur." Juvenal, he concludes, is not a "classic of moral satire" but a "classic of wit." [17] Mason's judgment depends on a distinction between "moral satire" and "wit," between declamation and seriousness. But one does not have to adopt Mason's distinctions, or his implicit definition of satire. One can agree with him about the characteristics of Juvenal's style and yet assign a higher value to hyperbolic and belittling wit. One can agree that Juvenal puts on a dazzling display of wit and yet argue that in doing so, Juvenal is not so much compromising his satire as acting like a satirist. What Juvenal helps us see is the element of performance and entertainment in good satire. When rhetoric is deployed in the agora, the forum, the law court, or the senate house, it serves as a means to an end—some practical decision. But to the extent that rhetoricians on the platform, or declamatory satirists, are separated from situations calling for decisions, they become entertainers. That rhetorical appeal becomes a kind of fiction; this in itself introduces the element of performance and display.

A mediating position between the "moral" and "rhetorical" Juvenal has gradually been worked out by the classicist William Anderson in such a way as to allow both for wit and indignation, for sincerity and what I am calling display. Beginning in the 1950s Anderson presented a sympathetic reading of Juvenal as rhetorician, demonstrating that Juvenal was employing rhetorically correct means—according to Roman standards—to achieve his desired effect: moral indignation.[18] Later, apparently in response to Alvin Kernan's argument that in Renaissance satire we hear not the author but a created speaker, "the satirist," Anderson applied the concept to Juvenal and argued in the early 1960s that Juvenal presented "a dramatic character subject to criticism" for his exaggerations and insincerity (*Essays on Roman Satire*, p. 304). In still later essays, following Mason, Anderson concedes Juvenal's wit but tries to preserve his indignation, tries to maintain a distinction (denied by Mason) between witty amoral Martial and witty moral Juvenal. He finds a set of "tensions" between the sophisticated rhetorician and the plain-speaking, angry truth-teller.[19] The dramatized "satirist" may be overwrought, and we (along with the rhetorician) laugh at his "moral extremism," but this does not mean that we are "totally negating morality."[20]

Anderson's final position seems somewhat strained, as he tries to hold together the textbook rhetorician, the moralist, "the satirist," the wit, and the sophisticated manipulator both of rhetoric and of several roles. His dramatized "satirist" figure—the familiar persona of New Criticism—now seems an unnecessary interpolation. But his arguments remind us that we oversimplify satire if we think only of the moral fervor *or* the verbal art, the formal conventions *or* the social-political context. And they remind us that our reactions to outspoken anger or public indignation, whether in life or in literature, are likely to be complex: we are both attracted and put off, especially if we are aware of some artifice, some self-consciousness. Anderson also helps us to remember the audience for Juvenal's satire, and their likely reaction to it:

> When Juvenal recited Satire 3 to his first audience in Rome, it knew Umbricius's facts [i.e., the claims by the main speaker that Rome was "corrupt," "dangerous," etc.], but his indignation did not correspond to the attitude of sophisticated Romans to isolated episodes of vice. I imagine that, as Juvenal concluded, he smiled and bowed, was roundly applauded, and that, as the audience filed out to get a drink, conversation developed enthusiastically over this new literary sensation in Rome, not

so much about the moral charges of Umbricius as about the interesting way Juvenal achieved so convincing a presentation of a moral extremist. [*Essays on Roman Satire*, p. 392]

Or to put it another way, Juvenal makes use of moral commonplaces (his satiric raw materials) and rhetorical pyrotechnics to present a performance or display that simultaneously stirs the blood (as fervent speech or loud music will do) and brings smiles of detached amusement and admiration.

The founder of the verse satire tradition has also been seen in these terms. Lucilius, though not the product of the rhetorical schools, is not simply a rough-edged plain dealer. Horace's ambivalent praise has slightly obscured the point that Lucilius is, as Anderson put it, "a man of wit, cultivated, intelligent, penetrating, but essentially more interested in displaying his cleverness than in pressing far into any moral or poetic problem" (*Essays on Roman Satire*, p. 21). And even the sober moralist Persius has been accused (by Scaliger, a partisan admirer of Horace) of "a feverish display of erudition."[21]

In both main satiric traditions then—formal verse satire and Menippean satire—an element of declamatory display is prominent.[22] When those traditions were recovered in the Renaissance, the declamatory element was not forgotten, as we can see by looking first at Erasmus—surely one of the world's most playful rhetoricians—and the self-consciously Juvenalian satirists of the 1590s in England. Erasmus was one of Lucian's greatest admirers and imitators, and thus it is not surprising to find in him the same "delight in verbal and intellectual display."[23] In formal terms a mock-encomium, *The Praise of Folly* belongs to an old species of epideictic rhetoric, as Erasmus himself indicates in the prefatory letter to More, where he cites among other predecessors Lucian, Homer, and Virgil. His "little declamation"— another professedly oratorical term—may (he says) displease some readers, who will claim that the book is too trifling. But Erasmus writes primarily for an audience of discerning men who will appreciate jokes that "aren't lacking in learning and wit" and who recognize that literary trifling can lead to "something more serious."[24] *The Praise of Folly* is both a parody of a formal oration and a dazzling display of rhetorical skill. Modern readers perhaps tend to focus on the more serious matter to which his "trifling" leads, the paradoxes that force us to confront the necessity of folly. And because they no longer receive training in formal rhetoric, modern readers have largely lost the ear for it and are left with little more than the traditional suspicions about its artifice. But readers in earlier ages could equally appreciate the virtuosity and find no contradiction between the showy rhetoric and the seriousness.

Training in rhetoric was still part of every schoolboy's day when formal verse satire was revived in England in the 1590s. Kernan has noticed the similarity between much English Renaissance satire and the traditional school exercises, especially those in which the student is required to write a speech of praise or blame on a set topic. But Kernan's interest lies elsewhere—in the dramatized "satirist" created in formal satire—and he does little more than deplore the "declamatory tendency" or the "oratorical mode" that "threatens to overwhelm the dramatic elements" (*Cankered Muse*, p. 84). Perhaps, however, he is dismissing as a defect an element that is, and long has been, central to satire. To adopt a Juvenalian role—as Marston, Hall, and their fellow satirists so consciously do—already suggests a strong element of performance. When Marston steps forth as a "sharpe fang'd Satyrist" determined to "plague and torture whom I list," when he announces his intention to "purge the snottery of our slimie time," the reader knows that the fierce anger is a pose, that the overstatement is both calculated and wonderfully excessive.[25] Our reaction is not to think we are in the presence of a truly angry man or a committed moralist but to watch and listen with amusement to the "rhetoric."[26] Hall's "six books" of satires often seem just that—bookish exercises.[27] His "Tooth-lesse Satyrs" comprehend the "Poeticall," the "Academicall," and the "Morall," and his targets (or topics) include the various kinds of poets (love poets, tragedians, sonneteers), a variety of traditional butts (lawyers, simoniacs, astrologers), and some obvious and traditional abuses (pompous gravestones, lavish dinners, boasters). One often has the sense that Hall is simply mustering the commonplaces. Sometimes he writes a variation on an old theme: the world has declined from the golden age (*Virgidemiarum* 3.1); everyone is discontented with his lot (4.6).

The claim that Hall's satires are not primarily a rhetorical performance but are aimed at real contemporary abuses is based largely on his Book 5, the only truly topical satires.[28] There Hall attacks the greedy landlord, the end of housekeeping, enclosure, and the wasteful spendthrift. These are perennial themes, though they may have been topical in the 1590s. It is significant that though Hall's entire *Virgidemiarum* fell under the Bishop's Ban in 1599, his "Tooth-lesse Satyrs" (bk. 1) were allowed to be reprinted almost immediately. Perhaps the bishops recognized the rhetorical element. It is significant too that Hall went on to write a Menippean satire, *Mundus alter et idem* (1605), a Lucianic fantastic voyage that shows he had absorbed the work of Lucian, More, and Rabelais. Written in Latin and designed not for publication but for a learned university audience, Hall's satire assumes considerable knowledge of philology. Its footnotes and mock-apparatus make it a parody of scholarly disputation. Inverting Juvenal's progress from rhetorician to satirist, Hall begins as satirist and ends as rhetorician: he was elected twice to lectureships in rhetoric at Cambridge. In later battles with the antiprelatical Smectymnuans (who remembered that he had been a satirist), one of the rhetorical tools he put to good use was the speaker's "ethical proof," the presentation of self as reliable and authoritative. Hall was derided for what his opponents considered "massive displays of self-righteousness."[29]

To circulate his early satires in manuscript may well have served to win Hall a reputation for wit. Though he did not admit to the charge, there is reason to believe that he and his fellow satirists in the 1590s had been motivated by a kind of vanity. Sir John Harington later confessed that he had written *The Metamorphosis of Ajax* (1596) "because I had layne me thought almost buryed in the Contry these three or foureyeere; and I thought this would give some occasion to have me thought of and talked of."[30] Donne, in a palinodic mood, observed in a later sermon that satirists write "*Satyrs*" in order that "the world" should find them witty.[31] One suspects likewise that in his youth Donne and other young men wrote paradoxes not simply to explode falsehoods and sharpen their sense of truth but to exhibit their wit.[32] John Oldham, in affecting the ranting, raging style of the Elizabethan "satyrist," proudly declared that writing satire was for him a means to show off: "I seek occasions, court Abuse, / To Shew my Parts, and signalize my Muse."[33]

But there may well have been a very practical reason for Elizabethan satirists to display their rhetorical abilities. They designed their satires, so John Wilcox suggested some years ago, as "the vehicle of youthful self-exhibition," at a time when such rhetorical display testified to the credentials that a patron would look for in a private secretary, a diplomatic aide, or a courtier.[34] Donne's fifth satire, as I have noted, was in fact addressed to his patron, Egerton, Lord Keeper, whom he served as secretary. Titled in one manuscript "Of the miserie of the poor suitors at Court," it works a series of witty variations on an old set theme.

With the great eighteenth-century satirists, patronage from the court became a fading prospect; Swift and Pope were in opposition to the ruling ministry after 1714. Yet the element of display remains prominent in their satire. Swift's early *Tale of a Tub* (1704) may in fact have cost him a bishopric, if we are to believe the report that Queen Anne, upon reading it, determined that the author was no proper defender of her faith. Ostensibly a satire on abuses and excesses in religion and learning, and an endorsement of the moderate Anglican *via media*, Swift's *Tale* has long been judged to be anything but moderate. Its ebullient (and sometimes bullying) rhetoric and wild inventiveness suggest in fact that Swift's real imaginative sympathies are with the extremists, not with Martin's "flegmatick and sedate" nature but with Jack and Peter's mental energy. Johnson wrote memorably that the book "exhibits a vehemence and rapidity of mind, a copiousness of images, and vivacity of diction such as [Swift] afterwards never possessed or never exerted."[35] Written at the beginning of Swift's satiric career, it seems a young man's book, an exhibition of the satirist's varied powers, and a bid for attention. As Tuveson has suggested, the *Tale*'s "main function" seems to be not to attack abuses but "to delight the rational imagination with its dazzling display."[36]

The *Tale* is filled with dizzying catalogues and extraordinary metaphorical richness. Indeed, it is Swift's constant habit to take his metaphors literally. This is a matter partly of discovering the material origins of "spirit"—all inspiration becomes windy vapor—and partly of pursuing them to ingenious lengths: "Therefore hospitably considering the Number of my Guests, they shall have my whole Entertainment at a Meal; And I scorn to set up the *Leavings* in the Cupboard. What the *Guests* cannot eat may be given to the Poor, and the Dogs [i.e., "common injudicious Criticks": Swift's footnote] under the Table may gnaw the *Bones*; This I understand for a more generous Proceeding, than to turn the Company's Stomachs, by inviting them again to morrow to a scurvy Meal of *Scraps*" (sec. 10). Tuveson suggests that the *Tale* "belongs to an older form of satire, that of the Renaissance—learned, brilliant, and exhibiting an endlessly varied wit."[37] Tuveson may here have in mind the so-called "tradition of learned wit" from Rabelais and Burton down through Sterne, in which the scholastic materials of cosmology, medicine, law, and religion afforded opportunities for ingenious speculations, chop-logic and paradox, or playfully perverse manipulations of a systematic body of knowledge.[38] The satirist does a kind of vaudeville turn for a knowing audience.[39] And as several critics have suggested, there is something almost akin to late or decayed metaphysical ingenuity in Swift's learned wit. His special genius is to apply untrammeled rationality to mundane (and often vivid or vulgar) details, as in the famous passage urging that readers inspect beyond the surface: "*Wisdom* is a *Fox*, who after long hunting, will at last cost you the Pains to dig out: 'Tis a *Cheese* . . ., a *Sack-Posset* . . . a *Hen*" (sec. 1), and so on.

Sometimes Swift's several rhetorical tricks are combined in a single passage, as in the "*Metaphysical* Conjectures" of the "Bird of Paradise" (sec. 9), or the account of the modern way of using books "without the Fatigue of *Reading* or of *Thinking*":

> The most accomplisht Way of using Books at present, is twofold: Either, first, to serve them as some Men do *Lords*, learn their *Titles* exactly, and then brag of their Acquaintance. Or Secondly, which is indeed the choicer, the profounder, and politer Method, to get a thorough Insight into the *Index*, by which the whole Book is governed and turned, like *Fishes* by the *Tail*. For, to enter the Palace of Learning at the *great Gate*, requires an Expence of Time and Forms; therefore Men of much Haste and little Ceremony, are content to get in by the *Back-Door*. For, the Arts are all in a *flying* March, and therefore more easily subdued by attacking them in the *Rear*. Thus Physicians discover the State of the whole Body, by consulting only what comes from *Behind*. Thus Men catch Knowledge by throwing their *Wit* on the *Posteriors* of a Book, as Boys do Sparrows with flinging *Salt* upon their *Tails*. Thus Human Life is best understood by the wise man's Rule of *Regarding the End*. Thus are the Sciences found like *Hercules's* Oxen, by *tracing them Backwards*. Thus are *old Sciences* unravelled like *old Stockings*, by beginning at the *Foot*. [sec. 7]

The passage accomplishes its ostensible satiric business in the first sentence, by laughing at modern readers who don't read more than the index (while incidentally comparing the use of books to the use of lords—not much to the credit of either). In the rest of the passage Swift amasses a series of analogies by which his mock-scholastic world of correspondences is parodically governed. His real satiric business here is to display his wit: the reader is delighted by the ingenuity, the ransacking of natural history, military science, medicine, folklore, philosophy, and myth to produce an interrelated series of puns. It is a bit like a virtuoso performer's cadenza, a jazz musician's improvisation, or the entries in some mad thesaurus under the heading "Regarding the End" or "Get In by the Back Door."

Pope's kind of satire has little in common with that of his friend Swift. Indeed, it has become commonplace to contrast the two: Swift unsettles, Pope reaffirms; Swift has doubts about satire's moral mission, Pope has none or few; Swift has doubts about satire's effectiveness, Pope often seems confident that he will "touch" or "hurt" the wicked and the proud. But in one respect they share a feature that may be common to all satirists: a taste for display—not so much self-display (though Pope does indeed love to pour himself out plain) as a display of satirical skill. The best instance in Pope is no doubt *The Dunciad*, in which he dramatizes and enacts the differences between a masterful satirist and a rabble of low-born, illiterate, and venal dunces. The poem affects to declare the triumph of Dulness but in fact declares her defeat: "Whatever inclination they might have to do mischief," the sons of Dulness "are generally render'd harmless by their Inability; . . . it is the common effect of Dulness (even in her greatest efforts) to defeat her own design" (Pope's own note to 4.584).

In part the *Dunciad* celebrates the triumph of wit.[40] In part it is a poem of warning: the dunces may be nothing more than water rats, but even a lowly rodent can burrow through the dike that holds back the waters of darkness (see Pope's note to 3.333). But we must also attend to the element of display that manifests itself here as a kind of satiric exultation. As Johnson put it, the poem is one of Pope's "greatest and most elaborate performances" (*Lives of the English Poets*, 3:145); in it he "shewed his satirical powers." The *Dunciad* is a kind of assertion of potency, a demonstration that though unlaureated, Pope is not only the head of his tribe but a masterful satirist who will put the dunces in their deserved places.

One recent critic, pointing to this element in the *Dunciad*, suggests that the poem is finally about itself. It is, in Michael Rosenblum's words, "a culminating work of the satirist's art, a virtuoso demonstration of how the apparent limitations of the genre can be converted to artistic gain." The poet shows how "he can make a beautiful and enduring poem out of the ugly and transient materials with which he is forced to deal."[41] Pope himself had in fact hinted as much. In the prefatory letter signed by "William Cleland," Pope observes that those readers alone are able to do justice to his poem who "know how hard it is (with regard both to his Subject and his Manner), Vetustis Dare Novitatem, Obsoletis Nitorem, Obscuris Lucem, Fastiditis Gratiam" (to give novelty to what is old, brilliance to what is commonplace, light to the obscure, attraction to the stale).[42]

Though Rosenblum is concerned only with Pope, he takes a hesitant step toward generalizing his claim by offering the view "that satire flaunts its own artifice rather than conceals it, and that it is concerned with the powers of the satirist and the act of satire rather than with any situation which exists outside the satire." Rosenblum's only other example is Swift's satiric predictions of the death of Partridge the almanac maker: "The real object is not to discredit Partridge so much as to show what the ingenious satirist can accomplish."[43] But in the light of the long history of satiric display—for the purpose of winning the applause of the witty or the informed, if not the attention of a patron—perhaps Rosenblum's view should be boldly generalized: the satirist is always a performer. What satirists display are their rhetorical skill, their wit, their erudition, their power.

Byron, the last of the English writers still part of a living tradition of generic satire, is in his ottava rima satires above all a performer. Anyone who reads *Don Juan* is aware of the self-conscious Byron displaying his apparently effortless command over the dynamics of his complex stanza, producing comic, deflationary rhymes as a kind of signature-tune and engaging in an almost continuous commentary on his own satiric narrative. In my next canto, says *Don Juan*'s narrator breezily, "I shall / Say something to the purpose, and display / Considerable talent in my way" (14.98.6-8). In a poem whose decorum permits Byron to do without any particular "purpose" (like Montaigne, he is always in his way, never out of it), we may suspect that the "display" of "talent" is what engages us (and him).

This feature has long been observed by Byron's readers. Frye notes that we "simultaneously read the poem and watch the poet at work writing it" (*Anatomy of Criticism*, p. 234). Hardly a page passes without some knowing, self-conscious, or even self-mocking remark from the Byronic narrator, sometimes in large-scale digressions, sometimes in a single parenthesis. What is worth emphasizing is that in conducting his satiric narrative in this way, Byron is not being impudently innovative; he is working in a long satiric tradition of self-conscious rhetoric and display. His example may serve to remind us of the credentials of another master of satiric narrative: Laurence Sterne, who in *Tristram Shandy* (like Byron in *Don Juan*) wants all eyes on him as he tries to tell his cock-and-bull story.[44]

Satiric Play

I cannot claim that *display* and *play* are etymologically related: to display is (radically) to unfold; to play is (radically) to engage in

some joyous exercise or movement.[45] The former requires an audience; the latter can take place without one. Yet there is a relation, for
what a satirist displays can be his playfulness. And play, like display,
takes place in an arena that is in some sense marked off from business or serious purpose, reserved for self-delighting activity that has
no concern for morality or for any real-world consequences save the
applause of the spectators.[46] The player nonetheless follows some set
of rules; his exercise often requires or tests some skill; it can attract
admiration. George Kennedy, historian of Greek rhetoric, calls epideictic speeches "playful exercises by an oratorical virtuoso."[47]

All literature is in one sense a form of rhetorical play: imitated
speech, not real speech; "ornamental rhetoric," not "persuasive
rhetoric." Poststructuralists have insisted on the free play of signifiers
in all poetry, and critics for at least thirty years have widely acknowledged the "element of playfulness in art."[48] To claim that satire is in
part playful is thus to claim little more than satire's artfulness, a point
worth remaking, since we often think of satire as primarily concerned
with honesty, morality, truth-telling, or "real life." But we can go a
little further and define the special nature of satiric play. *Allusion* is
(radically) a form of play (*ludo, lusus*) on words, a gamesome playing
with traditional or inherited materials. Satire has no monopoly on
allusion, of course, though it has a special fondness for epic allusion
that is in part sharply purposeful and in part a kind of literary playfulness or shared joke. From its beginnings satire has had an association
with food and festivity, from the overflowing *lanx satura*, the Roman
saturnalia, the symposium or philosophical dialogue, and the conviv-
ial banquet or Petronian *cena* to Pope's "feast of reason, and flow of
soul." We need to remember that context of festivity, an occasion
marked off from business for the play of wit. We have long recognized
the "playfulness" of Swift's mind[49] but have not yet adequately inte-
grated that recognition in our reading of Swiftian satire to see how
"savage indignation" and playfulness can cohabit. We can look at
satire itself as a kind of play in several distinct but related senses—the
largely purposeless or gratuitous verbal play of the type found in *A
Tale of a Tub*;[50] play with moral ideas that do not have the same status
they have in philosophical discourse; play with real people who are
transformed into something else when they enter the satiric game;
playful insult and invective that is teasing, competitive, or even genial;
and the intellectual play of irony and fantasy.

Very little has been written about the playfulness of satire.[51] Indeed, in the ususal view, playfulness is assumed to be foreign to satire.

Anger, as W.H. Auden said, is of all emotions "the least compatible with play."[52] Marston could even attack his rival Hall with the claim that his satires were *non ledere, sed ludere*," "not harmful, but playful."[53] One of the few brief discussions of play in satire is that of Gordon Williams in his book *Tradition and Originality in Roman Poetry* (1968). His immediate purpose is to redefine the moral dimension in Horace as something other than straightforward "didacticism." Though he does not say so, Williams in effect tries to get at what the Augustans meant by praising Horace's "delicacy." He imagines a "moral" poet who treats moral ideas personally, in relaton to himself and his addressee: "The artistic intention is to explore the potentialities of the situation in its dramatic conjunctions of personalities and topics. . . . Always humour is close at hand; always the tone is that of discussion, of playing with ideas, never of dictation or sermonizing" (pp. 599-600). "Playing with" here suggests a kind of ease and freedom in which moral sandards, while assumed, are not allowed to dominate. The poet is concerned not with the importance of the moral abstraction (in any case only a commonplace) but with the integration of moral concerns into the subtly woven texture of a life of shifting situations and moods. He is also concerned, as a poet, with finding some original way of using traditional materials. This kind of playfulness is perhaps especially characteristic of Horace's satires and epistles. It may distinguish him from Juvenal, a satirist far more interested in rhetorical display than in delicate playfulness.

Ludo is in fact one of the key words in Horace' satires. It is his verb for what the satirist does: *haec ego ludo*, "I play with these things," that is, my verses (*Sat.* 1.10.37); *illudo chartis*, "I trifle with my papers" (*Sat.* 1.4.139). He commends "play" to his friend Lollius (*Epist.* 1.18.66) and in his letter to the Pisos (*Ars P.* 405); he ranks it among his dearest losses to time (*Epist.* 2.2.56); he remembers the innocent gaiety of old Fescennine verses (*Epist.* 2.1.139ff.), or of Lucilius with Scipio and Laelius (*Sat.* 2.1.71-74). Lucilius himself had referred (in Book 30) to his own poems as *ludus ac sermones*, "playful conversations."[54] When Persius praises Horace's "sly insinuating Grace" (Dryden's translation), the ability to smile and at the same time teasingly chastise, he says Horace "plays" (*ludit, Sat.* 1.117). When he sets out to imitate Horace in his own *Satire 5*, Persius claims to censure faults *ingenuo ludo* ("in witty play," 5.16).

Although Juvenal does not share Horace's light, trifling, playful spirit, he often engages in a rhetoric that we know not to take *au pied de la lettre*. Even in his most virulent satire, Juvenal's denunciation is designed (to whatever degree it conveys hostility) as playful abuse. Consider, for example, *Sature* 6, against women: In the opening lines Juvenal paints a comic picture of pristine chastity, when "unpolisht Matrons, Big and Bold" gave suck to "Infants of Gigantick Mold" (Dryden's translation). They keep house in a "narrow Cave" and grow fat from eating nuts and acorns, and belching their "Windy Food." This may be primitivism, but it is hardly of the sober doctrinaire sort. (For another example, see the comical treatment of the Golden Age in *Satire* 13). Juvenal (in Dryden's reading) takes the idea of original Roman vigor and purity with a grain of salt: he *plays* with it. We might well compare the famous opening to Dryden's own *Absalom and Achitophel*, another playful use of the "pious times" topos. Later (in *Sat.* 6.370), when the female fencer rests after strenuous exercise, Juvenal says he laughs (this is the reader's cue) to see her "Call for the Pot, and like a Man Piss Out." Dryden seems to have responded heartily to this jaunty element of playful exaggeration in Juvenal and to have accentuated it in his translation. Thus Juvenal's aroused *adulter*, hiding behind the curtain (237) becomes in Dryden a "Panting Stallion at the Closet-Door" (335).[55] The gods, addressed without ceremony in Juvenal as *vos* (395), become "Your Godships" (516). In Juvenal, the wife's night cream sticks to the husband's lips when he kisses her goodnight. But in Dryden, "He takes fat kisses, and is stuck in Glue" (596). This is neither morality nor declamation but witty play.

A taste for play has always been part of the Menippean or Lucianic tradition, with its fantastic invention, its exaggerations, and its tongue-in-cheek manner. In the opening of his *True History* Lucian speaks of the importance of "exercising" and "relaxing" for both athletes and "book enthusiasts": "After poring over a lot of serious works, they ought to give the mind a rest to get it into even better shape for the next workout." He recommends "light, pleasant reading" which entertains and "furnishes some intellectual fare as well."[56] The Humanists, who admired and imitated Lucian, inherited and developed this taste for play. Erasmus called his *Praise of Folly* a "play of wit" (*lusus ingenii*),[57] and elsewhere (with Lucian in mind) described the mock-encomium as a form that both exercises and relaxes the mind: "vel exercendi, vel laxandi ingenii gratia."[58] *Exercendi* involves practicing and training the wit; *laxandi*, the slackening or releasing of tension. The apparent paradox (only apparent, because exercise can also be play) reminds us that, as many have noticed, play in Erasmus can also be serious.[59]

Play of wit keeps the faculties sharp. But the great Menippean satires do more than that. In Bakhtin's terms, they test or explore an idea. With More, that exploration might better be called a play of ideas, in which the point is not to arrive at a conclusion but to let ideas of high principle and worldly accommodation, community good and individual good, liberty and equality jostle against each other in an open and free-wheeling contest. In his *Utopia* the playground is the conversational circle in Peter Giles's garden, where thought is free and nobody—least of all More—really expects the ideas discussed to be implemented in the real world. Significantly, Utopia is an island, cut off (like most utopias) in time and space from the real world, constituting a world of its own, a *spielraum* for speculation. As Michael Holquist has pointed out, More in his account of Utopian customs models the kind of play in which he wants the reader to engage. Among the amusements of the Utopians are two games "not unlike our own chess." One is a battle of numbers. "The other is a game in which the vices fight a battle against the virtues. The game is set up to show how the vices oppose one another, yet readily combine against the virtues; then, what vices oppose what virtues, how they try to assault them openly or undermine them in secret; how the virtues can break the strength of the vices or turn their purposes to good; and finally, by what means one side or the other gains the victory."[60] The Utopians, like the reader, reduce "life" to a set of abstractions, stick figures, and pawns; they consider the complex interactions of vice and virture and play out the struggle by which one side or the other wins. The point is not so much that even games—in Utopia or in satire—are moralized, devices for inculcating good principles, but rather that moral discourse is cast in the form of a game. Thus Utopia itself—like most utopian fictions—is a kind of game, a staged opposition of ideas, and (as Holquist says) the utopist "leaves it up to the reader to decide who lost, who won."[61]

Swift engages in the same kind of game, but with a twist. It is striking to recall that his Houyhnhnms, in contrast to More's Utopians, play no games. Indeed, they seem without a sense of mental play altogether. Their only games are physical exercise. Because they are endowed with pure reason, they always arrive at the truth "with immediate conviction." They cannot understand the word "opinion" or how a point could be disputable; they find it ridiculous that Gulliver's compatriots might value "the knowledge of other People's Conjectures," since knowledge, "if it were not certain, could be of no use." Unlike Europeans—and Swift's readers—Houyhnhnms cannot "argue with

Plausibility on both sides of a Question." Gulliver's Houyhnhnm master has "no Conception of any Country beside his own" (*Gulliver's Travels* 4.10). He would make a dull companion at a symposium. The point is not that Swift devalues the process of intellectual game playing. It is rather that making the Houyhnhnms into a race without the capacity to play with ideas foregrounds the very process that Swift wants to urge upon his reader. Houyhnhnm woodenness forces us to be supple—or else to end up like Gulliver himself, dazzled by moral absolutes and talking to horses. It is a sign of Swift's own suppleness that he can joke at the expense of his moral exemplars.

Elsewhere in the *Travels* Swift gives games another satiric twist. As John Traugott has argued in a speculative and wide-ranging essay, Swift in the *Voyage to Lilliput* invokes in his reader a "nostalgia for the freedom of childhood games"—Gulliver as master of the dolls— but goes on to transform such innocent games as tightrope walking into the "bitter charades" whereby those in political power maintain themselves and discipline their underlings, the "diversion" or "entertainment" whereby candidates for office are "allowed" or even "commanded" to cut capers on a high rope.[62] In similar fashion but in a lighter mood, Pope sets his dunces to play at games of running, tickling, vociferating, and diving. In his narrative the dunces are wholly absorbed in play. Meanwhile, the footnotes direct the reader not only to the parody of Homeric epic games but also to the discreditable practices of contemporary booksellers, dedicators, fustian poets, and "profound, dark, and dirty Party-writers" (*Dunciad*, Argument to bk. 2).

Another element of playfulness in satire, involving both hostility and competition, appears most clearly in the long tradition of flyting, in which two satirists take turns abusing each other. The tradition probably goes back to the earliest forms of satire (there is an abuse contest between a Paphlagonian and a sausage-seller in Aristophanes' *Knights*). Anthropologists have often reported on the stylized exchange of insults in primitive cultures.[63] It is not clear, however, that insult competition performs the same function in sophisticated court-based cultures. Dryden cites both Casaubon and Horace in locating the "original" of satire partly in the Romans' holiday custom of "reproaching each other with their Faults, in a sort of *Extempore* Poetry" (4:30). Such "Fescennine verses," exchanged in "occasions of merriment," appear in Horace's own satires. In *Satire* 1.5 he narrates, in mock-heroic style, the battle (*pugnam*) of words between two "Tongue-combatants,"[64] one a coarse rustic and the other a professional jester (*scurra*). The battle, like the one in *Satire* 1.7, is a source of laughter for Horace and his well-bred companions. Such verses represent an early instance of competitive invective matches that would in the medieval period be called flytings and that survive even today in popular culture.

The *Fescennina Carmina* of Erasmus and the *Gargantua and Pantagruel* of Rabelais show that the delight in an exchange of abuse, under conditions suggesting friendly competition, remained strong in the Renaissance. Thus in the latter (bk 3, chap. 38) Pantagruel and Panurge trade abusive epithets—"A fatal fool." "A high-toned fool." "A natural fool." "A B-sharp and B-flat fool"—not in order to attack each other but to describe Triboulet as sufficiently a fool to preside over their deliberations. Panurge and Dingdong engage in a vehement quarrel—*Dingdong*: "Where do you come from, you goggle-eyed son of Antichrist? If you're of God's party, answer me." *Panurge*: "Answer me, you ram-dealer, you son of Mahomet. For I'm sure you're of the devil's party"—but all their anger is expended in their ritualized exchange of words, and they readily patch up their quarrel and drink each other's health "in sign of perfect reconciliation" (4.5). Compare the exchange of abusive gestures between Panurge and Thaumaste, in parody of formal scholarly disputation, before an audience of spectators (often a key element in the invective contest, suggesting performance, or a rivalry in pleasing). After vanquishing Thaumaste by placing "his two forefingers at each corner of his mouth, drawing it back as wide as he could and showing all his teeth" and "with his thumbs, [drawing] down his eyelids very low, making rather an ugly grimace," Panurge receives polite thanks and high compliments for his skill in "disputation by signs" (2.19-20).

Ludic combat of this kind answers well to Huizinga's classic description of the "play element" in culture. The invective contest takes place in a metaphorical field, marked off in time and space from ordinary life. It is both "serious" in that the participants are very determined to best the opponent, and yet "playful" in that the exchange of insults has no other consequence in ordinary life than a cordial celebratory dinner. Satiric play also follows prescribed rules. As in theold Fescennine verse, the "taunts" are "alternate."[65] In a typical wit battle you must pay attention to your opponent's words and match them, or overmatch them. Just as Pantagruel and Panurge punningly play off each other's epithets ("A natural fool" suggests the musical theme, and leads from "A" to "B" and from "natural" to the "B-flat and B-sharp fool").[66] Playful emulative abuse survives today in such un-

likely places as the following bare, stripped-down exchange in Samuel
Beckett's English version of *Waiting for Godot*:

> *Vladimir*: Moron!
> *Estragon*: That's the idea, let's abuse each other.
> (*They turn, move apart, turn again and face each other.*)
> *Vladimir*: Moron!
> *Estragon*: Vermin!
> *Vladimir*: Abortion!
> *Estragon*: Morpion!
> *Vladimir*: Sewer-rat!
> *Estragon*: Curate!
> *Vladimir*: Cretin!
> *Estragon (with finality)*: Crritic!
> *Vladimir*: Oh! (*He wilts, vanquished, and turns away.*)
> *Estragon*: Now let's make it up.

The string of insults is in fact a linked chain. Vladimir begins
with "moron" and Estragon counters with "vermin" (implicitly accepting Vladimir's "rule" that the epithet contain two syllables, —
r—n. Vladimir returns with "abortion," a new variation on the —
r—n formula, and Estragon answers with "morpion," again accepting
Vladimir's suggestion that they move to three syllables. "Morpion,"
meaning "crab-louse" and commonly used in French as a term of
personal abuse, derives as it were from "vermin" and in turn suggests Vladimir's "sewer-rat," an emphatic and challenging return
from French to English. Estragon puns on "sewer-rat" with "curate"
(sounding like cure-rat—. Vladimir accepts the challenge of c—r—t,
and produces "cretin," a reprise of his own earlier "moron" (but
suggested too by the bilingual pun on crétin/chrétien).[67] Estragon
caps him and gives the death blow with "crritic!" a bathetic conclusion, ironically apt for what has in fact been a verbal performance.
That the game is in some sense mere "play" is confirmed by its immediate aftermath: "Now let's make it up." "Your hand!" "Take it!"
"Come to my arms!"[68]
      Dryden claimed not to be amused by what he thought coarse
humor in Horace; he preferred "fine raillery."[69] But what one might
call the "Fescennine tradition" was very much alive in Restoration
and eighteenth-century England. In low-life London, watermen were
notorious for their volleys of abuse, directed at one another and at
their passengers. For an example from high life, one might cite the

sophisticated battle of wits between William Congreve's Mirabell and Millamant in *The Way of the World*.[70] A clearer example is Polly Peachum and Lucy Lockit in *The Beggar's Opera*, where the disputes between jealous operatic prima donnas of the day are parodically assimilated to the battles of the street and the river. John Gay's form, an air in which Lucy and Polly each sing a stanza, follows the old Fescennine lines of a ritual exchange of abuse and explicitly brings out the competitive element: "Why, how now, Madam Flirt? / If you thus must chatter; / And are for flinging dirt, / Let's try who best can spatter! / Madam Flirt!" Gay seems to have sensed and brought out into the open the "musical" quality of the insult contest, in which the satiric voices, as in two-part harmony, echo and answer each other.

The persistence of the verbal contest in eighteenth-century high art suggests that more often than we realize, abusive satire is a wit contest, a kind of game in which the participants do their worst for the pleasure of themselves and their spectators. To be sure, it is a dangerous game and succeeds in giving pleasure all around only if both combatants, together with the audience, in effect agree on the rules. If the exchange of insults is serious on one side, playful on the other, the satiric element is reduced.[71]

Although by the late seventeenth century Dryden and his contemporaries were beginning to feel uncomfortable about the ethics of such personal attacks, it would appear that the lampoons exchanged by Rochester and his court contemporaries Scroope and Mulgrave in part continued that old comic flyting tradition of impromptu, often obscene insult exchanged by acquaintances and social equals. In emphasizing the violence and cruelty of the Restoration lampoon, recent critics run the risk of overlooking the competitive element, which implies that the exchange of lampoons is a game.[72] When played well, it produces a keen pleasure on the part of the participants and their observers, as the flyting between William Dunbar and Walter Kennedy was said to have done at the court of James IV of Scotland.[73]

Many of Rochester's lampoons were composed impromptu (as the tradition has it). Wittily abusive lines of Louis XIV or on Charles II's court or on the king himself, they were first presented in a circle of courtiers. Charles, so more than one critic has plausibly claimed, tolerated and even enjoyed Rochester's satires on his court.[74] At the same court, Buckingham, according to his antagonist, did not resent the witty portrait of himself as Zimri.[75] And in the same age Boileau even suggested that Nero "gallantly" received the affronts of Persius.[76] At the English court, witty impromptu satires circulated by word of mouth and in manuscript copies. They frequently provided answers, often by other members of the same court. Thus Scroope's *In Defence of Satyr*, with its portrait of an ill-natured buffoon coward, was answered by Rochester's "On the Supposed Author of *In Defence of Satyr*": "A lump deform'd and shapeless wert thou born, / Begot in love's despite and nature's scorn" (11-12). Scroope responded with an epigram ("Rail on, poor feeble scribbler, speak of me / In as ill terms as the world speaks of thee"), and Rochester riposted with "On Poet Ninny": "The worst that I could write would be no more / Than what thy very friends have said before."

The quarrel has been described by some critics as bitter conflict between sworn enemies. But there is perhaps some room to suspect that we have mistaken the tone and real cultural significance of the exchange. The poems in question did not remain private documents but were copied, circulated, collected, and even printed for the enjoyment of the larger social circle of which the two wits were fellow members. To display one's wit was a social skill, no less important than dressing well or handling a rapier with grace (indeed, wit is itself both a kind of dress and a weapon). A member of that circle might then read a Rochester lampoon with wary admiration: this is a dangerously witty man; one pays a price in offending him. And one might try one's own hand: many lampoons against Scroope survive, written by various hands, not all of them his "rivals" or "enemies." It is as if they are trying their wit on a set topic (just as the Rochester-Scroope exchange works variations on the themes of failed lover and failed satirist, "harmless malice and hopeless love"), or even attempting to test themselves against Rochester by bending his Ulyssean bow. In a court-based culture where "work" is left to others, where "real life" consists largely of spectacle and intrigue, and where performance means power, satiric game and ordinary life can interpenetrate. As critics of Huizinga have suggested, the distinctions between play and seriousness, or play and "ordinary life," are often hard to draw and maintain.[77] The lampoon is a kind of serious play, competition that both provides amusement and exercise and at the same time establishes a pecking order in a world of court players.

Against this view of the lampoon as stylized theatrical violence, produced as a sign of one's verbal prowess for the amusement of the court, it might be argued that the lampoon was rather the displacement of actual combat. Rochester and his fellow courtiers might still meet each other with swords instead of pens. Verbal abuse might be revenged by an actual beating, as Dryden discovered when he was set upon by ruffians—presumably hired for the purpose—in Rose Alley. And lampoons were not tolerated without limit, as Rochester found out upon being banished from the court. Courts are notoriously riven with factions, and some of the exchanged lampoons, so it has been said, reflected literary alliances and rivalries for favor. So Rochester aligned with Shadwell, as against Dryden and Mulgrave.[78] But the evidence of these "alliances" is largely the poems themselves. And the lines allegedly separating factions were often crossed (as witness Rochester's unstable relations with Thomas Otway and Nathaniel Lee) or ignored (by dramatists such as Etherege and Wycherley, who seem not to have taken any sides). In sum, one hesitates to deny that Restoration lampoons expressed any bitter hatred for a rival poet, but a balanced account of the poems, and their pleasures, probably requires that we see them in part as stylized and even playful abuse, written to satisfy the somewhat course appetites of an age that tore its pleasures with rough strife.

The primitive satiric contest survives also in a more displaced form: the friendly, emulative rivalry between practicing satirists. Horace's "Journey to Brundisium" (*Sat.* 1.5), clearly modeled after Lucilius's "Journey to Sicily," is a form at once of homage and of competition.[79] Erasmus and More consciously competed in replying to Lucian's *Tyrannicide*, and in 1506 Erasmus celebrated their rivalry as "a bout in the wrestling-school of wit."[80] As late as the eighteenth century, satirists delighted in their rivalry. In March 1728 Swift reported with pleasure to Gay that "the Beggers Opera [then being performed] hath knockt down Gulliver [published in 1726]; I hope to see Pope's Dullness [shortly to be published] knock down the Beggers Opera."[81]

The idea of a boundary between the field of play and ordinary life—a boundary that is often porous—may help us to see the "play element" in two other common features of satire: its irony, and its use of fantasy. Insofar as irony (pretending to affirm something) enables the satirist to avoid committing himself, it creates a field of play in which the ironic satirist can revel at will. Hostile critics will call this irresponsibility; the sympathetic will call it "freedom"[82] or "the play of the mind."[83] But satiric irony also involves a reader. A.E. Dyson has called Swift's irony not only a "battle of wits" with his reader but also a "civilized game." It is an "intellectual game" that enables us to separate our enjoyment of the exercise of irony as pure technique from the appalling conclusions about human nature to which Swiftian irony presses us.[84] The ironist's game is an intellectualized combat in which we repeatedly jockey for position, so as always to be on the "inside," seeking always to avoid being "bit." If we wholly concentrate on the game, we can virtually ignore the ordinary world outside the field of play. But it is characteristic of satiric play that we cannot long remain within the field's boundaries. Play in satire is usually mixed with other elements—moral concern, or the unsettling rhetoric of inquiry and provocation. Byron could *claim*, in a letter to his publisher, that *Don Juan* is a "playful satire," and "never intended to be serious."[85] But his readers don't believe him. It's playful, to be sure, but ordinary life keeps breaking in.

A satirist who can manage to keep life from breaking in may remain in a world of pure fantasy—and pure play. Perhaps we should consider as play those moments in high Augustan mock-heroic when the satirist seems to pause from the work of ridicule to create and revel in an inverted world of delightful absurdity. MacFlecknoe is of course presented as a wretched poet, but neither Dryden nor his readers have ridicule or censure uppermost in mind when he describes the "Realms of *Non-sense*" that MacFlecknoe happily inhabits. As MacFlecknoe's "rising Fogs prevail upon the Day," and as his "goodly Fabrick fills the eye," so too does a delight in playful fantasy prevail upon our judgment and fill the eye of reason. If MacFlecknoe is "design'd for thoughtless Majesty," we ourselves are for a moment "thoughtless" as we contemplate the wonderful spectacle of the bulky poet's solemn state and supine reign (ll. 24-28). Ariel's airy field of "lucid squadrons" in *The Rape of the Lock* and the "jetty bowers" at the bottom of Fleet Ditch in *The Dunciad* define other sites where satirist and reader meet to suspend their normal standards. In the midst of powerfully judgmental satire, we playfully indulge the imagination's power to create.

4

Satiric Closure

A rhetoric of inquiry and provocation enables us to see more clearly that satire is often an "open" rather than a "closed" form, that it is concerned rather to inquire, explore, or unsettle than to declare, sum up, or conclude. Elements of playfulness and performance likewise shift our attention from satire's ostensible end to its means. "End," like "open" and "closed," here refer to the satirist's rhetorical purpose. But they can also point to formal features, to what happens at the "end" of that satire.

Beginnings do not present a problem for the satirist. "The opening is sudden and unexpected," says the sixteenth-century theorist Minturno, "since the satirist, driven by indignation and scorn, starts biting suddenly."[1] The world has always supplied such an abundance of vice and folly that satirists need only open their eyes, look about, and begin to speak. Words are drawn or even forced forth. It is hard *not* to write satire. Satirists need not stir, for the world of fools obligingly and disobligingly invades their quiet: "Shut, shut the door! good John," says Pope. "Fools rush into my Head, and so I write."[2] Once they have begun, it is easy for satirists to sustain their discourse. They will not lack for subjects: "All human endeavors, men's prayers, / Fears, angers, pleasures, joys, and pursuits, these make / The mixed mash of my verse" (Juvenal, *Sat.* 1). Digression is their delight. Like leisurely travelers, they will carry their company along with them to every pleasing or digusting "Scene in View, whether of Art, or Nature, or of both" (Swift, *Tale of a Tub*, sec. 9). Having well begun in anger or disgust, the satirist takes a kind of pleasure in going on, in letting the verse and the voice pour forth, as plainly spoken (says Pope), "as downright Shippen, or as old Montagne."[3] And having won the attention of their readers or listeners, satirists are reluctant to relax their "firm Hold": "It is with great Reluctance," says the narrator of Swift's *Tale*, "That I am at length compelled to remit my Grasp" (sec. 9).

But as Swift's satirist knows, "*Going too long* is a Cause of Abortion as effectual, tho' not so frequent, as *Going too short*" ("The Conclusion"). Satirists must stop speaking, and their satire must end. But how can they accomplish this so as to satisfy their own psychological needs, as they have represented them, and the aesthetic or formal needs of their readers for closure? Given the special decorum of satire—an aroused or a merely chatty speaker, a virtually unlimited subject matter—endings present a problem that satirists have historically had difficulty solving.

The problem of closure in satire needs to be seen ultimately as part of the more general problem of narrative endings that has drawn considerable critical attention since R.M. Adams's discussion of modern "open form" in *Strains of Discord: Studies in Literary Openness* (1958) and Frank Kermode's *The Sense of an Ending* (1967). More recently, critics have begun to explore the ways in which all narrative may be said to be open, or at any rate to note that *closed* and *open* are relative terms.[4] No doubt a critic with a taste for ambiguity, one who pushed hard enough, could find *open-endedness* or unresolved elements in virtually all fictional narratives. A deconstructionist would find that literary endings, like alleged literary wholeness, are always unraveling. Satiric endings, however, seem a special case. Many novels, when all is said and done, seem for most readers to end satisfyingly, to round off and tie up; but few satires do. Nor should we link satire too closely with narrative. Narrative is probably a necessary constituent of novels, but it is only incidental—and readily suspended or dispensed with altogether—in satire. Finally, satiric endings are often obtrusively open, not because the end of one story is always the beginning of another, or because literary constructions are subject to deconstructing or unraveling, but because the form and purpose of satire seem to resist conclusiveness.

The most spectacular examples of problematic endings are of course in those great European satires that were left unfinished at their authors' deaths: Rabelais's *Gargantua and Pantagruel*, Butler's *Hudibras*, Byron's *Don Juan*. Nor is it possible to imagine how these works *could* have concluded but with the deaths of their authors or perhaps of their protagonists. Each was published serially and might have been extended indefinitely. What Johnson said of *Hudibras* might be applied to all three sets of satiric adventures: they are—and if extended only could be—a "succession of incidents, each of which might have happened without the rest, and which could not all cooperate to any single conclusion."[5] Rabelais published four books of

Gargantua and Pantagruel during his lifetime. At the author's death in 1553, Pantagruel and Panurge were still sailing toward the Oracle of the Holy Bacbuc. Rabelais had intended to continue the story, for he left additional chapters that were posthumously published in 1562. Whether he had intended to "complete" the book is unclear. The "Fifth and Last Book," as it was titled when published in 1564, was compiled by an editor and perhaps "completed" by him as well. Byron was still writing stanzas of the unfinished Canto 17 of *Don Juan* less than two months before he sailed to Greece to die. Two years earlier he had told his publisher, John Murray, that he didn't know how many cantos he would eventually write, "nor whether (even if I live) I shall complete it." Earlier plans had called for Juan to continue his adventures after his stay in England (the subject of the final published cantos). Byron talked of sending Juan to Italy as a *cavaliere servente*, and even to Greece, and "had not quite fixed whether to make him end in Hell, or in an unhappy marriage."[6] But as Kernan notes, "it seems doubtful that it ever could have been finished, . . . for what 'conclusion' could there have been?" (*Plot of Satire*, p. 177).

That narrative satire perhaps doesn't want to conclude is suggested too by some examples of famous works *apparently* finished by their authors. About the *Satyricon* of Petronius one cannot speak dogmatically, since all we have are fragments, but we may reasonably doubt that the adventures of Encolpius were ever concluded in twenty books. Lucian's *True History* breaks off just as its hero survives a shipwreck and swims ashore on a "new continent." "What happened to us," he promises, "I will tell in the subsequent volumes." These volumes were of course never published. The promise of a sequel is perhaps only a hoary promotional device, or else another of Lucian's wonderful "lies." Swift's *Tale of a Tub* likewise claims that Peter, Martin, and Jack had many further adventures. In his papers, says the narrator, there was a full account of "how *Peter* got a *Protection* out of the *King's-Bench*: And of a Reconcilement between *Jack* and Him (sec. 11)," and so on. But it is plain that Swift had no intention of continuing the story, for he says that "the Particulars" of these adventures "have now slid out of my Memory, and are beyond all Hopes of Recovery."

It might appear that these narrative satires present a special case. The narrative satirist tells a story in order to mock, to expose, to subvert. The story is only a vehicle; it may be interrupted at will; it may be broken into episodes; it may be extended ad libitum or broken off (as Butler says) "in the middle" (Argument to *Hudibras* 1.1).

Since satirists are not normally interested in narrative wholeness, in character consistency, in drawing that Jamesian circle by which a particular set of human relations appears to be bounded, they will feeel no obligation to provide narrative closure. But in fact, as I propose to argue, narrative satire is in this respect typical of all satire, no matter what form it takes.

As a mode, satire can invade virtually any form. Even as a genre (my focus here) it can take a number of forms. Broadly speaking, one might distinguish three traditions: formal verse satire, the looser Menippean tradition, and the parodic tradition of mock-epic, mock-pastoral, mock-elegy, and the like. In each tradition satire tends to avoid or even to subvert formal closure.

Daniel Heinsius, a learned Renaissance commentator, defines satire as "a kind of Poetry without a Series of Action." As Dryden says, this definition distinguishes satire from drama, which consists of a single continued action with a beginning, middle, and end.[7] Satire then does not contain a plot in the rudimentary Aristotelian sense. Nor can we find a new-Aristotelian plot as Ralph Rader and others have described it: the convergence or divergence of a character's fate and his deserts.[8] In the classical tradition satire takes the forms of a diatribe or a *sermo* ("conversation" or "little chat"), for which there is no obvious or conventional means of closure. Juvenal called his satire a *farrago*, remembering the conventional derivation from *lanx satura*, and often seems ready to add one more topic to his full platter. In his first satire he rails that "today every vice / Has reached its ruinous zenith," and the structural principles of the poem appear to be little more than repetition and association. In his sixth satire, further examples of vicious women could always be added to his catalogue (as Pope added portraits of women to later editions of his "Epistle to a Lady, of the Characters of Women"). Horace's famous meeting with the bore or climber (*Sat.* 1.9) ends only when his interlocutor is hauled off to court: "And thus I was saved by Apollo." Juvenal's third satire ends not because Umbricius has concluded his tirade ("There are many other arguments I could adduce") but because night is falling and the muleteer who will carry him into voluntary exile is anxious to get started.

With no plot or conventional ending, formal verse satire must achieve whatever sense of closure it attains by means of the satirist's own rhetoric. Barbara Herrnstein Smith has suggested that poets make use of a number of "closural devices," both thematic and formal, to give their work that "sense of conclusiveness, finality, or 'clinch'" that we experience when our anticipation of a "terminal event" has been gratified. Among "formal devices" (arising from the physical properties of language) she includes terminal modification, as in the series AAAAAB; and the return to a norm after a deviation such as a syntactic suspension or a metrical departure). Among "thematic devices" (arising from the conventional and symbolic properties of language) she includes allusions to the "natural stopping places of our lives" (sleep, night, death), references to finality, and, especially, absolute or unqualified statements.[9] As an example of thematic closure one might cite the closing line of Pope's "Epistle to Arbuthnot"—"Thus far was right, the rest belongs to Heav'n"—which combines, through the pun on "rest," both a reference to sleep as finality and a summary declaration of a dependence on providence. As a general rule, only those satires in which the moral standards are clear and clearly applied display unqualified closure. Pope's "Epistle to Bethel" (*Hor. Imit.* Sat. 2.2) also displays strong thematic closure: "Let us be fix'd, and our own Masters still," where fixity and stillness (another pun) suggests a kind of stability and self-mastery that contrasts effectively with the ebb and flow of wealth and property ownership.[10]

Pope's satires typically draw clear distinctions between vice and virture, moral heroes as opposed to fools and knaves, but even Pope frequently chooses to end his poems by gently or ironically undermining the stance of the heroic satirist. The "Epistle to Bolingbroke" builds to a celebration of "that Man divine whom Wisdom calls her own" (180), a model of integrity and self-possession.

> Great without Title, without Fortune bless'd,
> Rich ev'n when plunder'd, honour'd while oppress'd,
> Lov'd without youth, and follow'd without power,
> At home tho' exil'd, free, tho' in the Tower.
> In short, that reas'ning, high, Immortal Thing,
> Just less than Jove, and much above a King,
> Nay half in Heav'n—
>
> [181-87]

Mounting idealization ("Immortal Thing . . . half in Heav'n") without parallel in the Horatian original sets up a ringing conclusion—or an ironic fall. Pope brings the Man of Wisdom back to the ground of common humanity: "Nay half in Heav'n—except (what's mighty odd) / A Fit of Vapours clouds this Demi-God." The calculated infor-

mality, even slanginess, and ironic use of "mighty" (a traditional divine attribute) and "clouds" (which traditionally veiled the gods
from human sight) make Pope's deflationary ending wittier than
Horace's.[11]

The two dialogues of Pope's *Epilogue to the Satires* likewise build
the satirist into a hero or prophet, but they do not conclude without
implicitly questioning the effectiveness of their own moral stance.
Each is calculatedly anticlimactic. Dialogue 1 ends, to be sure, with
strong closural force: after surveying the triumphal procession of Vice
in England, Pope sees its virtual deification: "Nothing is sacred now
but Villany" (170). The climactic line, with its absolute statement and
its summary character, has strong closural force. Against such apparent finality Pope props a couplet which in some ways displays equal
force: "Yet may this Verse (if such a Verse remain) / Show there was
one who held it in disdain." The solitary defiance is impressive, but
the words encourage us to see too an ineffectual gesture (the conces-
sive parenthesis, the self-regarding aloofness of "disdain").

Dialogue 2 presents an apparently opposite case. The poem concludes with a lofty celebration of the defiant satirist in the last days.
Pope looks beyond a corrupt world to the "Temple of Eternity"
where truthful verse is "Immortal." Until then the poet will stand
firm: "Yes, the last Pen for Freedom let me draw. . . . Here, Last of
Britons, let your Names be read." We are plainly led to expect a
resounding end. Again Pope provides an ironic anticlimax. The interlocutor impatiently breaks in: "Alas! alas! pray end what you began, And write next winter more *Essays on Man*." The call for an
"end" of satire and a renewal of didactic writing (less biting, less
discomforting) imposes an abrupt and enforced closure on the satirist's efforts. It also patently attempts to cool the apocalyptic fervor
and remind poet and reader alike of the satirist's alienation from a
hostile and cynical audience.[12]

One common closural device in satire is a combination of what
Smith calls formal and thematic devices. In some formal verse satire
the satirist presents a series of "negative" moral examples concluded
by a single "positive" example, so that the form can be represented
as AAAA . . . B, where A and B stand not for formal but for thematic elements. Juvenal's tenth satire is organized on this principle.
Most of the poem is taken up with a series of examples of what men
foolishly wish for. Only the last twenty lines (out of 366) are devoted
to what men *should* pray for—a sound mind in a sound body.[13] But

it is notable that Juvenal undercuts the force of his thematic closure in advance by mocking the very idea of prayer to the gods: "If you insist on offering up the entrails and consecrated sausages from a white pigling in every shrine, then ask for a sound mind in a sound body."[14] His subsequent declaration that "what I've shown you, you can find by yourself: there's one path, and one only, to a life of peace—through virtue" serves not as compelling climax but as a kind of throwaway line, an offhand reference to a Stoic cliché, not a philosophical conclusion but an effective polemical device.[15] Readers who complain that the ending of Johnson's imitation of Juvenal's poem, "The Vanity of Human Wishes," is somehow unpersuasive, merely "tacked on," should consider that the alleged "weakness" is to be found in the Latin original. They might then go on to consider that such a conclusion need not, in satire, be a weakness.[16]

Other examples of the Juvenalian priamel can be found in Pope's *Moral Essays*. The second essay ("To a Lady") contrasts the inconsistencies of a "whole Sex of Queens" with the best kind of contradictions, found in Martha Blount, the subject of the final paragraph.[17] The fourth essay ("To Burlington") varies the form slightly, but Pope retains the examples of bad taste (Villario and Timon) and closes with Burlington himself, the model builder; this closural device can also be used to call attention to its own inefficacy. The first essay ("To Cobham") concludes with a series of seven satiric exempla of the ruling passion, and one final example, Cobham himself, who illustrates the principle with the virtuous ruling passion of patriotism.[18] But Pope's perfunctory four-line tribute seems almost designed as a hapless ironic gesture toward compliment and closure. The third essay ("To Bathurst") does not even pretend to close. After a series of misers and prodigals we find in terminal position not the Man of Ross but Sir Balaam. His tale closes emphatically—"Sad Sir Balaam curses God and dies"—but the poem as a consequence remains radically open, its moral vision clear but its confidence in the triumph of moderation and the "True Use" of riches manifestly shaken. Indeed, a strong argument might be made that all four Essays are open in that the inconsistencies or follies exposed in the early parts of the poems overwhelm the neat normative conclusions.

In some few cases, it is true, formal satire seems to display strong closure. The purest example is perhaps the lampoon, in which the satirist sets out to destroy, even to annihilate, a victim. The primitive curse or spell ends when the victim has been magically "killed":

"Evil, death, short life to Caier! / Let spears of battle wound him, Caier! / Caier . . . Caier . . . Caier under earth, / Under ramparts, under stones be Caier!"[19] The Restoration lampoon ends when the victim's dignity has been symbolically and definitively destroyed:

> Half-witty, and half-mad, and scarce half-brave,
> Half-honest (which is very much a *Knave*.)
> Made up of all these Halfs, thou can'st not pass,
> For any thing intirely, but an *Asse*.[20]

> But 'tis too much, on soe dispis'd a Theame;
> Noe Man, wou'd dabble in a dirty Streame:
> The worst that I cou'd write, wou'd be noe more,
> Than what thy very Friends have said before.[21]

In the first example, "half, half, half, . . . intirely" builds (cumulatively) to an effective conclusion. In the second, the search for "the worst" insult concludes (in ironic reversal) with what the fool's own friends will say of him. We often suppose that more sophisticated satire is built upon the same base as the lampoon, that all satire is designed to denounce, expose, or ridicule, and that satirists set about the task vigorously and single-mindedly until they stand triumphant over their fallen victims. But in fact, the lampoon is unrepresentative. As formal verse satire increases in length and looks beyond the single victim, it tends (as I have argued) to find it more difficult (or less appropriate) to conclude with summary dismissal.

Consider next a second formal tradition in satire, where the satirist invades a form or parodies it (not necessarily in order to mock it). Such forms include the verse letter, the scholarly disputation, the projector's pamphlet, the travel narrative, and the epic. Here the satirist takes over an existing form, and whatever sense of closure it carries. What commonly happens is that the sense of closure is deliberately weakened. Rochester's "Letter from Artemiza in the Towne to Chloe in the Countrey," for example, literally takes the form of a letter, from its abrupt salutation ("Cloe . . .") to its formal close ("Farewell.") Artemiza's letter ends as a real letter might end:

> But now 'tis tyme, I should some pitty show
> To Chloe, synce I cannot choose, but know,
> Readers must reape the dullnesse, writers sow.
> By the next Post such storyes I will tell,
> As joyn'd with these, shall to a Volume swell,

As true, as Heaven, more infamous, then Hell;
But you are tyr'd, and soe am I. Farewell.[22]

The gesture of closure is unmistakable, but the ending is in fact quite arbitrary. Rochester's deliberately artless transition—"But now 'tis tyme"—mocks the very idea of conclusion. Artemiza closes her letter not because her story is completed (indeed, the "fine Lady" whose conversation she has been recounting when last seen is still running on) but because she is tired. Her story has simply been suspended; it will be continued by the next post. Morally too the poem is obtrusively "open" rather than "closed." Having been introduced successively to three quite different women—Artemiza herself, the "fine Lady," and "that wretched thinge Corinna"—the reader is left with no clear set of standards by which to judge them. Is Artemiza a clearsighted idealist or an impertinent? Is Corinna a sordid courtesan or a practical and plucky survivor? The poem ends without answering any of these critical questions.[23]

Rochester's "Satyre against Mankind" also borrows its structure from another form, in this case the scholarly disputation. Like the letter, the logically articulated formal argument would seem to have a built-in power of arriving at a conclusion. Rochester counts on the reader's expectation that the argument will lead to a definitive Q.E.D., yet in the end he arrives at a conclusion in which nothing is really concluded. The poem pretends to demonstrate the truth of the paradox that it is better to be an animal than a man. It begins by presenting the shocking thesis, entertains objections from an imagined adversary, and answers them, arguing that with respect to "wisedom" and to "Nature" an animal's principles are more "gen'rous . . . and just" than a man's. The final section of the poem, sometimes called the epilogue (174-221), may have been added later. With or without the epilogue the "Satyr" in one sense achieves a kind of closure and in another sense remains radically open. The shorter version ends with brisk suggestions of a debater's summation ("Thus Sir you see . . .") but wittily proposes that the original implied question (is it better to be a man or an animal?) be replaced by another (since I've shown you that all men are knaves, it only remains to ask "who's a *Knave*, of the first *Rate*?"). The version with the epilogue in effect promises to recant the impudent paradox on condition that one just man be produced in the court or the church. The condition will plainly go unmet. But even if it were met, this "*God-like*" just man would serve as the exception to prove the rule. Although the wittily reformulated para-

dox ("*Man* differs more from *Man*, than *Man* from *Beast*.") gives the
"Satyr" one kind of closure, through epigrammatic compression and
a return to the poem's opening point, the reader knows that the conclusiveness is deceptive. The conclusion is both inescapable and absurd, obviously not to be taken seriously but just as obviously not to
be dismissed as a trick of logic. Likewise, the one "just man" is at once
a fantasy and an idealized image that neither satirist nor reader wishes
to abandon.[24] As with Juvenal's tenth satire, this is the conclusion of a
rhetorician—whose mission is to strike and even challenge—and not
of a moralist.

A more famous satire whose structure from beginning to end is
based on carefully reasoned consecutive argument is Swift's *Modest
Proposal*. Perhaps because Swift parodies so closely the tone and rhetoric of contemporary projectors, his *Proposal*, more than most satires, seems to come to a strong and "natural" end. Swift's projector
presents first the problem, then a proposed solution, the advantages of
his proposal, possible objections, answers to those objections, and a
final disavowal of any personal interest. By its close we sense that
there is nothing more for the satirist to say on the subject. We are left,
in Barbara Herrnstein Smith's terms, with "the expectation of nothing."[25] But if we look more closely at the last two paragraphs of the
Proposal we can see that the rhetoric is carefully calculated to offer
and ultimately to subvert closure.

The climax of the argument, the sharpest sting of the satire,
comes in the penultimate paragraph. In answer to his objectors,
Swift asks how else than by his proposal will food and clothing be
found for "a hundred thousand useless mouths and Backs." He goes
on in a single terrifying sentence, which in nearly two hundred words
provides a panorama of the problem he addresses, to suggest that
even the parents of the proposed victims would have preferred his
proposed solution of institutionalized cannibalism to the present
"perpetual Scene of Misfortunes" they have endured "by the Oppression of Landlords; the Impossibility of paying Rent, without
Money or Trade; the Want of common Sustenance, with Neither
House nor Cloaths, to cover them from the Inclemencies of Weather,
and the most inevitable Prospect of intailing the like, or greater Miseries upon their Breed for ever." The familiar Swiftian catalogue of
horrors works here not simply to oppress the reader with its burden
but to reduce the Irish poor, step by inevitable step, to naked shiver-
ing victims of inclement weather. It also leads the reader, step by
inevitable step, to accept the logical conclusion of Swift's proposal:

they would be better off dead. By unobtrusive technical means Swift builds the intensity and the persuasiveness of his peroration. The four phrase units ("the Oppression . . ., the Impossibility . . ., the Want . . ., the inevitable Prospect . . .") steadily increase in length and syntactic complexity and suggest a linked chain of increasing deprivation: cruel landlords, no rent money in any case, not even shelter or clothing. The chain leads inexorably not to death but (worse) to *endless* misery.

Surely this is a masterful moment, one of the most stirring climaxes in all Swift's work or in any satire. The relentlessness of the rhetoric impresses us equally with the satirist's power—his controlled rage, his ability to compress, his acuteness of focus—and with the utter impotence of the Irish victims, their devastated lives offering them only the "inevitable Prospect of intailing [a painfully ironic verb] the like, or greater Miseries upon their Breed [a last reminder of their subhuman status] for ever." Swift seems to have made a definitive and unanswerable satement of the case, leaving himself and his opponents nothing to say and his readers nothing to expect. All passion is spent.

But Swift chooses not to end *A Modest Proposal* here. The final paragraph, with the profession of sincerity and disinterestedness, deliberately undercuts the sublimity of the climax: "I PROFESS, in the Sincerity of my Heart, that I have not the least personal Interest, in endeavouring to promote this necessary work; having no other Motive than the publick Good of my Country. . . . I have no children, by which I can propose to get a single penny, the youngest being nine Years old, and my Wife past child-bearing." The drier, more detached tone is restored, implying both the blindness and impersonal heartlessness of the typical projector as well as Swift's own comic control of his material and of his own rage. The final paragraph closes the satire only in the sense that it restores the frame, returning to the tone of the beginning. In other respects it opens the satire for our speculation. The disparity between the fervor of the penultimate paragraph and the dry mockery and modesty of the final one provokes our reflections on the character and motive of the speaker and on the problematic relation between professed sincerity and genuine compassion, blind rationality and humane insight. The final paragraph also brings us back from a simulacrum of reality to obvious artifice, from tragedy to satire, from unrelieved despair to the self-conscious and self-critical emotions prompted by effective satire. In leaving us with the burden of further speculation, it refuses to end.

By contrast, *Gulliver's Travels*, which takes its narrative shape from the contemporary travel book, seems emphatically closed in the sense that we do not imagine Gulliver taking a fifth voyage. Numerous details prepare us for the book to "end." The last chapter of the fourth voyage is presented as a farewell to the reader. The prefatory "Letter to Sympson" and the "Publisher's Letter to the Reader" confirm Gulliver's retirement. After years as a blind and undaunted admirer of human nature, Gulliver undergoes such changes in the country of the Houyhnhnms ("I began to view the Actions and Passions of Man in a very different Light") as to induce in us a sense of imminent closure. But as many commentators point out, Swift carefully forestalls any novelistic conclusion. The famous "Sinon" passage—which reminds us that Gulliver may be a liar ("splendide mendax") or else Swift's puppet and satirical device—may well have been included in the final chapter in order to open the conclusion and to encourage the speculation and controversy about Houyhnhnms, Yahoos, and Gulliver that has raged ever since.

Consider finally some examples of mock-epic that borrow whatever closural force they have from the narrative forms they parody. Traditional epic ends firmly in death, restoration of order, or establishment of empire. But, as in other parodic forms, the mock-epic satirist seems bent on subverting this tendency toward closure. Dryden's *Absalom and Achitophel* builds (as Johnson noted) toward an epic confrontation between the friends and enemies of the king but concludes with an anticlimactic speech from the throne and confirmatory "peals of thunder" to signal wittily that David's power as king and Dryden's power as satirist are supreme. *MacFlecknoe*, a mock-coronation episode, ends abruptly as old Flecknoe, "yet declaiming," is dispatched through a trapdoor. With such formal "conclusions" Dryden mocks the idea of closure. In one case we have a *deus ex machina* and in the other its witty obverse.

Pope's mock-epics offer similar instances of foiled closure. Both the *Rape of the Lock* and the 1728 three-book *Dunciad* end with a vision that effectively suspends the narrative. In *The Rape of the Lock* the vision of the lock "amidst the stars" acts as a kind of *deus ex machina*: it enables Pope to break off the mock-epic battle of belles and beaux just as it reaches a peak of intensity. It also enables him to compliment Belinda by turning loss into gain, a ravished and irreplaceable lock of hair into a sign of her glory, a perishable "lock"—which, as Clarissa says, "will turn to grey"—into a poetic "*Lock*," which will forever shine. Even as we sense the arbitrariness of the poem's end, we appreciate Pope's deftness and ingenuity in diverting our eyes from the potentially disagreeable scene of acrimony, division, and disorder, drawing our eyes and those of the whole "Beau-monde" upward in a moment of communal admiration. Let us join together and put the foolish incident behind us, says Pope, who has been asked to laugh the quarreling families together again. The case is apparently closed. But some nagging questions remain to make us suspect the pretty artifice. Was not Belinda, when last seen and heard, shrieking "*Restore the Lock*" (5.103) no less fiercely than Othello "roar'd for the Handkerchief"? Is not the significance of the stellified lock as likely to be misinterpreted as was the real value of the lock when it graced Belinda's neck? Pope says that "some" will think it "Mounted" to an Ariostan "Lunar Sphere," that the "Beau-monde" shall consider its ray "Propitious," that unhappy lovers shall think it Venus, that the ridiculous Partridge by its appearance shall foretell the fate of kings and empires.[26] "Belinda's Name" will be inscribed "midst the stars," where most interpreters will be simply bemused by its metaphoric appearance. But Belinda herself might well be distressed if she could know her ambiguous reputation—for beauty, coquetry, folly, and pride—among readers with "quick poetic eyes."

In the third book of the 1728 *Dunciad* the vision of the future triumphs of Dulness is modeled upon the vision vouchsafed to Aeneas in the sixth book of the *Aeneid*. If the action of the 1728 *Dunciad* is the crowning of a new king, ensuring the succession and the wonders that Theobald is "himself destin'd to perform" ("Argument" to Book 3), then the vision is a satisfactory narrative conclusion. But Virgil's hero proceeded from vision to performance of epic deeds. Pope's hero never wakes from his vision at the end of the poem. Contemporary complaints that the hero of the poem never "did" anything point to a feature of the *Dunciad* that Pope may well have intended. Just as the actions of the dunces tend toward inertness and sleep, so the poem is deliberately left unconcluded. Most obviously, its narrative climax— "And universal Darkness covers all"—is subverted in the final line, when the vision flies "thro' the Ivory Gate." The vision is in some sense a "falsity," though Pope does not make clear in what way it is false. Presumably the satire on contemporary dunces is "true"(despite Scriblerus's mock-disclaimer), and the prophesied triumph of Dulness "false." Whether or not, as Scriblerus says, we should read the vision as "no more than a Chimera of the Dreamer's brain" (note to 3.5, 6), the final effect is deliberately deflationary and inconclusive. There is still more for Pope to say. The Argument to Book 3 intimates as much when it notes that "the present Action" gives only a "Pisgah-sight" of Dulness's full glory, "the Accomplishment whereof will, in all probability, hereafter be the theme of many other and greater Dunciads." Pope in effect serves warning to the dunces that the *Dunciad* might be indefinitely extended.

The fourth book of the *Dunciad* was in fact Pope's only continuation, and it promises, in the terms of its argument, "to declare the Completion of the Prophecies mention'd at the end of the former" (that is, Book 3) and thus to give the poem a definitive ending. If any satire is closed, one would think it the four-book *Dunciad*. A version of the concluding lines of the fourth book had of course appeared, as prophecy, at the end of the three-book version, but for several reasons the fourth book seems more conclusive. First, the couplet framing the vision of Darkness as a false dream is absent. Darkness does not "cover" all as in 1728 (a cover is removable, and may only be temporary, as the dark of night covers the earth). In the 1742 *New Dunciad* it "buries" all. The vision is given as an accomplished present, in the poet's own voice, not as prophecy of future events in the voice of Father Settle. It now follows a long fourth book in which, by critical consensus, Dulness is presented as more seriously threatening, universal (that is, not limited to literary matters), and furthermore the "principal Agent" of the poem.

But even here, closure is deceptive. Dulness, says Pope, would have continued speaking at line 605, but her own yawn prevented it. Pope would relate, with the Muse's help, "who first, who last resign'd to rest" (621), but that narrative, like Dulness's speech, is foreclosed: "in vain, in vain"—the poet cannot conclude. Instead, he narrates the arrival of Chaos and Night, the definitive event that must end his poem. But in two ways the arrival of old Chaos is hardly definitive. First, it is simply one more in a series of strikingly similar "endings" scattered through all four books of the poem:

And heavy harvests nod beneath the snow. [1.67-68]

And all be sleep, as at an Ode of thine. [1.318]

Th'unconscious stream sleeps o'er thee like a lake. [2.304]

So from the mid-most the nutation spreads
Round and more round, o'er all the sea of heads. [2.409-10]

And all the nations cover'd in her shade. [3.72]

And all the western world believe and sleep. [3.100]

'Till one wide conflagration swallows all. [3.240]

While the long solemn unison went round:
Wide, and more wide, it spread o'er all the realm. [4.612-13]

Art after Art goes out, and all is Night. [4.640]

And Universal Darkness buries All. [4.656]

In each of these "endings" a muffling cover of some kind (snow, water, fire, darkness) brings oblivion, darkness, or sleep to "all" (the word "all" appears in eight of my ten examples). It might be argued that each of these endings is an anticipation of the final end. We might thus read the action of the *Dunciad* as one long day's journey into night and sleep; from the beginning of the poem the dunces incline toward their end. But perhaps we should read the final line as one more repetition of what has already been said many times over; the narrative mode conceals the fact that the dull do not enact dullness or improve in their art; they simply *are* dull. By the same token, the poem could be said to be a gradual exfoliation, by means of narrative, of the true nonprogressive nature of dullness. Each book reveals the same "story"; each ends in sleep, and the fourth is no more conclusive than the first.

Furthermore, although the poem appears to end at 4.656, the 1743 volume in which the complete poem first appeared in most emphatically does not end. As the "all-composing hour" falls, Pope is still composing and rearranging some forty pages of appendixes, including (in ironical juxtapostion to the alleged end) a "Preface" to earlier editions of the *Dunciad*, and a "continuation" of the *Guardian* discussion on pastorals.[27] Life goes on.

The third formal line of satire—the Menippean tradition—is not always readily distinguishable from the parodic tradition. Is *Gulliver's Travels* a parody of a travel narrative, or a Lucianic imaginary voyage?[28] But in general we can say that the Menippean satirist selects forms that display relatively weak closure: the catalogue, the dialogue, the symposium or conversation, the imaginary voyage, the picaresque narrative, the anatomy, the allegorical vision. These forms are in principle infinitely extendable. There can always be another story or adventure; the conversation can always take another turn. What Kernan says of *Don Juan* may be applied to all Menippean fictions: the pattern is always "but then . . ." (*Plot of Satire*, p. 178). In the European Menippean tradition, which borrows these and other forms, formal closure is very uncommon, as a brief survey will recall.

More's *Utopia* makes use of two forms: the traveler's narrative

(Hythloday's account in Book 2 of the island of Utopia), and the symposium (the conversation among "More," Hythloday, and the others in Book 1). More began work on *Utopia* with the traveler's tale, the present Book 2 (c. 1514-15), a potentially closed form, but proceeded to reduce his reader's sense of closure by adding a frame, the symposium of many voices in Book 1 (1516). Hythloday concludes the inset narrative with a panegyric on the wealth, justice, and harmony of the Utopians, but we are not permitted to rest with his firm conclusion of their superiority to the Europeans. "More" speaks the last words, signaling briefly that he has a number of "objections" to the Utopian system which he does not elaborate. The book concludes with repeated signs that nothing has really been concluded. Hythloday is "tired with talking" and besides is not likely to accept "contradiction," so "More" will not pursue the discussion. But he says to Hythloday that they must find some other time for thinking about these matters more deeply and for talking them over in greater detail. "More" then in effect turns to his reader to say he hopes "such an opportunity will present itself some day"—that is, he alerts us that there may be a sequel (if only in our continuing thoughts). For now, "More" says, he "cannot agree with everything" Hythloday has said but finds "many things" in the Commonwealth of Utopia worth imitating. Even this hope of future closure is dashed, for More doesn't really expect that England will ever imitate the offered model. Utopia remains no-where.

The contemporary *Praise of Folly* is built upon a frame with a powerful potential for closure. The classical oration is designed to close with a *peroratio* in which the speaker both recapitulates his argument and seeks to arouse his audience in a direct emotional appeal. When Folly has offered, in her most powerful argument, an account of Christian folly, she arrives at the moment for summation. But she plainly refuses: "I see that you are expecting a peroration, but you are just too foolish if you suppose that after I have poured out a hodgepodge of words like this I can recall anything that I have said." And the book closes with a perfunctory "farewell." It is as if the logic of satire has made Erasmus hold back.

Burton's *Anatomy of Melancholy* presents a curiously similar case. In his first edition (1621) Burton in fact supplied a formal "Conclusion of the Author to the Reader." But after the first edition Burton dropped the "Conclusion" and used much of its contents in the *prefatory* "Democritus Junior to the Reader." To defer premature conclusion in this way was perhaps an appropriate gesture for a writer who continued to revise and enlarge his book through five editions for the rest of his life. His anatomy is in principle infinitely extendable, and his subject infinitely divisible into further partitions, sections, members, and subsections.

Eighteenth-century Menippean satires are notoriously inconclusive. Johnson's *Rasselas* of course ends with a "Conclusion, in which Nothing in Concluded," and *Tristram Shandy*—heir to Rabelais, Burton, and a long tradition of "learned wit"—comes to a mock-end after nine volumes. It leaves many readers assuming that the book does not go on for one main reason: the author died. Blake's *Marriage of Heaven and Hell* closes not with a recapitulation of its opening "Argument," but with one more "Memorable Fancy." Blake sees an angel "who stretched out his arms, embracing the flame of fire, and he was consumed, and arose as Elijah." This seems a promising apocalyptic ending, but Blake adds a footnote to report that the angel, now become a devil, is Blake's particular friend, and to promise that there is more to come. In our own day, Thomas Pynchon's novels (late exemplars of Menippean fictions) tend not to conclude conclusively.[29]

One of the most obvious ways in which a poem can indicate its own conclusion thematically, as Smith says, "is simply to say so." But such "explicit self-closural reference," she notes, "is in fact uncommon."[30] For satirists, as we have seen, ending cleanly and firmly seems either difficult or undesirable. Even when employing conventional closural devices, they find a way to keep such devices from exerting their full power. With few exceptions, satirists want to keep their work open, ambiguous, unresolved, even when declaring that they have finished. *A Tale of a Tub*, one of the most pointedly open of eighteenth-century satires, is also one of the most self-conscious about the business of closing. Swift's allegory of the three brothers breaks off in section 9, where as I have noted he pretends to have mislaid or lost "the remaining part of these Memoirs," consisting of the further adventures of Peter, Martin, and Jack. The section begins with indications that the "End" of the narrator's "journey" is in sight, and Swift hastens (reluctantly and self-consciously) to provide that end, "the Ceremonial Part of an accomplish'd Writer and . . . least of all others to be omitted."

Although wary of the dangers of "*Going too long*," Swift has grown "very loth to part" with his "old Acquaintance," the reader: "So that I have sometimes known it to be in Writing, as in Visiting, where the Ceremony of taking Leave, has employ'd more Time than the whole Conversation before." Although he knows that he has nothing more to say, he will not willingly put down his pen. In describing his current experiment "to write upon Nothing"—"When the Subject is utterly exhausted, to let the Pen still move on; by some called the Ghost of Wit, delighting to walk after the Death of its Body"—he refers not to another project but to his present words. In part Swift parodies the garrulousness of modern hacks whose egotism, deficient sense of form, and fee per page keep them scribbling and from "Discerning to have Done." But he exercises too the characteristic doggedness of the satirist, reluctant to "remit [his] grasp" on the reader. Finally, he resolves to leave off, knowing that he has left his reader with "sufficient Matter to employ his Speculations for the rest of his life" (sec. 10).

What can we conclude from satire's tendency not to conclude? First, that it is simply difficult to close because there is no "natural" end to the satirist's anger. Perhaps, like the wife of King Midas in the *Epistle to Dr. Arbuthnot*, the satirist discovers some temporary relief by letting the secret pass to each fool "that he's an ass" (80). The satiric "truth once told," says Pope, "the Queen of Midas slept, and so may I" (81-82). But the calm is only temporary, and the rhythm of the poem *Epistle to Arbuthnot* is an ebb and flow of satiric resentment. There is always more for the satirist to say, further examples to be supplied.

Second, to whatever degree satirists are drawn toward a single pattern that will explain and contain the vice and folly they see, they know the pattern is an oversimplification and that the farraginous nature of experience resists our categories. A.B. England has shown that Swift characteristically refuses to reduce the miscellany of irreducible particulars in the world to any "ordering design."[31] Irwin Ehrenpreis has noted that Swift refuses to unify the satirical thrust of *Gulliver's Travels*. Instead of providing "structural coherence," he prefers to "push separate arguments to extremes without regarding the inferences that persistent and learned readers might draw from them."[32] Or as Byron flippantly says, "If a writer should be quite consistent, / How could he possibly show things existent?" (*Don Juan* 15.87). The satirist, like Byron, pursues conflicting arguments and expresses conflicting opinions. A satirist's final word, as Harry Levin deftly observes, is likely to be "But."[33] Though Levin has Voltaire in mind, he might have cited a more famous example from *A Tale of a Tub*. At the climax of the brilliant passage about credulity and curiosity in the "Digression on Madness," Swift disposes of the satirical anatomist but then icily exposes his opposite, the Epicurean projector, as a "Fool among Knaves." Most rhetoricians would have been content with this shattering conclusion as a kind of triumphal exit line; Swift, however, doesn't miss a beat: *"BUT to return to Madness."*

It appears that the satirist's instinct is not to close off an argument but to think of another example, or a qualification, or a digression. The point is to keep moving, and the satirist is supple enough to do so. If this is true, then we will have to modify Kernan's influential thesis that the "plot" of satire is stasis, "in which the two opposing forces, the satirist on the one hand and the fools on the other, are locked in their respective attitudes without any possibility of either dialectical movement or the simple triumph of good over evil." Kernan sees in satire not a change, either in the world or the satirist, but "mere intensification of the unpleasant situation with which satire opens." [34] Kernan's is a dramatic model in which the satirist is a dramatized character, "locked" in anger. But if we shift to an expository model in which the satirist and author are one, the plot of satire is rather movement than stasis: an ever shifting scene beheld by a supple satirist who keeps changing perspective and rhetorical purpose. Perhaps Byron is in this respect the archetypal satirist. As Kernan himself says elsewhere, in *Don Juan* every conclusion is only "momentary"; what Byron presents is the "constant flow of life leading on from change to change" (*Plot of Satire*, p. 182). In Bakhtin's terms, satire is a carnivalesque genre and shares with carnival an attitude toward closure: "The carnival sense of the world . . . knows no period, and is, in fact, hostile to any sort of *conclusive conclusion*: all endings are merely new beginnings" (*Problems in Dostoevsky's Poetics*, p. 165). Menippean satire is particularly resistant to closure. In the words of Philip Holland, commenting on Bakhtin: "As tragedy and epic enclose, Menippean forms open up, anatomize. The serious forms comprehend man; the Menippean forms are based on man's inability to know and contain his fate. To any vision of a completed system of truth, the menippea suggests some element outside the system." [35]

Perhaps this slightly overstates the fluidity of satire. A fuller account would have to acknowledge that satire's flow is punctuated by moments of epigrammatic force and even thundering climax. Like the heroic couplet, of which satirists have been so fond, satire is a mix of witty closure and forward movement. End-stopped couplets permit the satirist to write with what used to be called *point* (which Johnson defines as "the sting of an epigram; a sentence terminated with remarkable turn of words or thought"). But they also permit a satirist to resist closure, because the tension of the individual couplet sends us back to its internal parallels and contrasts, and because the march of successive couplets keep us moving forward. So too satire as a form builds to *moments* of narrative, moral, or rhetorical closure. But the moments pass and turn out to be pauses. Even in the final sentence of "The Conclusion" to *A Tale of a Tub* Swift cannot bring himself to end: "I shall here pause awhile, till I find, by feeling the World's Pulse, and my own, that it will be of absolute Necessity for us both, to resume my Pen."

5
Satiric Fictions and Historical Particulars

At the opening the fourth book of Pope's *Dunciad* the several muses lie in chains below Dulness's throne. The triumph of Dulness seems complete, except that "sober History" attends on Tragedy, promising "Vengeance on a bar'brous age," and "Satyr" holds up the head of her sister, Comedy. In Pope's allegory History and Satire then work together to keep alive some spirit of opposition to Dulness.[1] Six years earlier, in his "Character, Panegyric, and Description of the Legion Club" (1736), Swift invokes Clio, the muse of history, who conducts him to the door of the club (representing the Irish House of Commons) but flees at the stench that comes from within; the satirist "resolves to stay" (131). As these two instances remind us, satire and history are often thought to be near allied. Proxies or substitutes for enfeebled tragedy and comedy, they work in tandem and perform similar functions, "recording the crimes and punishments of the great" and "exposing the vices or follies of the common people" (Pope's note to *Dunciad* 4.39).[2] But as Swift suggests, sometimes history itself lacks the requisite nerve, and satire had to take over its function. Pope and Swift here provide an occasion for reassessing an often canvassed topic: the relationship between the "fictions" of satire and the "real world" outside the text. We may begin with the familiar assumption that satire refers to people and events in the world of history.

Satire and Referentiality

Editors of satire have long taken as one of their responsibilities the identification of historical references, names, and events that time has darkened, or that the satirist themselves darkly or incompletely identify in their texts. Some Renaissance commentators thought Juvenal and Persius were deliberately obscure—perhaps to protect themselves from retaliation or censorship, perhaps to follow satire's proper style as they understood it. But Marston argues that if his readers had lived in the days of Juvenal and Persius, they would not have found Roman satire difficult to understand. Present-day readers, he says, simply don't know the "private customes of the time" that the satirists attack.[3] Seventeenth-century editors of Juvenal and Persius provided lengthy notes, both to help the reader and to "clear" their authors from unfounded charges of willful obscurity. Sir Robert Stapylton's *Juvenal* (1660) is accompanied, according to its title page, by "a Large Comment, Clearing the Author in Every Place, wherein he Seemed Obscure, Out of the Laws and Customes of the Romans, and the Latine and Greek Histories." Holyday's 1673 commentary is designed to "illustrate" Juvenal and Persius. The assumption is that satire derives its strength and its very life from its grounding in a certain time and place. Thus Henry Higden, in his 1687 translation of Juvenal, declares: "All *Satyrs* [have] a strong taste of the Humour and particular Hints of the Times wherein they were writ, which is indeed the Life and Beauty of *Satyr*."[4]

Editors since the seventeenth century have continued to provide necessary "historical" information. Pope's Scriblerian apparatus to the 1729 *Dunciad* provides the sort of annotation that Swift predicted the poem would need to identify the obscure and forgettable dunces.[5] Johnson's "Life of Butler" (1779) in effect explains *Hudibras* by recreating for his reader the forgotten "opinions" on which the manners of the poem are founded. The Twickenham editors, beginning in 1938, elaborated Pope's own notes for an audience that needs even more help. The explicit assumption behind such annotation and explanation is that satire is a topical art. The present-day reader, in the Twickenham view, needs to know not only where Pope refers to the South Sea Bubble or to Walpole's mistress but that Addison stands behind Atticus, and Hervey behind Sporus, since Pope expected his first readers to see the originals. The implicit philosophical assumption is of course that satire, by its very use of the medium of language, is a mimetic and *referential* art, that it imitates and *refers* to people and events outside itself. This is an assumption that, until very recently, nobody would have thought to question.

With the flowering of the New Criticism in the 1940s and 1950s came a new emphasis not on satire's historicity but on its autonomy. Like all poetry, it was seen as a self-contained verbal order. Satire makes use of "fictions." It is concerned with universals, not particulars—not finally with particular scoundrels and ministers but with the timeless war of good and evil. There are probably historical reasons for this emphasis. In rescuing satire as art, the New Critics not only advanced their own case for a critical formalism but rehabilitated writers who had fallen into some disfavor (such as Pope) by combating the old charge that satire is too mired in particulars. This charge dates back at least to Johnson, who thought much of *Hudibras* was "perishable," and to Thomas Warton, a harbinger of future taste: "Wit and Satire are transitory and perishable, but Nature and Passion are eternal."[6] The prominent theorists of satire in the 1950s and 1960s—trained in New Criticism at Yale, or practicing it there— argued in response that wit and satire, because embodied in fictions, are themselves eternal.

Such a reading of satire does not deny the presence of particulars but reinterprets them as symbols, representatives, or fictive re-creations. Dryden's "Sh—" is in one sense the historical Thomas Shadwell, in another sense a wholly re-created or fictional figure: a Bad Poet. Colley Cibber in the *Dunciad* is in one sense the actor, playwright, and buffoon whom we know from his autobiographical *Apology*. But more important, he is symbolic of what is wrong with the state of literature, akin to all bad poets and even akin to Milton's Satan. As Aubrey Williams says of the *Dunciad*, the poem "simultaneously affirms and denies its historical connections at every moment."[7] This New Critical view extended beyond the high art of mock-heroic to formal verse satire and even lampoon. George Lord, who as editor of the densely topical *Poems on Affairs of State* might be expected to make room for history, declared that "the richest satire . . . is that which transmutes concrete historical realities into universals. Its fictions include but transcend historical fact."[8] The critic's emphasis, in this view, clearly falls not on historicity but on universality or on fiction. Thus Kernan sees Hall's satires as purely conventional, not social-historical documents (*Cankered Muse*, pp. 85-86n). Such critics in effect join forces with Northrop Frye, who declared in the major 1950s document on literary theory that all literary statements are "hypothetical" (*Anatomy of Criticism*, p. 74).

Even though the sun of New Criticism is long past its noon, and critics of Pope have reintroduced biography and social context, the New Critical or "formalist" reading of satire persists. In some cases history disappears altogether. Michael Rosenblum argued in 1972 that satire is concerned not with the outside world, but ultimately with itself. The *Dunciad* transcends its occasion, and substitutes for history. "The Lord Hervey of history is unimportant; it is only when he completes the quire, enters the pages of Pope's book, that he has any significance. Pope and the reader are not interested in who the dunce is, but only in what can be made of him."[9] In this view, the satirist uses historical data as raw material to be re-created or transformed into a fiction. In other cases, the emphasis falls not on the fictionality of satire but on its universality. Even a formalist can make room for history by what has been called a "generality theory of value."[10] Satires that transcend their immediate occasion and circumstances are judged by most readers to be of greater value than those that remain topical and occasional. Such readers in effect agree that satire refers to the world of history but does so in a powerfully generalizing way: it refers to "the way things are" (and always have been), to historical universals, and thus gains a kind of autonomy from history (most historians nowadays would call this a denial of history).

In recent years, literary theory has challenged the old logocentric mimeticism and encouraged critics to think of literature as constituting a purely verbal world. Deconstruction, as many have suggested, is a more insistent formalism. In a deconstructive spirit, Fredric Bogel has proposed that we now need to renew the formalism of 1960 in a more intense way and to "continue the dehistoricizing that the formalists began." He wants to see referentiality and factuality as *conventions* of satire, "products of certain rhetorical strategies." Bogel distinguishes between the *fact* of "reference" and the "textual gesture" of "referentiality," that "repertoire of namings, pointings, allusions, and presuppositions that constitute one of the central conventions of satire [and all 'factual' genres]: the assumption that there exists a historical world, 'out there,' elements of which are both solidly specifiable and distinct from the order of discourse in which they are specified." What interests Bogel is not the *fact* of reference, but its structure and function in satire (as acts of casting out, or exclusion). If satire is only language, and "reality" is constructed in language, then we misplace our emphasis if we try to look "outside." What we do *not* need, he argues, is an effort to "interpret a text or passage by detailing the historical circumstances that may have surrounded or given rise to it."

Simultaneously with New Critical emphasis on satire as self-contained rhetorical art, the so-called "Chicago critics" (Sheldon Sacks, Edward Rosenheim, A.R. Heiserman) beginning in the early 1950s emphasized referentiality as the key feature of satire.[12] Whereas the

New Critics were anxious to distinguish satire from "sociology, biography, or other kinds of non-aesthetic history," the Chicago critics—as I suggested in Chapter 1—sought to distinguish satire from other genres. In their view the distinguishing feature of satire is that it refers (in Rosenheim's words) to "discernible historical particulars"—like Butler's Puritans.[13] Satire operates by ridiculing "particular men, the institutions of men, traits presumed to be in all men": that is, by sending us back to the "external objects of the satire" in the external world outside the text.[14] In such a view of satire, so Michael Rosenblum notes, we must "translate the fictions back into the world which they in some way comment on. . . . Satire tries to make us move back to the world."[15]

The "Chicago" or historicist camp, like the "Yale" formalist school, has its latter-day supporters. Reacting against Rosenblum's formalism, Malvin Zirker argued in 1972 that "great satire . . . cannot exist apart from a successfully achieved sense of moral indignation that inevitably depends in considerable degree on our sense of the rightness of the attack on those conditions in the real world to which our attention is called." More recently R.B. Gill has insisted that personal satire has to do with "interactions between real people." Reacting against the tendency to fictionalize satire, he claims that the "confrontation with historical people in occasional literature enlivens it and gives it a biting edge."[16] Satire, says another recent critic, is "the mode of 'reality,' of the actual, of things as they are."[17]

We thus have two incompatible accounts of satire's relationship to an external world. Both the Yale and Chicago accounts now seem partial—partial in the sense that they are incomplete and in the sense that they are dictated by larger theoretical considerations. Thirty years later, in a different critical climate, the Yale formalists of the early 1960s now seem to have insisted too much on satire's transcendence of the particular. Today we are readier to see that literature of any kind is always implicated in its time and place, and more hesitant to speak about art and universals. The older Chicago historicist claims about "discernible historical particulars," unable to account for a satire as canonical as Gulliver's fourth voyage, now seem based on a narrowly positivist view of historical "facts." The latter-day proponents of the formalist and historicist positions seem likewise to advance their claims too far. Bogel's "intenser formalism" would subsume history and the world "out there" to the formal order of satire. But historical particulars do not go along peaceably. They insist on their historicity and on bringing the world of history

into the poem. Satire likes to name names; it attracts "keys." As a
Renaissance epigram put it, satires "father themselves";[18] that is,
they entice us to identify the masked targets and to apply the conclusions to the external world we live in. We supply those names and
events from our stock of information about the "real world." We do
not simply enter the satirist's linguistic order and play the verbal
game by his rules. By the same token, Zirker insists too much that
the satirist be "right" about the conditions he attacks. But do we
really care whether Dryden is "right" about Shadwell, Swift about
Temple and Bentley, Pope about Walpole and Theobald? Does it
matter to us as readers of Juvenal's satire whether or not the empress
Messalina was an imperial whore? Is there a "right" or "wrong"
view about the alleged (and much debated) "dignity of human nature" or the "rational nature of man"?

On the other side, Gill grounds personal satire too firmly in the
world of "real people" when he insists that the "structure of persuasion" depends on our prior and independent knowledge of the satirist and his real-life adversaries. In all forms of literature we tend to
accept the judgment of the narrator, unless we are given a reason not
to. We are persuaded in part by the bill of particulars the satirist
presents, in part by the sheer wit and force of the attack. We do not
always need to know historical details to be persuaded (or entertained), nor do we have to know who the author is "in real life" in
order to admire the skills of a satirist, even when they are self-
consciously displayed. And insofar as a satire serves not to attack an
adversary but to unsettle its readers, conduct an inquiry, or explore a
paradox, it draws those readers into a space defined for the purpose
and relies little on their specific knowledge of the external world.

The debate about satire's link to the external world, it would
appear, has reached a deadlock. One way out is to look more closely
at satiric texts and to remember that satires vary, in the degree and
kind of referentiality, far more than the competing theories acknowledge. The debate has become stalemated in part because the terms in
which it is conducted are too crude.

Some of the difficulty lies with the term "referential," which can
be used to suggest several different relationships between satire and
the external world. Some critics use the term to mean that satire *represents* the real world and thus *includes* it, brings it into the text. In can
do so by means of Johnsonian "just representations of general nature," which "recall the original to every mind" (cf. Sacks's "traits
presumed to be in all men"). Or it can allude to real particulars. In

each case *representation* can, but need not (depending on one's theory), imply a real link to the external world. In the older understanding, a representation not only resembled the original but bore its character or power.[19] For some recent theorists, a representation is *only* a text, a linguistic re-presentation. To "refer" is sometimes taken more literally, in the sense of *redirecting* the readers' attention, or even sending them back from satire to the world outside, where they will find the very fools and villains that the satirist has named. In this case, as Rosenblum has noted, the text of satire is only a middle term between the provocation or occasion and the real-world consequences; it thus tends to disappear once it has performed its referential function.[20] So long as sharply opposed assumptions are hidden in the same word, we are (like Sterne's Walter and Uncle Toby) unlikely to clarify our differences, much less arrive at consensus.

Even if we agree on a definition of "refer," we still have to remember that satire refers to different kinds of "objects": sometimes to particular people (such as Shadwell or Cibber) or classes of people (upstart "gentlemen" in the Renaissance, the Greeks in Juvenal's Rome); sometimes to specific political issues (English colonial policy toward Ireland in the eighteenth century, the South Sea Bubble); sometimes to more generalized period issues ("corruption" under Walpole, the decline of housekeeping in the sixteenth century); sometimes to universals (pride in reason, loss of ancestral virtue). Referentiality comes also in varying degrees, from full proper names to intials or asterisks (we must count syllables being represented, and then supply an appropriate name), to type names that carry associations (Timon, for example), to invented or borrowed type names (such as Hall's "Labeo"—taken from Persius—which seems to refer to "any bad poet"), to historical parallels and allegory.

Some satires are of course more topical then others. At one extreme is the lampooning attack on an individual, at the other a "satire on mankind." Late Pope poems are liberally studded with proper names, Donne's and Hall's marked with type figures. Juvenal is more topical than Horace. Gulliver's fourth voyage is considerably less topical than the third. Clear reference to historical particulars thus seems to be true of some satire but not essential in all satire. Nor is it a feature that distinguishes satire from other genres. Panegyric (such as Dryden's "Astraea Redux") and historical poems (his "Annus Mirabilis") are crucially tied to specific people and events.[21]

Even when a satirist appears to "refer" to historical events or persons, the reader does not always make the identification. Sometimes this is deliberate: the satirist teasingly offers initials, or a name or other specifier that might fit more than one target (for example, Pope's "Timon" in the "Epistle to Burlington," the unnamed "Rev'rend Atheists" and "poisoning Dame" in the *Epilogue to the Satires*).[22] The reader, even while encouraged to supply a real name, is uncertain whether the name refers to a type or an individual. Some satiric allegories are readily deciphered, (as are Dryden's *Absalom and Achitophel* and Samuel Garth's *Dispensary*); others (such as *Hudibras*) are not, even with the help of a published key (whether authorized or unauthorized).

Most satire, furthermore, tends to lose referential power over time. This may or may not be a limitation on its effectiveness as satire. Readers either find the references obscure (as in Persius) or assume they are reading general rather than particular satire (in which case the identity of named individuals is simply unimportant). It is sometimes argued that satire loses some of its sting or bite if it does *not* confront historical particulars. But Gulliver's fourth voyage, without particulars, scathingly indicts European colonialism (pretending to exempt only England); and the third voyage, which contemporaries would have recognized as a particular reflection, remains a powerful satire on political tyranny even to readers who know nothing about English-Irish politics in the eighteenth century.

We do not really need to know Simon Patrick, Nathaniel Ingelo, and Richard Sibbes (or, in one version, Richard Stillingfleet) in order to feel the satiric impact of Rochester's "Satyr against Reason and Mankind" in which they are named and derided.[23] One might argue that a few satires have actually gained in referential power over time. Eighteenth-century imitations of Juvenal acquired additional bite through their reflections on the parallels between past and present corruption. As Lord Chesterfield remarked, while arguing that the proposed Licensing Act could not be effectively enforced, old plays can sometimes be given topical application, if not by the actors or manager, then by an audience that will "apply what never was, what could not be designed as a Satyr on the present Times."[24] Those who have lived through the special tyranny of twentieth-century totalitarianism are perhaps able to see in *Gulliver's Travels* a strange prophecy come true. Pope observes ironically that even when he exaggerates or invents in satire, eventually some "real" fool comes along and "sins up to my Song" (*Epilogue to the Satires* 2.9). To combat the loss of topicality, however, he updated the names in the *Dunciad* to keep it current, as the dunces of 1743 replaced the forgotten (or deceased) dunces of 1728. So too Young revised his *Love of Fame* in later editions, perhaps because he felt the original lines had become ineffective as satire.[25] And Garth updated the historical references in *The Dispensary* in successive editions from 1699 to 1714.

Even when satire is as "referential," as directed at particular people, as Pope's later work, we should remember that historical particulars in satire always have a curious in-between status, neither wholly fact nor wholly fiction. Once inserted into a satire, the particular becomes the satirist's thrall, to use as he wishes: perhaps to be comically abused, perhaps to stand as an example for the deterrence of others. Cibber in the *Dunciad* is not simply the historical Colley Cibber. He is given a much larger role to play than Laureate, actor, apologist, and theater manager. In a playful distortion of history, Pope assigns him two bronze brothers—perhaps because of euphony ("brazen, brainless brothers"), perhaps to bring out Cibber's own moral brazenness, perhaps even to draw Cibber into the protest that the brothers were "not *Brazen*, but *Blocks*."[26] But Cibber also recognizably remains Colley Cibber (1671-1757), and his authentic history cannot easily be excluded from the poem. Thus we cannot say that particulars are utterly "transformed" or "transcended." Satire remains a radically impure art, both contaminated and energized by the world outside itself.

"Referential" is not the only term that needs to be sharpened. We also need to interrogate the very word "history." At a time when professional historians are rethinking what it means to "write" history, it is well for literary critics and theorists to look again at their casual assumptions about history. To do so is to discover that satire has prospered most when it regarded history, and history regarded it, with suspicion and rivalry.

History and History-Writing

The idea that history is "what actually happened" and that history-writing is properly a full recovery and authentic recording of "how things really were" (as Leopold von Ranke put it) is an old ideal of nineteenth-century positivist history that still survives in the general mind. Such history is a fixed order of events, waiting to be discovered by the persistent and objective researcher. It once supplied the literary critic with a conveniently fixed reference point outside the literary work, from which that work was insulated or to which it referred (depending on one's theory). The key point is that history in this view is fixed and accessible to us. Thus Rosenblum says that "the satirist's efforts are tied to history," Sitter that "satiric poetry is nearly always highly *historical* poetry."[27] But what if "history"—as some would now suggest—is only a sophisticated kind of "fiction"?

Our naive and unhistorical view of satire and history finds them similar because they both deal in "facts" and "identifiable historical particulars," or find them divergent because one finally deals in facts and the other in fictions. But some philosophers of history have recently urged historians to acknowledge that "the presumed concreteness and accessibility of historical milieux" is constructed by the historian and not found in the documents. History-writing, they argue, is not the discovery of objective truth but a construction, a story, the imposition of an interpreter's grid or template on an undifferentiated "historical field."[28] In such a climate the literary theorist can better recognize that the historian and the satirist are akin, but in some unsuspected ways.

In one tradition, the historian and the satirist are akin in sharing a rhetorical purpose: to assign praise or blame. In classical antiquity history was still closely allied to epic (in its subject matter) and to rhetoric (in its power of moving or persuading). For Aristotle, history, poetry, and philosophy are three branches of learning; they differ not in their subject matter but in their manner of teaching. Philosophy teaches by precept, and history by example. A latter-day Aristotelian such as Sir Philip Sidney could argue that poetry was superior to the other two branches because it combined the general notion with the particular example and was thus at once less abstract than philosophy and more general than history. But history had its own champions who claimed it to be more certain than poetry, which dealt not with the actual but the ideal or the possible, and more useful than philosophy, which lacked the power to enliven and enforce its precepts.

The Renaissance inherited this "exemplary" theory of history. One of the last inheritors was Bolingbroke, for whom history was still (in the words of the old commonplace) "philosophy teaching by example how to conduct ourselves in all the situations of private and public life."[29] As the theory of examplary history is defined by its exponents, it sounds remarkably like the theory of satire advanced at the same time by Dryden and his followers.[30] Like the satirist, the historian distinguishes between the virtuous and the wicked, and perpetuates the memory of both. As in satire, such examples serve as inducements to virtue. Historical justice, says Bolingbroke, brands the name of a villain with "infamy" and celebrates the honest man "with panegyrics to succeeding ages." Good men are encouraged with the promise of "a bright and lasting reputation," and evil men threatened with "the terror of being delivered over as criminals to all posterity."[31] Students of history will know that Bolingbroke here draws on a storehouse of commonplaces (to be found in contemporary French and English writers),[32] but the student of satire will hear the accents of Pope's late Horatian satires. A late eighteenth-century translator of Horace claimed that stire, "perhaps more properly than even History, may be termed 'Philosophy teaching by example.' "[33]

Exemplary history aims not at particular truths but at general truths, at the universals of human nature and social or political conduct. Because it teaches "the general principles of virtue, and a general system of ethics and politics," history is the proper training ground for magistrates and statesmen.[34] It is also a means of commenting on the political world in one's own day. Bolingbroke was not only a philosopher of history but also a practicing politician, one of the guiding spirits behind the opposition to Walpole, and one of the leading contributors to its chief newspaper, the *Craftsman*. Like many papers in its day, the *Craftsman* made use of "parallel history" to argue its case against Walpole. Events drawn from classical or earlier English history might be surveyed to produce a warning against the dangers of wicked ministers and of "Corruption." Parallel history was designed to achieve the same end as political satire. Like satire, it often focused on Theophrastan types and exemplary or cautionary figures (Pericles, Sejanus, Wolsey) and made use of selected historical particulars to establish a general proposition (about avaricious or overweening ministers, for example), which might then be given particular application.

Bolingbroke's friend Swift, though he did not write for the *Craftsman*, had engaged in a similar kind of parallel history in his early career. *The Contests and Dissensions . . . in Athens and Rome* (1701) belongs to the same tradition of exemplary history turned to partisan political ends. The occasion for Swift's work is the threatened impeachment of the Whig leaders, which he seeks to avert. To this end Swift ostensibly reviews the political conflicts in Greece and Rome which disturbed the "Ballance of Power" between the people and the nobles. What he is in fact concerned about is imbalance in one direction only—popular excess. "The People" are portrayed in a consistently bad light, repeatedly harassing and accusing their leaders— "the best men"—through their own "rash, jealous, and inconsistent Humour" and ultimately through their "Tyranny" (*Prose Works*, 1:209). History itself, so the work implicitly claims, will demonstrate that popular power must be curbed. But Swift goes on to make direct application in "some particular Remarks upon the present Posture of Affairs" (I:228).

Exemplary historians and moral satirists were thus engaged in the same enterprise and shared common ground.[35] But as the older tradition of exemplary history was coming to a close in the eighteenth century, it was competing with a younger tradition of "critical" history, which in some respects made an enemy of satire. This newer tradition is especially associated with Pierre Bayle and his late seventeenth-century *Historical and Critical Dictionary*, but we may perhaps see Francis Bacon as a forerunner. Poetry for Bacon is still an "imitation of history." But poetry acts by supplying the deficiencies of history, feigning acts "more heroical" and providing for poetic justice, "accommodating the shows of things to the desires of the mind." History, by contrast gives us "ordinary events" and works by "buckling and bowing down the mind to the nature of things." Though less gratifying to the mind, history is at once the most dignified and difficult of human writings. It is difficult to write, he says, and is often done badly, because it is difficult to ascertain the truth about the past, and dangerous to tell the truth about the present.[36] Though Bacon perhaps anticipates later conceptions of history as objective truth awaiting discovery by the diligent investigator, he still understands (what we sometimes forget) that history is a powerful instrument for illumination. Like truth (or like satire) it is dangerous—because it can reveal "secrets" and "pretences" that some will not wish revealed.

Bayle builds on Bacon's point that it is sometimes difficult to get at the truth, often because previous authorities and witnesses cannot be relied on; they are partisan, credulous, and uncritical, and the true historian must submit all reports to critical scrutiny in order to determine their value. From this perspective, satire and panegyric are two of the kinds of sources that must be used very cautiously: "Satire and flattery are the two plagues of history, two sources that poison the relations of human events; but we may say, that the contagion of a detracting writer, who is governed by hatred and resentment, is more pernicious to history, than the contagion of those who write panegyrics."[37] Here we have the beginning of a split between satire and history: the former is calumny, partisanship, mere prejudice or opinion; the latter is a judicious and critical report of the facts.[38] Thus Bolingbroke, touched by the newer history, wrote to a colleague: "In whatever I write that is historical, I will be neither apologist, panegyrist, nor satirist."[39] And modern historians use with great caution the "evidence" from satire about corruption in Elizabethan London or Domitian's Rome,[40] or, like Johnson, dismiss the testimony of Pope and Swift about the alleged "ignorance and barbarity" of their age.[41]

But we should not assume that "critical history" immediately won the day and displaced the claims of satire. On the contrary, partisan history (whether panegyrical or satiric) continued to thrive, often by assuring its readers that it was telling the unvarnished truth. Swift, for example, claimed in his *History of the Last Four Years of Queen Anne* that as a "faithful historian" he wrote "with the utmost impartiality . . . in order to undeceive prejudicial persons at present, as well as posterity" (*Prose Works*, 7:xxxiv). In fact, as his excessive protestation suggests, Swift's *History* was quite plainly a "party piece" and was recognized as such by his friends and enemies. Swift will be "faithful" to the truth ("I cannot suffer falsehoods to run on any longer") but also to the queen and her ministers, from whom he hoped for preferment.[42] He declares that he is neither satirist nor panegyrist: "I shall strictly follow Truth, or what reasonably appeared to me to be such, after the most impartial Inquiries I could make. . . . Neither shall I mingle Panegyrick or Satire with a History intended to inform Posterity," for, after all, "facts truly related are the best Applauses, or most lasting Reproaches." But he gives the game away by offering to "discover the Designs carryd on by the Heads of a discontented Party Faction." "Discontented" is not just a neutrally descriptive adjective; it implies that the Whigs are murmuring malcontents and that the Queen's "faithful Friends" (the Tories) signal their virtue by their "faith" (*Prose Works*, 7:1) Swift is in effect writing satire under cover of history.[43]

The increased prestige of impartiality and "critical history" did not leave the job of truth-telling in the hands of the historians. Just as historians denounced satire and claimed to offer a more justly based reproach, so satirists have long denounced history as little more than flattering lies by hired writers. "What are most of the Histories of the World but Lies?" Fielding asks rhetorically in the *Covent-Garden Journal* (No. 12): "Lies Immortalized, and consigned over as a perpetual Abuse and Flam upon Posterity!"[44] Fielding comes at the end of a long tradition that reaches back at least to his favorite, Lucian, whose dialogue *How to Write History* complains that historians forget the difference between history and panegyric, indulging in flattery of the leaders on their own side and in disparagement of their enemies; his own *True History* mockingly supplants the "lying" tales of travelers and of historians like Herodotus. "What lies the Greek historians dared to tell!" says Juvenal (*Sat.* 10.174-75). Though as historian Swift repudiates satire, as satirist he corrects history. Gulliver's report of a session with the magicians of Glubbdubdribb is titled "Antient and Modern History corrected" (*Travels*, 3.8). When Gulliver asks to see the famous ancients, he discovers that the "World had been misled by prostitute Writers" and by the "Roguery and Ignorance of those who pretend to write *Anecdotes*, or secret History." By means of the necromantic power of calling up the dead (a metaphor for satire?), Gulliver penetrates history's lies and is at last "truly informed." Pope's satire too is offered as a corrective to the propaganda "history" being purveyed by Walpole's *Daily Gazetteer*. His *Epilogue to the Satires* (1738) was originally titled "One Thousand Seven Hundred Thirty Eight," as if it had been designed as an unadorned chronicle. It draws a picture of an England almost completely drowned in corruption and vice. As "evidence," the poem—like many of Pope's later satires—offers a full supply of proper names and explanatory footnotes.

Critics have sometimes suggested that Pope's footnotes in effect do provide documentation for his charges and give the poems the status of history. Thus Sitter speaks of Pope's "determination to leave a record—the true record—for posterity, a record often spilling over into footnotes meant to outlast the pseudohistories of Walpole's propagandists." But we should not be taken in by the professions of a satirist any more than we should naively accept a historian's account at face value. Pope's history is usually just as partisan as that he claims to explode. His evidence is carefully selected, his portraits heightened, his very footnotes a sly mixture of truth, exaggeration, and invention, a prosecution of satiric war by other means.[45]

The satirist's "truth" has sometimes proved to be extraordinarily persuasive. In some cases, satire succeeds in constructing and perpetuating an image that manages to override the "facts" and in a sense to supplant "history." Thus Dryden's portrait of Shimei in *Absalom and Achitophel* has been so successfully painted over the original Slingsby Bethel that it has virtually obliterated the memory of the former sheriff of London.[46] That Shaftesbury's name has been "to all succeeding ages curst" is in large part the work of Dryden's satire. That Shaftesbury conspired with Monmouth to put the latter on the throne and that Buckingham (the Zimri of the poem) was in any sense a major figure in the Exclusion Crisis are "unhistorical" insinuations that must be patiently unlearned by anyone who investigates the poem's relation to the "facts" of Restoration political history. Perhaps the most obvious instance of satire supplanting history is Dryden's portrait of Thomas Shadwell as "Sh—," or "MacFlecknoe." When critics of satire comment on the point, they usually applaud Dryden for his power to "transcend" history or to re-create the local as the archetypal. But we should perhaps acknowledge that satire's supplanting power is not simply innocent. For every hundred readers of poetry who now know "Shadwell" from Dryden's poem, perhaps one specialist in Restoration drama knows that Thomas Shadwell (1642-92) was in fact a very successful and talented comic playwright—indeed, a better comic dramatist than Dryden. As satirist, Dryden has created not a universal but a new particular, not an image of the archetypal bad poet but an enduring image of Thomas Shadwell. It is Dryden's hostile image and not Shadwell's own claims for himself (in critical prefaces to his plays) that occupies our minds.

Swift and Pope likewise demonstrate satire's ability to *displace* history. Swift predicts that the foolish astrologer Partridge will die and announces that the prophecy has been fulfilled. By vainly protesting that he is still alive, the hapless Partridge only prompts Swift's warning about impostors and confirms his satiric power. The *Dunciad*, Pope said, "was not made for these Authors, but these Authors for the Poem." [47] It is usually assumed that Pope thereby "asserts the priority of the poem over history," [48] treating the dunces as so much raw material for his satire. But this is to assume a wholly aesthetic attitude toward Pope's victims. We should not forget that the dunce does not spend the remainder of his life in Pope's poem; he must reenter the world of "history," where he is sentenced to wear the new identity that Pope's satire has assigned him. On a larger scale, Pope and the other Tory satirists, with the help of the *Craftsman*'s partisan history, created so convincing a picture of cultural corruption and tyranny under Walpole that historians then and now must labor to show that Walpole was in fact a masterful administrator, and that England under the new financial capitalism was basically strong, confident, prosperous, and healthy. Even Johnson, who "corrected" Pope's partisan history, in his "Vanity of Human Wishes" inadvertently fixed an inaccurate reputation for beauty on "Vane" and "Sedley," two rather uncomely royal mistresses. [49]

But if satire and history usually made competing claims about particular truth, they found themselves in agreement about general truth—particularly in times widely regarded as corrupt. Even Bayle, though wary of satire, had to concede the resemblance between faithful history and sharp satire: "The Corruption of Manners has been so great, as well among those who have lived in the World, as

among those who have lived out of it, that the more a Person endeav-
ours to give faithful and true Relations, the more he runs the hazard
of composing only defamatory Libels." In bad times an unadorned
account of the simple "facts" speaks for itself; judgment is unnecessary. As Edward Young put it: "Historians themselves may be considered as satirists, and satirists most severe; since such are most
human actions, that to relate, is to expose them."[50]

Insofar as history is understood not as particulars but as general
truths, it seemed to practicing historians of the period—who were
attracted to themes of degeneration—that history and satire con-
verged. Bayle quotes a historian of the Middle Ages to the effect that
the title of Orosius's treatise *De miseria hominum* is "agreeable to
History in general": "History is the mirrour of human life; now the
condition of human life is such, that the number of wicked and impious men, as well as that of fools must be infinite; history is nothing
else but a representation of the misery of mankind."[51] It is not surprising to find Edward Gibbon, occupied with the long decline of the
Roman Empire, uttering very similar sentiments. History, he agreed,
"is, indeed [as Voltaire had said], little more than the register of the
crimes, follies, and misfortunes of mankind."[52] Readers of Gibbon
have often thought that his cool irony about the triumph of fanati-
cism over urbanity made him seem at least half a satirist. If the historian's "duty" is to "discover the inevitable mixture of error and corruption which [Religion] contracted in a long residence upon earth,
among a weak and degenerate race of beings," then the historian
must be a satirist.[53]

Strictly speaking, satirists are free to express their indignation at
corruption. Historians should restrain themselves. "Doubtless," says
Bayle, "there is a great Difference between History and Satire," but
one can easily "metamorphose" into the other:

> If on the one hand, you take from Satire that Spirit of Sharpness, that Air
> of Anger, which discovers that Passion has a greater Share in the Scan-
> dals reported, than a love of Virtue; and if you add the obligation one is
> under, of relating indifferently the good and the bad, it is no longer
> reputed Satire, but History. Let a Historian, on the other hand, faithfully
> relate all the Crimes, Weaknesses, and Disorders of Mankind, his Work
> shall be reputed rather a Satire, than a History, if he discover but even so
> little Emotion in himself at the thought of so many condemnable Facts
> which he exposes to public View.

After carefully drawing that fine line between history and satire,
Bayle then crosses it: "I do not believe That Coolness of Temper with

which a Judge ought to pronounce Sentence against Robbers and
Murderers, is always to be exacted from a Historian. Some pointed
Reflexions do not become him ill."[54] In other words, let the histo-
rian speak out like a satirist.

Upon occasion the similarity between the historian and the satirist extends even to the use of particulars, not just of ancient exemplars but of modern figures too. Readers of Voltaire's *History of
Charles XII* (1732) and Johnson's nearly contemporary *Vanity of
Human Wishes* (1749) would have found very similar observations
about Charles's folly in seeking military glory.[55] Voltaire uses Bayle's
license to make "pointed Reflexions." Johnson assembles famous examples of the vanity of human wishes—Wolsey, Alexander, "Swed-
ish Charles," Xerxes, Charles Albert of Bavaria—content to "let
hist'ry tell" (93), and thereby "point a moral" (222).

Exemplary history gradually gave way at the end of the eighteenth century to a newer "objective" history in which the historian
no longer sought to teach general truth. It is plausible that the
change in history-writing and the simultaneous decline of great satire
can be attributed in part to the same cause: a gradual loss of the idea
that human nature is the same in all times and places.[56] The old
universalism had served the satirists well. Even an atack on a particular instance of vice or folly could be enjoyed for its own sake and at
the same time (since the victim could be regarded as typical or representative) seen as an instance of a general truth. But when historians
on the one hand claimed to limit themselves to "objective narration
and analysis" and on the other abandoned the attempt to arrive at
general truth, the gap between history and satire opened up again.

From our perspective, we can see that nineteenth-century historians were in their various ways still highly partisan. Their deeper
intent, some would argue, was to generate national stories or myths
in order to create national identity to suit the new nation-state—
even in England, with its long political tradition. Macaulay and the
other "Whig" historians are in their way just as "unreliable" in their
accounts of the court of Charles II and the reign of Walpole as were
the Restoration court satirists or the Tory satirists of Pope's day.

Wariness about historians' claims to truth has been accentuated
in recent years by theorists who have challenged the status not only
of the documentary novel but even of the Holocaust narrative as a
"factual" report uncolored by the literary and narrative medium in
which it must be encoded.[57] The effect of such a challenge is to discover the "textuality" of all narrative, whether "fictional" or "factu-

al," "documentary" or "imaginary." We should see a continuum, not a gap, between the interpretive descriptions of the novelist and documentarist and the work of the satirist. But satire proper, unlike "factual" genres, rarely offers itself as "objective" or documentary, and it thus presents the interpreter with special problems. Alerted by its generic signals, we are not likely to mistake a satire for fact, not likely to overlook its avowedly "rhetorical" nature. To understand satire we need a model in which the writer is felt to have a palpable design on us and to offer us a frankly partisan view. Furthermore, the writer of satire makes no simple binary division of statements into "fact" and "fiction," truth and distortion, evidence and innuendo. Satirists are released from certain restraints—about violating particular truth or fairness, about exaggeration or bias or evidence, whether in drawing or in applying a character. They have a license to lie. Yet they do not simply create a world of make-believe. The excitement of satire (its bite) is based on our knowledge (or just our suspicion) that the victims are "real," even if we can't always identify them. Our interpretive task as readers is not simply to identify the victim; it is also to identify the principles of selection and distortion that shape the satirist's "facts," and the ideological bias—perhaps invisible to the satirist—that undergirds the enterprise.

A better rhetoric of satiric fact might enable us to define more precisely the nature of satire's relation to history. To do so it would have to recognize that the events and persons in satire are raw historical data that are given some shape, just as they would be in a historical narrative. It is naive, we can now see, to declare either that satirists simply use preestablished historical "facts" or that they "transform" events and people into "fictive" creations.[58] Satirists do not simply name names and point fingers. Satirists, no less than historians, must construct their characters, in the sense that they must decide what attitudes and responses they wish to evoke, what aspects they choose to bring into focus. To assume that a satirist *or* a historian is simply referring to "truth" or to "history" is to be persuaded by that writer's version of events.

6

The Politics of Satire

Having concluded that "reference" *to* a world of "history" is problematic, we can now look more closely at satire *in* history. What is the effect of satire on the world outside the text and, in particular, on its political order? Is satire essentially conservative, or subversive? Does it have any effect at all? These questions have received various answers from theorists and commentators. At present there is no clear consensus, and my earlier claims about satire may not appear to bring us any closer to one. If satire is inquiry and provocation, it bears directly on our real moral beliefs; insofar as it is display or play, perhaps it does not touch our everyday lives. Even if we cannot provide definitive answers to these old questions, we need to go on to ask new questions: under what historical conditions does satire typically thrive? Who writes satire, and who typically does not? Whose interests are served?

The Conditions for Satire

When we think of satire as a genre, we must guard against the idealist notion that the genre exists apart from its exemplars: satire always emerges at particular times and places. Commentators have in fact long noted that satire seems to belong more to some times than others. It is a commonplace that satire flourished in first- and second-century Rome (at the time of Persius and Juvenal), briefly in the late sixteenth century in England (Donne, Marston, and Hall), the seventeenth century in France (Regnier and Boileau), and the eighteenth century in England (Pope, Swift, et al.). It is also regularly conceded that satire in English declined in the late eighteenth century, that apart from Byron we have had little significant satire proper since about 1750. Can we go beyond the commonplace and, by a process of induction, discover the historical conditions that favor the rise of great satire? The attempt to explain the flourishing of any art by reference to determining historical factors is notoriously risky: great art must involve unaccountable factors such as individual genius and sheer luck. But perhaps we can distinguish the less adequate from the more adequate explanations.

We can readily dismiss the idea that great satire appears as a direct result of egregious corruption in the writer's social world. Juvenal may have claimed that he was driven to speak out by the spectacle of vice, but satirists always say that the times have never been worse. One critic has suggested that satire rose to prominence in eighteenth-century England because of the widespread longing for "moderation" after a half-century of political and religious extremism, together with a confidence that "men are free and responsible beings, who can set about improving themselves and their society by the exercise of reason" (Elkin, *Augustan Defence of Satire*, pp. 6-9). But this explanation too is open to some objections: it is probably the case that *all* ages have shown a longing for moderation and have (at least officially) assumed that humans are responsible for their conduct and are capable of reason (or at least common sense) and of self-correction. It is also a dubious claim—if one remembers Swift— that satirists are moderate persons or have confidence that people *will* correct themselves by means of reason if only satire will gently remind them.

Other universalist explanations are sometimes given for the appearance of satire. It arises, some say, at a time when moral norms are so firmly fixed that the satirist can freely and confidently appeal to them. On the contrary, say others, it arises at a time when moral norms are being called into question and must therefore be reaffirmed with some force to prevent further breakdown of moral order. A third view asserts that satire arises "when there is little credence in public standards of morality and taste." [1] In a judicious attempt to find some middle ground, Elliott suggested that "the greatest satire has been written in periods when ethical and rational norms were sufficiently powerful to attract widespread assent yet not so powerful as to compel absolute conformity." [2] At this point the skeptical observer would argue that a society's moral norms are *always* being simultaneously challenged and affirmed, that generational conflict (being constant) always sets new idea against received opinion, young against old.

Some have sought an explanation for the appearance of satire not in broad cultural conditions but in more narrow *literary* conditions. Satire, it has been suggested, tends to arise in reaction to other, usually higher, literary forms. Richard Helgerson, for example, has argued that for up-and-coming writers inthe 1590s, satire was a way of "relocating poetry," since the aureate or golden verse of the Elizabethans was no longer available to them as inspiration. Why not? Because the higher forms of epic, romance, pastoral, and even sonnet sequence had been used up or "exhausted" by Sidney and Spenser.[3] Helgerson's claim is based on the same notion of belatedness that was made popular by W.J. Bate in *The Burden of the Past* (1970): there is little left to do, so the argument goes, that one's great predecessors have not already done, and of course one cannot simply do the same thing they have done, or hope to do it better. The choice of satire by the generation of Donne, Marston, and Hall is thus a way to mark their difference from the previous generation, especially since the satirist was already conventionally opposed to the amorist: "The historical dynamic that opposes generation to generation and the literary system that sets genre against genre sufficiently explain their choice."[4]

Helgerson's argument has sufficient plausibility for us to take it seriously, especially since a version of the argument has long been an unspoken assumption about eighteenth-century satire. Dryden and Pope turned to mock-heroic and satire, so it has been assumed, because Milton had used up epic and pastoral. The Augustans turned to an outward-looking public or social poetry (especially satire) in reaction to the more inward-looking or private poetry of the seventeenth century. One might even try to extend the argument to Juvenal: he flourished as a satirist in a self-consciously post-Virgilian and post-epic age.

But Helgerson's argument will not finally hold up, either with the Elizabethans or the Augustans. The evidence he offers is largely a deduction from his theory of generational conflict. Hall, it is true, attacks all kinds of poetry except satire in Book 1 of his *Virgidemiae*. But Helgerson misreads a contemporary contrast between the sharpness of satire and the "surfeit of excess" in other poetic forms: the "surfeit" is not aureate fullness but lasciviousness. And his claim that the aureate style was no longer available is complicated by Samuel Daniel and Michael Drayton, who carried on older poetic traditions after 1600. Helgerson must say that they simply "did not realize that an independent poetic career could no longer be made with the materials that had served Sidney and Spenser." He would have to claim too that many popular early seventeenth-century poets—the sonneteers and neo-Spenserians among them—"did not realize" that what they were attempting was impossible.[5]

More generally, Helgerson's explanation for the outburst of satire in the 1590s fails because his model for generational conflict is too crude. It assumes that writers arrive in generations every fifteen to twenty years, when in fact new writers arrive continually. Some new writers will feel affinity with their elders and some with the younger generation. The model also assumes a simple action-reaction pattern: if the previous generation did *x*, you must do not-*x*. But the filiations and affiliations among writers are surely more complex. Pope followed Milton and also departed from him. He likewise followed and modified Dryden and Abraham Cowley. Satirists, like all writers, make many predecessors their mentors or masters but do not simply take their direction from the preceding generation of poets in their own language. Wyatt's satire has something to do with Alamanni's satire in sixteenth-century Italy, Pope's with Boileau in seventeenth-century France and with the long traditions of Roman verse satire descending from Horace, Juvenal, and Persius. Finally, the generational model will not account for the emergence of Swift and Pope as the greatest satirists of their age. Swift began his career as a satirist with a dazzling work that signaled his affiliations with the learned wit of the late Renaissance (no reaction there). Pope did not come to satire until relatively late in a career that took him through a variety of traditional forms, from pastoral to epic, which (so he apparently thought) were far from exhausted.

If the internal dynamics of literary history do not account for the rise of satire, we can still (proceeding inductively) look for some more specific factors, both literary and cultural, that seem to be present when satire has risen to prominence. Several elements would appear to be necessary. The first is a knowledge of the conventions of satire as first practiced by the Romans and by Lucianic writers—the commonplaces, the stances and situations, the tones of voice—for satires are written in large part out of earlier satires. The reappearance of verse satire in the Renaissance is very likely linked with the republication of the works of Horace and Juvenal, and their part in the standard classical education of the day. Renaissance Lucianic fantasies are in part a result of Lucian's installment in the sixteenth century as a school text for learning elementary Greek.[6] If modern writers do not know Horace and Lucian, they are less likely to write verse satire than those few (such as Robert Lowell) who do.

The second necessary element is some tolerance for, even taste for, ridicule among readers. Where ridicule is thought to be cruel, unfair, unmanly—as it came to be in the "Age of Sensibility"—satire will tend to soften or to change form.[7] This factor is commonly cited by writers attempting to explain the decline of satire in the later eighteenth century, but it is easily overstated. As the examples of Oliver Goldsmith, Laurence Sterne, and Robert Burns suggest, there is no necessary conflict between satire and sentiment.

The third and probably more important factor is the presence of a fairly small, compact, and homogeneous reading audience (virtually by definition aristocratic rather than bourgeois) located in the cultural and political capital. Satire, it is commonly said, is an urban form: it thrives in Juvenal's Rome, Boileau's Paris, Pope's London, but not in the English Lakes or the American South. It needs a milieu in which the major writers all know each other, take part in the capital's public and political life, and are not removed from centers of learning. It needs an audience that is interested in literary rivalry and gossip, that appreciates innuendos, allusions, in-jokes of all kinds. It perhaps thrives best in conditions of oral performance, whether in formal recitation (as in the case of Juvenal) or informal delivery (as in the case of Scriblerians); or in societies where satires circulate in manuscript or literally grow out of collaborative efforts (as with the coterie around Buckingham that produced *The Rehearsal*). Such conditions prevailed in second-century Rome, the Elizabethan Inns of Court,[8] the courts of Charles II of England and Louis XIV of France, and the fashionable Westminster of Pope and Swift. They were less and less prevalent after about 1750, when the court ceased to be the cultural center of the nation, when writers were less likely to be located only in London, when reading audiences grew and diversified, when writers began consciously to think of themselves as alienated artists and of art as autonomous, cut off from the worlds of politics and ordinary life. It would appear in fact that satire thrives in a culture whose basis is aristocratic rather than bourgeois. Are not satirists themselves somewhat aristocratic in their sympathies and prejudices if not in actual social status—disdainful and imperious, intolerant, sharply aware of social differences, sensitive to style, suspicious of the mob? When Francis Jeffrey looked back at Queen Anne's days, he saw wits who wrote "in a tone that was peculiar to the upper ranks of society, and upon subjects that were almost exclusively interesting to them"[9] (though to be sure, the gentleman-satirist was a kind of fifth column: he took delight in ridiculing a vapid or corrupt nobility, and in incorporating the unclean and "low" into his "high" discourse).[10] As the base of English culture shifted from aristocratic to bourgeois in the late eighteenth century, satire declined. Fittingly, the lordly Byron was chief satirist among the Romantics, and the last great English satirist. Although he was contemptuous of English high society, Byron's tone—his recklessness and irreverence, as Leavis called it—is that of an aristocrat. If satire staged a brief recovery in the London of the 1930s—with W.H. Auden, Wyndham Lewis, and Roy Campbell—perhaps it was because some of the old coterie conditions were temporarily reestablished.

Great satire furthermore appears ironically to depend on some resistance to itself. Although it is sometimes argued that satire requires "freedom of speech" as its "essential condition" (Hodgart, *Satire*, p. 77), it would seem on further reflection that what is required is only some minimal freedom, with limits and penalties set by political authorities. If it prospered under political liberalism and toleration, one would expect to find satire increasing throughout the nineteenth century and flowering in the twentieth, especially in Western Europe and America. And one would expect that it would not be found in repressive conditions. Thus, Matthew Hodgart argues that a "conservative attitude" defending the monarchical system as "established with divine approval and support" is "not conducive to political satire" (*Satire*, p. 52). In fact, the greatest satire was written under the Roman emperors and under kings of England and France who would have resisted any challenge to the "monarchical system." In the late twentieth century it has appeared not in the liberal West but in Russia and Eastern Europe.[11] The work of Horace, Juvenal, and Persius appeared at a time when the satirist at least nominally risked lawsuits, exile, imprisonment, or even death.[12] Donne wrote as a Catholic in the 1590s, at a time when his coreligionists were under close scrutiny. Pope's *Epistle to Fortescue*, based on Horace's *Satire* 2.1, assumes that the old Roman laws against *mala carmina* are still in effect in Walpole's England.[13] As indeed they were: English governments in the seventeenth and eighteenth centuries employed licensers and censors, imposed penalties for sedition, and put a price on the head of the writer of the *Drapier's Letters*. Jacobites were virtually proscribed: Pope (a Catholic, a suspected Jacobite, and friend of the political opposition) was driven into innuendo, and Swift's printer had to suppress an episode in Gulliver's third voyage—the Lindalino (that is, Dublin) revolt—which appears to reflect on English tyranny over Ireland. Augustan critics routinely referred to Roman and English libel laws and acknowledged that legal and political constraints influenced the design and even the style of satire.[14]

The idea that satire thrives in the face of—and because of—threatened censorship or political reprisal is easy to overlook at a time when the press is free. But writers who had to fear licensers and censors understood the point very well.[15] Defoe in 1711, writing at a moment that ostensibly enjoyed "liberty of the Press" and implicitly arguing against reimposed censorship, recalled "the Days of King *Charles* II when the License Tyranny Reign'd over the Press." The result of licensing was not to control dissent but to redirect it from print into "Lampoons, Pasquinades, and Inveterate Satyrs, . . . whose Darts will be keener, and Poisons stronger than any Thing Printed."[16] Shaftesbury, Defoe's contemporary, observed: "'tis the persecuting Spirit has raised the bantering one. The greater the Weight is, the bitterer will be the Satire. The higher the Slavery, the more exquisite the Buffoonery."[17] Anthony Collins, another contemporary, quotes Shaftesbury's observation and notes that in Italy, where "Spiritual Tyranny is highest," one finds buffoonery and burlesque not only in writing and the theater but in conversation and in the street. But if men were allowed "Liberty to examine into the Truth of Things" they wouldn't need to take refuge in irony.[18] In other words, it is the limitation on free inquiry and dissent that provokes one to irony—and to satire. If open challenge to orthodoxy is freely permitted, then writers will take the most direct route and debate the ideas and characters of political leaders openly in newspapers, protected by guarantees of free speech. It is difficult, or unnecessary, to satirize our political leaders when the newspapers are filled with open attacks on their integrity and intelligence. But if open challenge is not permitted, writers will turn to irony, indirection, innuendo, allegory, fable—to the fictions of satire.[19]

Indeed, satirists would seem to *prefer* indirection to frontal attack, and thus to be spurred to do their best work by restriction. As Freud said, comparing the satirist and the dreamer, "the stricter the censorship the more far-reaching will be the disguise and the more ingenious too may be the means employed for putting the reader on the scent of the true meaning."[20] In his essay "The Calling of the Tune," Kenneth Burke once threw off the remark that "the conditions for satire are 'more favorable' under censorship than under liberalism—for the most inventive satire arises when the artist is seeking simultaneously to take risks and escape punishment for his boldness, and is never quite certain himself whether he will be acclaimed or punished. In proportion as you remove these conditions of danger, by liberalization, satire becomes arbitrary and effete, at-

tracting writers of far less spirit and scantier resources."[21] Although
Burke does not elaborate, one imagines he means here that the satirist is not so much a dedicated guerilla intent on overthrowing injus-
tice as he is an impudent and daring mocker (like Lord Rochester at
the court of Charles II), seeing how much he can get away with but
not really believing that authority will be shaken.

Donne gives a strong impression of the climate of oppression
under which a Renaissance satirist operated. In his second satire the
"huge Statute lawes" threaten the satirist with their "vast reach"
(111-12). In the famous third satire he criticizes an uncritical adher-
ence to the established church. As a recent critic has put it, by rejecting the Oath of Allegiance as a kind of idolatry, Donne came close to
treason and risked political reprisal.[22] In his fourth satire the "Giant
Statutes" (132) against treason will devour a man for loose talk, or
even for listening to it. Pursuivants stand ready to accuse you of
popery, and informers of treason. The satirist disdains the court
world but is nevertheless dangerously drawn to it. Is Donne's interlocutor merely a hanger-on, a political climber, or a spy seeking to
entrap the satirist into a libelous, disloyal, or papist sentiment? And
yet Donne the satirist returns in Satire 4 to the dangerous world of
the court after escaping it, perhaps because it stimulates his wit and
spleen and moral intelligence.[23]

That satire thrives under limited repression or censorship is plausible enough, even commonsensical. And it is worth observing that
such an idea accords well with the history of satire. Its first great age
was in classical Greece, when Aristophanes and his fellow dramatists
were permitted to ridicule individuals by name, but as Swift notes,
"the least reflecting word let fall against the *People* in general, was
immediately caught up, and revenged upon the Authors, however
considerable for their Quality or their Merits" (*Tale of a Tub*, "The
Preface").[24] Erasmus and More lived at a time of great intellectual
ferment, but it is a mistake to think they wrote under conditions of
"Humanist freedom of thought."[25] Erasmus was attacked by the
Roman Catholic Church, and More was put to death because he
refused to bend to the will of his king on a matter of conscience. The
great age of French satire is not after the Revolution but under the
ancien regime: La Bruyère, La Rochefoucauld, Regnier, Cyrano de
Bergerac, Molière, and Boileau in the seventeenth century, Diderot
and Voltaire in the eighteenth.[26] Satire had a vigorous life in pre-1914
imperial Germany[27] and nineteenth-century Czarist Russia, where

writers employed an Aesopian language that the censors understood and agreed to tolerate.[28]

The question "Under what conditions does great satire arise?" leads, then, to some tentative conclusions about the nature and function of the form: that it involves bantering exchanges among or for the amusement of a small and sophisticated circle, under the eye of a government closely watching for the satirist to overstep his permitted bounds. Can we discover more by asking more specific questions? For example, within such a satiric community, who are the satirists? What are their social and economic status? Whose interests do they serve? Do they assert an ideology?

The Satirist's Social and Economic Status

In Ben Jonson's *Every Man out of his Humour* (1599) the satirist Macilente is presented as "well parted, a sufficient Scholler" who lacks "that place in the worlds account, which he thinks his merit capable of" and as a result falls into "an envious apoplexie" against the world, complaining about "these mushrompe gentlemen, / That shoot up in night to place, and worship."[29] We can recognize the hostile caricature of the satirist as mere malcontent; critics in all ages have charged that the satirist is motivated by little more than envy. But if we focus on the sociopolitical instead of the moral details, Jonson's dramatic caricature may point to an interesting truth about the writer of satire. The satirist in fact tended to be classically educated, university trained (unless a Roman Catholic in Protestant England, like Pope and Ben Jonson), and therefore (at least through the eighteenth century) by definition a gentleman, who turned to writing not as a profession but as an amusement or a means to patronage or political advancement. This was true of Donne, Marston, and Hall in the 1590s: their satire reflects the coterie worlds of Cambridge and the Inns of Court.[30] They wrote about and for a small and intensely competitive world in which they hoped to find a place—as private secretary to a powerful peer and, ultimately, as a courtier or servant of the queen.

Recent analysts have argued that at the end of Elizabeth's reign bright young men of talent were underemployed and "impatient for preferment," held back by an older generation; that it was in part the "high rate of unemployment among university and inns-of-court men" that prompted them to castigate abuses in satire.[31] As Arthur Marotti has suggested, satire in the 1590s was a "literary form practiced by those whose ambitions were frustrated and who yearned to involve themselves more deeply in the social environments they pretended to scorn."[32] Donne succeeded in becoming private secretary to Egerton but rose no higher. Like Hall and Marston he ultimately made his career not at court but in the church. Jonson himself, a professional dramatist whose early plays have been called "staged satires," is only apparently the exception to the rule. Although a talented satirist, he forsook "comical satire" after his early years, or rather redirected it into comic dramatic poems and classical epigrams as he built a "laureate" career that was at once a profession and a vocation.[33]

When satire again rose to prominence, in the late seventeenth century, its practitioners again tended to be amateur gentlemen rather than professionals or writers who aspired to a laureate career on the Virgilian model. Rochester, Dorset, and Buckingham were all titled aristocrats. Marvell, a Cambridge man, later a private tutor in the service of Fairfax and Cromwell, is one of the few satirists to build a successful political career, first as Latin Secretary and then as member of parliament. The other gentleman satirists were markedly less successful: Samuel Butler served as private secretary to several patrons and was finally pensioned for *Hudibras* at the end of his life. Oxford-educated John Oldham, who began as a schoolmaster and private tutor, sought preferment at court and spent his adult life for the most part as a dependent in the households of various patrons.[34] Swift's career was to him a disappointment: his service as Sir William Temple's private secretary did not lead to a political post, just as his service under Robert Harley and Henry St. John did not lead to a bishopric. In a perverse parody of the conventional appeal for notice, he published *A Tale of a Tub* (announcing his arrival as a satirist) in 1704 and probably marked himself forever as a dangerous wit, unsuitable for any high position in the church. Rabelais was luckier: son of a wealthy lawyer and landowner, trained as a priest, he served as secretary to a powerful Benedictine abbot (and tutor to his nephew), then as physician to the Bishop of Paris (later a cardinal), who protected him from attack.

As late as the eighteenth century the satirist was likely to be a gentleman in search of preferment. The obvious examples in England are Edward Young and (if we may consider him a satirist) John Gay.[35] Young as a verse satirist stood second only to Pope in his age. Son of a clergyman, product of Winchester and Oxford, he spent an entire life, as George Eliot put it, "angling for pensions and preferment."[36] Each of the satires that was to make up his *Love of Fame* (1728) was dedicated to some man of wealth and influence, including Walpole himself. Already chaplain to Queen Caroline, Young was rewarded with a pension of £200 in 1726 and named chaplain to King George II in 1728. "Poor Gay" never rose so high in the world. His life was passed in the vain pursuit of preferment at court, but he was never offered any position higher than that of Gentleman Usher to the infant Princess Louise in 1727. His *Shepherd's Week* (1714) was unluckily dedicated to Bolingbroke, who immediately fell from power and could do little for him thereafter. His *Poems* were successfully published by subscription in 1720, but he lost £1000 when the South Sea Bubble burst. Despite his apparent failures, however, Gay was supported by a steady line of generous private patrons, for whom he served as domestic steward, secretary, and amiable house guest.

It is significant that of the major satirists only Dryden and Pope were in any sense professional writers. But Dryden's satire, with the exception of *MacFlecknoe*, reflects the servant of the king (Laureate and Historiographer Royal) rather than the professional dramatist, and even *MacFlecknoe* was written for private satisfaction: it circulated in manuscript for six or seven years before receiving unauthorized publication in 1682. Pope was likewise a professional but preferred to think of himself as a gentleman-author who wrote satire to settle differences among neighbors or to amuse himself and compliment his friends.[37]

To put it another way, since the satirist was not a professional writer but a talented gentleman—usually without independent income—he was typically a *client*, whose talents and service were rewarded by wealthy patrons or protectors (even the titled Rochester was an impoverished aristocrat who depended on the favor and the generosity of his king).[38] This was eminently true of Juvenal, whose first satire wittily laments the plight of the client who must compete for the attentions of wealthy patrons. Indeed, it has been strongly argued that the point of view Juvenal most clearly articulates is not that of the fierce moralist or the celebrant of lost Roman virtue but that of the class of dependent and often disappointed and humiliated clients.[39] It was true of Horace, who won the patronage of Maecenas and the protection of Augustus himself, and of Lucilius before him, who enjoyed the friendship and protection of Laelius and Scipio (see Horace *Sat.* 2.1.65-72). Even Lucian was given a minor bureaucratic post in Roman Egypt.

Donne offered compliments—and an implicit appeal for continued favor—to his patron Egerton in Satire 5.[40] Dryden was on the payroll of Charles II (though irregularly paid), and Boileau was both pensioned by Louis XIV and protected by the king against attacks from his literary enemies.[41] It was the rare satirist who achieved genuine financial independence or abandoned all hope for favor: even Swift was still dreaming of preferment in the late 1720s.[42] Pope seems to have received £200 from Walpole for his *Odyssey* in 1725, and he had the *Dunciad* officially presented to the king and queen by the prime minister himself.[43] Despite his proud claims of independence ("Un-plac'd, unpension'd, no Man's Heir, or Slave"), Pope carefully sought to maintain civil relations with Walpole and his supporters (including Fortescue) as late as the 1730s.[44] He could count on an extensive network of landed aristocrats to cushion any blows (Oxford, Bathurst, and Burlington held the copyright of and legal responsibility for the *Dunciad*) and provide him solid comforts during his summer rambles.

Client status imposed some limits on the satirist's freedom: he had to take care not to bite the hand that (so he hoped) would feed him.[45] Juvenal limited himself to naming the dead. Trebatius warned Horace (*Sat.* 2.1) not to offend his great friend (*maiorum amicus*). And Horace, Dryden notes, "as he was a Courtier, comply'd with the Interest of his Master, and avoiding the Lashing of greater Crimes, confin'd himself to the ridiculing of petty Vices, and common Follies" (4.68). Even Pope was cautious not to publish some satirical portraits (of Atossa, for example, the Duchess of Marlborough) until (as Johnson noted) it was "safe" to do so—that is, after her death. Nor did he publish the four-book *Dunciad*, with its bold allusions to Walpole, until after the minister's fall from power. But (not surprisingly) satirists have occasionally overstepped the mark: Juvenal made dangerous reflections on an emperor's taste in male dancers and may have been exiled for it; Rochester got himself banished from the court for similar literary indiscretions.

The worldly constraints on the satirist's independence are perhaps nowhere better illustrated than in the case of Thomas Wyatt. Delighting like Pope in simple country pleasures, in his affinities with the rural gentry, in his refusal to comply with the corrupt ways of the court, the Wyatt of the satires was probably making a virtue of necessity. In the summer of 1536, when the satires were apparently written, Wyatt was "in Kent and Christendom" not by choice but in internal exile. Arrested in May of that year and briefly imprisoned, he was released on condition that he remain on his father's rural estate. To "flee the presse of courtes" (*Sat.* 1.3) is not so much to choose virtuous retirement as to acknowledge the power of those "to whome fortune hath lent / Charge over us, of Right, to strike the stroke" (8-9). Despite the bravado of "No man doeth marke where so I ride or goo; / In lusty lees at libertie I walke," Wyatt is too honest to conceal his constraints, even if the "clogg [that] doeth hang yet at my hele" is only metaphorical (prisoners in Wyatt's day were "clogged" to prevent escape). The series of "I cannot" clauses—I cannot lie, I cannot flatter, and so on—of which the poem largely consists emphasizes Wyatt's principled refusal but also his powerlessness: he *cannot*; he is disabled. Even in minimizing the effects of the restraint—"No force for that for it is ordered so, / That I may lepe boeth hedge and dike full well"—the satirist ruefully emphasizes the restraining orders: the line with its grimly ironic impersonal construction says "I have so ordered or arranged my life that I am free to do as I like," but it also recognizes that it is the king who has *ordered* Wyatt to remain within appointed bounds. And the king's deadly *force* stands behind his order.[46] Even the final address to his friend John Poins recalls the judicial circumstances of his imprisonment and his sentence: "Thou shalt be judge how I do spend my tyme"—that is, the prescribed term and conditions of exile.[47]

It is striking to note, finally, that with few exceptions the great satirist (despite aspirations to position) remained what Marotti calls Donne, a "political outsider" with little real power and influence.[48] More precisely perhaps, the satirist was a "marginal insider,"[49] standing *near* the center of power but usually standing by as the rewards went to others, often to the "new men" who were better able to thrust their way up from below. Even Dryden, though he has been described as the last satirist to serve as a king's spokesman and to "stand beside the throne,"[50] could not get his royal salary paid. The typical satirist had about as much access to power and license to speak as that archetypal railer, Homer's Thersites, who was tolerated by the other warriors unless he spoke too boldly.

Satirists have tended since Roman days to think of themselves as persons of breeding and have looked with disapproval and some snobbery at the successful upstarts: this is Juvenal's attitude toward the mushroom millionaires or the tricky Greeks; it is Donne's attitude toward the jumped-up newly made gentlemen at the Elizabethan court; it is Pope's attitude toward the new men whose wealth is based not on land but on commerce and money. There is perhaps some truth beneath the old charge of envy: to adapt Pope's line, satirists find themselves "out," and "would be in" (*Epilogue to the Satires* 2.123). George Orwell suspected (not altogether unfairly) that Swift's "debunking of human grandeur, his diatribes against lords, politicians, court favorites, etc., has mainly a local application and springs from the fact that he belonged to the unsuccessful party."[51] Satire's one real insider is probably Horace, who "lived among the great." But he never pretends to have acquired any real power from the association. Pope, in his imitations of Horace, sometimes implies that his villa at Twickenham is somehow the real center of wit and virtue, if not of power. It takes the demythologizing perspective of Johnson to see that Pope and Swift were not as important in the scheme of things as they imagined.[52] Given the restraints on satirists' power and freedom, however, it is worth remarking how much they neeeded to preserve the idea (was it only a fiction?) that their pens or their silence had not been bought. In the famous epistle to Augustus (2.1) Horace declined to celebrate the emperor in heroic strains. Shaftesbury argued that in his late epistles Horace successfully established his independence from "Maecenas and the Court's desires, who would have kept him."[53] Boileau, as Pope noted with admiration, though "pension'd" could still "lash in honest Strain" (*Imitations of Horace*, Sat. 2.1.111).

The satirist's need to declare independence from a patron perhaps sounds most clearly in Horace's epistle to Maecenas (1.7), explaining the refusal of an invitation to return to Rome. The poem is often described as Horace's "manly" and "dignified" reply to what must have been an implicit reproach, but we can observe a mixture of firmness and caution. Horace in fact begins by admitting that he has been false to his word (*mendax*) and, pleading fears for his health, acknowledges he can remain absent only through Maecenas's indulgence, his *venia* (which combines ideas of permission and forgiveness). The refusal to return until the following spring is carefully softened: "Te, dulcis amice, reviset / cum Zephyris, si concedes, et hirundine prima" (you, dear friend, he will revisit, if you permit, with the west wind and the first swallow; 12-13). Maecenas has the prominent position in the sentence. Even the assertive "I" disappears as Horace, earlier "your poet" (*vates tuus*), is now simply "he."

Having uttered the refusal, Horace quickly slides into four entertaining and illustrative stories, first of the importunate Calabrian host, then of the fox in the corncrib, of Telemachus's refusal of a gift from Menelaus, and finally of Volteius Mena, whose life is made miserable by the generosity of his insistent patron, Phillipus. And Horace concludes with safely general reflections: one must beware of gaining one good if it means giving up a greater; it is reasonable for every one to measure himself by his own standards. Running through the stories, however, is Horace's willingness to give up everything Maecenas has granted him. "I call you patron [*rex* and *pater*], but I stand ready to give back your gifts [*donata reponere*], if necessary, to preserve my ease and freedom." With tact born of knowing his audience, Horace manages to discharge at once the obligations he owes to Maecenas and to himself.

Few poets have been as lucky as Horace. Most would have gladly traded their patron (if they had one) for a Maecenas. But when they found it necessary to refuse a patron's wishes or to lodge a complaint, several later satirists—Ariosto in sixteenth-century Italy, Swift and Pope in eighteenth-century England—remembered Horace's epistle to Maecenas. Ariosto also refused a request from his patron, Cardinal Ippolito d'Este, to accompany him on an extended stay in Hungary. The satire (his first) is addressed not directly to the patron but (more cautiously) to his own brother, also a member of the patron's entourage. Ariosto offers Horace's excuse—fear for his health—but goes on to complain that he has not been well rewarded for his service. He worries that the patron might withhold his favor but prefers a life of peace and liberty to the distasteful life of a retainer. A version of Horace's fable of the fox in the corncrib leads to an emphatic conclusion that (as with Horace) it would *not* be bitter and harsh (*acerbo et acro*) to return the cardinal's gifts, and recover his freedom.[54] Ariosto was not simply imitating Horace as a literary exercise. One of the ten children of a minor courtier, "forced to live at another's cost" (*a spese altrui*—Satire 3.24), all of his seven satires are written from the point of view of the dependent courtier who resents the "servitude" of living at court. Satire 7, in the words of one critic, "presents in tone and content Ariosto's final renunciation of the life of ambitious striving after recognition, preferment, benefices, and sinecures. It is his final statement of disgust with the patronage system."[55]

Swift too was bitterly aware of his impotent dependence on his political masters. His "Libel on Dr. Delany" (1730), alluding to the afforts of a fellow clergyman to secure patronage, reflects the mortifying plight of all "deluded" dependents "summoned" to a patron's table. Perhaps, the poem suggests, "men of wit" are no more than "a

kind / Of pandar to a vicious mind; / Who proper objects must provide / To gratify their lust of pride." The client is inevitably disappointed to discover that the patron will not talk of "business" (that
is, preferment). For his literary talents the poet can expect no more
than a dinner. Of his fellow writers, only Pope (says Swift) seems to
have escaped the client's fate: "His heart too great, though fortune
little, / To lick a rascal statesman's spittle."[56] Years earlier, while still
in service to Harley and Bolingbroke, Swift addressed to the former
an imitation of Horace's epistle to Maecenas. Written shortly after
Swift had been installed as Dean of St. Patrick's, the poem casts Harley as Phillipus and Swift as Volteius. In Swift's version, Harley extends his favor merely as a "jest." Tellingly repeated three times (15,
81, 136), the word carries a range of meanings from the bitter (you're
just playing with me; this must be some kind of cruel practical joke)
to the cautious (I know you didn't *mean* to hurt me). In any event
Swift the gudgeon "takes the bait" (80) and soon discovers that the
promised "plenty, power, and ease" are vexation, frustration, and
debt. He returns to his patron and begs to be released from favor:
"Since you now have done your worst, / Pray leave me where you
found me first" (137-38). The tone remains light and facetious, but
given Swift's known disappointments and resentments, we can hear a
reproach beneath the joking.[57]

Twenty-five years later, in very different personal circumstances,
Pope took up Horace's epistle and imitated it "in the Manner of Dr.
Swift." Pope's motives may simply have been to extend an imitation
that Swift had left incomplete. Swift imitated only lines 46-95 of
Horace; Pope takes up the opening forty-five lines of the epistle and
imitates them not in his own pentameters but in Swift's tetrameters.
Commentators can find no clear parallel in Pope's life to Horace's
refusal of Maecenas's invitation. It is very likely that Pope at some
time declined or deferred *some* lord's invitation to visit. But after his
successful Homer translations, Pope was never as dependent upon
patronage as Horace was upon Maecenas. His declaration of independence is thus made at little cost to himself. With no real equivalent to
Horace's offer to return the patron's gifts, Pope can only counter with
"South-Sea Subscriptions take who please, / Leave me but Liberty and
Ease" (65-66). But Craggs, long dead, had made the gift of South Sea
stock some seventeen years earlier. Pope's claims that he is ready to
"retrench," live on "Bread and Independency," and "Shrink back to
my Paternal Cell" sound hollow coming from a man of independent
means. Perhaps, however, we should interpret them as signs of the

quick sensitivity that Pope—like many satirists before him—displayed at any hint of a wealthy friend's claim on him.

Satire and the World of Politics

Is satire essentially conservative or radical? Does it serve to defend traditional values, support the established order, and "safeguard existing boundaries"?[58] Or does it serve instead to challenge authority, to question or subvert conventional values, to disrupt and even tear down foundations?[59] Ronald Paulson has suggested that there are indeed two kinds: "Depending on its emphasis—whether it is on the noncomformity and deviation of the false society from old norms, or on its rigidifying of the old ways—the satire can be conservative or revolutionary, its aim to attack release or to use it as a foil to stultification."[60] Juvenal is for Paulson an example of the conservative and Lucian an example of the revolutionary satirist.

Paulson's observation has probably seemed so sensible that the question of the satirist's political stance has not been opened since the 1960s. In the 1990s, however, when literary critics are again pondering the relationship of literature to its cultural contexts and the ways in which literature sustains or subverts a dominant political system, Paulson seems vulnerable to several objections. First, there is the matter of terms. As many have observed, the conservative and the revolutionary are more akin than they may realize. The conservative wants to conserve the best of tradition, the radical or revolutionary wants to return to the *roots* to find a purity that has been corrupted. Each is oriented toward an ideal in the past. Second, even assuming that we can distinguish between the two, it is very difficult to agree whether we should place a particular satirist among the conservatives or the revolutionaries. Where do we put Horace? or Rochester? or Donne? or Rabelais? Some satirists, like Swift, would appear to be sometimes "conservative" (as in certain parts of *A Tale of a Tub*) and sometimes "revolutionary" (as in the *Modest Proposal* or the *Drapier's Letters*). It is very difficult to distinguish satirists by subject matter, by the techniques they use, or by the effects they achieve. Both the "conservative" and the "revolutionary" censure, attack, and ridicule; both display their wit, playfully explore a topic, provoke or challenge complacency.

Third, there is little evidence that a satirist is typically motivated by clearly articulated political principles, or even by what might now be called political ideology, that "system of interlocked ideas, sym-

bols, and beliefs by which a culture . . . seeks to justify and perpetu-
ate itself; the web of rhetoric, ritual, and assumption through which
society coerces, persuades, and coheres."[61] Indeed, it is likely that
satirists' concerns are more *literary* than political, that they write
satire because they think it will advance their careers by winning
audiences or patrons. Thus, as one critic recently argued, Hall's *Virgidemiae* was designed not as social criticism but as a "literary de-
but."[62] And Fielding's apparently shifting political allegiance can be
explained as his taking advantage of satiric opportunities in his pursuit of a literary career. As Fielding himself wrote: "Why is an Author obliged to be a more disinterested Patriot than any other? And
why is he, whose Livelihood is his Pen, a greater Monster in using it
to serve himself, than he who uses his Tongue to the same Purpose?"[63] Though we often casually assume that "political satire" is
written from a clearly defined political position, we should suspect
that what looks like principle is often a blend of literary and political
opportunity, personal circumstance, and an attempt to discredit a
particular person or party or to advance a literary career. "If the
Public will feed a hungry Man for a Little Calumny," says Fielding,
"he must be a very honest Person indeed, who will rather starve than
write it."[64] The satirist's primary goal *as writer* is not to declare
political principles but to respond to a particular occasion and to
write a good satire. A quick review of the major English satirists
from Butler to Swift confirms the suspicion.

   Butler in the 1660s writes *against* the defeated and discredited
Puritan party. Of that much there is no dispute. But critics of Butler
have found it very difficult to define what it is that Butler is *for*. He
does not clearly write from a Cavalier/Royalist point of view. Nor
does he celebrate the town or the court, or some unspoiled traditional rural culture. Rochester, for all his interest in "affairs of state," is a
curiously apolitical poet. His poems do not reflect or seek to influence the great political events of the day. Indeed, he looked on politics, and on politicians, with considerable contempt. Dryden, on the
other hand, would appear to be a strongly political writer in the
public sense, writing on behalf of the king and the court party; the
political principles implicit in *Absalom and Achitophel* have been
summarized as the "conservative myth."[65] But Dryden was not simply a Tory ideologue or defender of Stuart monarchy. At a crucial
moment in *Absalom and Achitophel* he weighs the claims of competing principles—a republican or contract theory on the one side, and
a theory of absolute sovereignty on the other—and appeals at last

not to principle but to pragmatism: "What Prudent Men a setled Throne would shake?" Furthermore, the poem does not simply endorse Charles's skillful use of his authority. It may even offer a warning to the king that he runs a risk of being too lenient, too negligent.

Pope used to be thought of as a "Tory satirist," but recent studies have brought out how long he evaded partisan politics, preferring to appear all things to all men: "Tories call me Whig, and Whigs a Tory" (*Imitations of Horace*, Sat. 2). It was only in the closing years of the 1730s that Pope in any sense briefly joined the political opposition, when he became an outspoken critic of corruption. But it is difficult to find in his work a consistent political thread—not Jacobitism, not the "landed interest."[66] As Mack notes, Pope's politics were not "practical": they consisted of "a vision of a possible true community."[67]

Swift, by contrast, was in his early career associated with the Tory ministry, for whom he served as a political journalist. But despite recent claims that Swift's lifelong politics were "Tory,"[68] it is well known that as late as 1708 he called himself a Whig, and that he intended *Gulliver's Travels* to apply not to one country and one set of politicians but to all countries and all times.[69] The politically engaged *Drapier's Letters* are in Swift's career as a satirist the exception rather than the rule. Perhaps we should read them not as satire but as polemic that makes local use of satire. And even in that instance it is notable that Swift focuses his efforts to *defeat* a particular coinage measure and not to advance a political program. Despite the almost insurrectionist rhetoric of the Drapier's fourth letter, in which he appears to challenge the contemporary theory that Ireland was a "depending kingdom," Swift was no revolutionary. He was rather closer to what Orwell called a "Tory anarchist"—"despising authority while disbelieving in liberty, and preserving the aristocratic outlook while seeing clearly that the existing aristocracy is degenerate and contemptible." Orwell, from his own quite different political perspective, goes on to note that Swift ultimately has no basic disagreement with the political arrangements of his day: "His implied aim is . . . the world of his own day, a little cleaner, a little saner, with no radical change and no poking into the unknowable."[70]

I suspect that one could say as much for most of the great satirists. They are not really interested in fundamental rearrangements, only in minor adjustments. Swift would not in fact wish to bring back a "real" Christianity. Such a "wild Project" would be "to dig up Foundations; . . . to break the entire Frame and Constitution of

Things" (*Argument [against] the Abolishing of Christianity*). So too, as Erich Auerbach suggests, Molière "accepts the prevailing structure of society, takes for granted its justification, permanence, and general validity." Although he ridicules excesses, he does not challenge the status quo that defines them as excesses.[71] Juvenal is in no real sense a republican, for all his praise of old Republican virtue, and Lucian's devastating skepticism suggests cheerful resignation rather than any polemical urge to tear down the structure of superstition in his day.[72] Blake is perhaps the exception. Sufficiently eccentric, sufficiently remote from the common life of his day, he calls for the kind of revolution that would indeed "dig up Foundations." The Martin Marprelate tracts (a 1588-89 series of prose attacks on Anglican bishops) might seem another exception. But I would argue that—like the later Smectymnuan tracts in which Milton figured—they are not satire proper. They are polemical and controversial prose that makes use of satiric elements.

If satirists for the most part are not committed to a set of political principles, neither can their work be said to have had much effect on the world of practical politics, either to support tradition or to subvert it. Aristophanes' attacks on Cleon, it has been shown, never "diminished the demagogue's power or popularity"; Old Comedy did not "exert a practical influence on social and political life" in Greece.[73] The Roman emperors can have paid little attention to the political allusions or implications of Horace, Juvenal, Persius, and Lucian and were certainly not deterred or encouraged in their actions by the ironies or the declamations of satirists. Auden once said that poetry makes nothing happen; his rule may be extended to satire. The Puritan party was already thoroughly defeated when Butler wrote against it. Shaftesbury was *not* indicted by the grand jury that met as *Absalom and Achitophel* was published.[74] Shadwell was so little hurt by *MacFlecknoe* that he continued in his successful career as popular dramatist and went on to succeed Dryden as Poet Laureate and Historiographer Royal at the Revolution. Lord Petre did not marry Arabella Fermor, as the families hoped. Opera was already out of fashion when Pope attacked it in the *Dunciad*, and Walpole was already fallen when the four-book version of the poem appeared in 1743. Cibber was in no real way discredited (in the eyes of his contemporaries, anyway) by Pope's attack on him. And Pope's political campaign against corruption was only a "private satirist's war" against Walpole.[75]

That satire has little effect on the "real" world is borne out by

Bertrand Goldgar's study of the "actual relations of politicians and men of letters" during Walpole's ministry. The satirists of the day, he argues, "played no direct role in pressing measures in Parliament; one cannot imagine that their writing had any influence on the politics themselves in this crucial period." The satirists were not interested in the "details of the political struggle," unlike the pamphleteers and journalists, who constituted a more significant political force.[76] Goldgar quotes from a pro-Walpole writer who looks (perhaps a little defensively) at Pope, Swift, and their fellow satirists from the point of view of the real center of power:

> No man can be so weak as to think that a People of Good Sense, such as the English are, will ever be laughed into an Opposition to the Government. Believe me, Sir, these Writings and Sayings have not the Effect that we may imagine. They do indeed open a great many Mouths against the Government; [but] they are little to be regarded. The Men of Interest and Wealth in the Nation are they who make the least Noise; as they have a great deal to lose they are more cautious, and don't care to disoblige any Party by speaking too freely, and for this Reason all the Talkers and Laughers are on the Side of the Opposition.[77]

If satire has little power to disturb the political order, then why have governments thought it important to control? From the days of the Roman decemvirs to the twentieth century, laws imposing sharp penalties for sedition and libel have been used to threaten satirists. Acts mandating the prepublication licensing of books likewise testify to the belief that printed words are powerful and dangerous to authority. Perhaps governments are naturally suspicious and even fearful of dissent, and have thus been disposed to exaggerate the threat posed by dissenters and papists in Dryden's day, Jacobites in Pope's, or the American Communist Party in ours. Furthermore, the laws in question are not aimed primarily at satire. All governments seek to protect themselves against those they define as internal enemies. Sedition acts are designed to catch traitors and revolutionaries, bigger fish than satirists. All societies that enjoy the protection of a system of laws likewise protect citizens against what they define as libel. Libel laws are designed primarily to penalize direct defamation but are always available to restrain the publication of works of wit that ridicule or discredit.

But what of laws that specifically prohibit or restrain satire? Roman law prohibited *mala carmina*, abusive songs or poems. In 1599 the Archbishop of Canterbury and the Bishop of London ordered the burning of several works of satire. In the late 1720s progovernment writers in England urged that political satire be restrained. And in 1737 the Stage Licensing Act served to control the satirical tendencies of the London stage. Do such laws not constitute evidence that governments genuinely *believe* satire has the power to hurt? Hurt individuals, yes. Embarrass the government, perhaps. But seriously disturb the state—probably not. The old Roman law against satiric songs, dating from a time when in popular belief a curse still had a magical power to wound, may refer only to magical incantations, not poems. In any case, punishment for defamation was very rarely enforced in Rome.[78] The Bishops' Ban was probably aimed not at satire's social or political criticism but at its indecency. Various nonsatiric works of sedition and libel were also called in for burning.[79] The Stage Licensing Act, as a recent study shows, was the product of a convergence of several forces, including traditional moral disapproval of the theater and the attempt by licensed theater managers to preserve their lucrative monopoly. One progovernment writer warned that "to turn [government and religion] into Ridicule, is to unloose the fundamental Pillars of Society, and Shake it from its Basis."[80] But such testimony about the threat that dramatic satire really posed is rightly discounted as "self-serving" and thus suspect.[81] The act implicitly distinguished between satire or innuendo on the stage and satire on the page, regarding the former as more dangerous, perhaps because an eloquent actor might arouse several hundreds in a single theater audience. Books—so the act implies—have less power to corrupt.[82] Even so, Chesterfield ridiculed the idea that the government might be "overturned by such licentiousness, even tho' our Stage were at present under no Sort of legal Controul."[83]

Despite the fears of political authorities from ancient to current times, it has not been convincingly shown that satire has the power to encourage the actions or alter the attitudes of its readers. Voltaire once noted that since few members of the populace read, "sedition is produced by speaking to assemblies of the people rather than by writing for them."[84] Even among those who do read, satire does not often *persuade*. Modern sociologists have attempted to determine whether or not satire measurably influences opinion. What evidence has been collected suggests not only that satire does not change attitudes but that many readers even have difficulty determining whether or not a given work is intended as satire or what its author's attitude or intention may be.[85] Defoe's *Shortest Way with the Dissenters* and Swift's *Modest Proposal* both demonstrate—by the misreadings they have received—the danger an ironic satirist runs in overestimating the acuteness of his audience.

Political satirists have sometimes persuaded themselves that if they could not reform the wicked, they could at least deter them by striking fear into their hearts. Pope boasted that men who were not afraid of God were "afraid of me"; though unrestrained by bar, pulpit, or throne (the law, the church, the state), they were "touch'd and sham'd by *Ridicule* alone" (*Epilogue to the Satires* 2.208-11.) But in the final note appended to the poem Pope conceded that "bad men were grown so shameless and so powerful that Ridicule had become as unsafe as it was ineffectual." Swift shared a similar sense of the satirist as vigilante, supplying a "defect in the law." He entertained the idea that satire might shame from further ills those Whigs who voted themselves a "General Act of Indemnity" to block scrutiny of their conduct of the war with France. But Swift too yielded to doubts about the possibility of restraining "such hardened and abandoned Natures." If you cannot tame or bind a "Savage Animal," he concludes, "the best Service you can do the Neighborhood, is to give them Warning, either to arm themselves, or not come in its Way."[86]

This is not to say that satire has no effect at all on its readers. F.P. Lock suggests that even if Swift's satire did not make any converts, its effect was to "keep up the spirit of its own side."[87] Swift designed the *Drapier's Letters* not to turn the tide—to dissuade people from supporting the English government's coining scheme—but to consolidate and strengthen already organized Irish resistance and to assure shopkeepers that it was legal (and therefore safe) to refuse the coins.[88] And Goldgar grants that given Walpole's personal unpopularity, Pope and the opposition satirists "played an active part indeed in keeping the public inflamed against the government."[89] Modern sociologists have gathered some evidence to suggest that even if satire produces no change of attitude in its reader, it reinforces existing attitudes. Furthermore, works not primarily designed as satire might become so in a highly partisan political climate, where hints will be seized by commentators, applications will be discovered, or imposed. Thus *Gulliver's Travels*, *The Dunciad*, and *The Beggar's Opera* were all exploited by the opposition to Walpole in order to embarrass his government.[90]

In some instances, keeping up the spirit of one's own side may serve to maintain the momentum of a political movement toward a political victory. But it is probably more common, as the early Soviet critic Anatoly Lunacharsky suggested, that satire provides a "moral victory" as a substitute for a "material victory." In a little-known review of a new Russian edition of *A Tale of a Tub*, Lunacharsky argued that the satirist's method is to "launch an attack against an enemy while simultaneously declaring him already vanquished and making a laughing-stock of him." But in fact the satirist is usually "sadly convinced that the evil he has challenged is very formidable, very dangerous." His purpose then is to "encourage his allies, his readers" that they and he are victors at least "in theory" or in "moral superiority."[91] In some readers (and satirists too) satire no doubt induces a gratifying sense of moral victory to compensate for their status as political underdogs or outsiders. Compensation combines the ideas of substituting for loss and conferring benefit. Literature is often said to promise, or to constitute, compensation for some defect or loss in our lives. The special compensations of satire have to do not with fame or immortality but with the sentiment it fosters of superiority in morality or in wit or in power.[92]

From the point of view of rulers, such compensatory satire would not be threatening. Indeed, since it would tend to keep the underdogs contented, it might be seen as a means of political control, a harmless way to allow the venting of dangerous steam. Monarchic governments, said Montesquieu, tolerate satire or impose only limited penalties so as to "give the people patience to suffer" and indeed to "laugh at their suffering."[93] If the licensed disruptions and misrule of pre-Lenten carnival, the medieval Feast of Fools, and the Ass's Mass serve finally to reinforce communal norms and established authority, perhaps we should view political satire as a similar kind of safety valve.[94]

Two examples suggest that we should. In sixteenth-century Rome a mutilated statue was disinterred and set up by Cardinal Caraffa at the corner of his palace. It became known as Pasquino or Pasquilo, and the custom gradually arose of affixing satirical Latin verses, often of a political or ecclesiastical nature, to the statue on St. Mark's Day. The anonymous poets signed themselves "Pasquino." It might be argued that such verses, known as *pasquinades* or *pasquils*, enabled satirists to lodge grievances. But we should also note that they enabled the church and state to channel protest into a controllable form, on a specified day and at a specified place, symbolically under the watchful eye of the cardinal and his successors. Pope Adrian VI reportedly tried to get rid of the statue but was persuaded not to by an official who said that if thrown into the Tiber, Pasquino "like a frog . . . will find a voice in the water," and if burned, he would become a martyr and the site "a place of pilgrimage for wits."[95] As Bacon later said, "despising" (that is, scorning, ignoring) libels against the state is a better policy than suppressing them: "The going about to stop them doth but make a wonder long-liv'd."[96] "Burning a book by the common hangman," wrote Swift, "is a known expedient to make it sell."[97] In other words, the interests of the state are better served by watchfulness and a calculated refusal to take offense.

My second example is from Swift. Does his riotous *Tale of a Tub* shake the foundations of decency and religion, as Wotton and others feared, or is it simply a wild speculative flight designed to preoccupy (and therefore divert, and thus defuse) a restless and thus potentially dangerous reader? Recall that Swift claims that the "sole Design" of his *Tale* is to "divert" the "terrible Wits of our Age" inclined to "tossing and sporting with the *Commonwealth*." Swift elsewhere showed himself slyly aware of the political utility of diverting dangerous wits (and aware too that satire's electricity can be harmlessly discharged). If "Great Wits" are not permitted "a *God* to revile or renounce, they will *speak Evil of dignities*, abuse the Government, and reflect upon the Ministry: which I am sure, few will deny to be of much more pernicious Consequence" (*Argument [against] the Abolishing of Christianity*). The anarchic energy of wit, in Swift's politics, is better (because more safely) redirected than repressed. "Great Wits," he goes on, should be "always provided with Objects of Scorn and contempt, in order to exercise and improve their Talents, and divert their Spleen from falling on each other, or on themselves." This political tactic is not merely Swiftian fantasy. Richelieu, as Swift probably knew, was said to have established a literary academy "to amuse busy & turbulent wits & divert them from speculating into matters of state."[98]

By tossing the wits a tub, Swift will "employ" their "unquiet Spirits" ("Preface"). That is to say, he will keep them busy.[99] Can we even go on to suspect that among the "unquiet Spirits" Swift (when disposed to promote stability in church and state) would include his own subversive or "speculative" side? His speaker calls himself "a Person, whose Imaginations are hard-mouth'd, and exceedingly dispos'd to run away with [my] *Reason*" (Sec. 9). He thus promises to "vent [his] Speculations . . . for the universal benefit of Human kind." "Vent" is nicely ambiguous: it can mean to let out either in the sense of to utter or publish, or in the sense of to release, discharge, get rid of. Pressure is vented to prevent an explosion, or grief vented (says Marston) to prevent the heart from bursting. Speculations, mere mental schemes not limited by the practical world, can be dangerous. Swift elsewhere asserts that dangerous, heterodox opinions cannot be forbidden but should be kept to oneself. In the *Tale*, on the contrary, he suggests that speculations, like vapors, should be "vented"—that is, safely released into the air, lest by being repressed or directed against the state they disturb the social order. This puts in a new light the common charge that the satirist merely "vents his spleen." Like his alter ego the "truly learned" reader, Swift too will find in his *Tale* "sufficient Matter to employ his Speculations for the rest of his life" (p. 185). Can we say that Swift as it were throws out his *Tub* to himself? If so, his work ultimately serves the interests of stability. It will "contribute to the *Repose* of Mankind in Times so turbulent and unquiet as these" (p. 208).[100] The darkest and most subversive suspicions are released as harmless intellectual speculation. To "vent" one's "spleen," as satirists conventionally do, may be no less harmless. Addison worried about the "angry Writer" who "vents his Spleen in Libels and Lampoons" (*Spectator* No. 451), but perhaps such a writer is only discharging anger that he cannot express in print. As Byron said, "All my malice evaporates in the effusions of my pen."[101]

Among other readers political satire may induce a kind of skepticism or detachment, even a weary cynicism, about politics and politicians. The reader of *Gulliver's Travels* is made wary about the promises of a minister of state: "The worst Mark you can receive is a Promise, especially when it is confirmed with an Oath; after which every wise Man retires, and gives over all Hopes" (4.6). On the one hand, such skepticism might concern a governing authority. In a famous 1704 English libel case the judge concluded: "If men should not be called to account for possessing the people with an ill opinion of the goverment, no government can subsist."[102] Perhaps Johnson, concerned about the dangers of unlicensed printing, had that in mind: "If every murmurer at government may diffuse discontent, there can be no peace."[103] But on the other hand, skepticism and discontent can lead to a kind of passive obedience (if politicians are "all alike," what's the use of trying to change things?) that permits a government to maintain its authority and to control dissent.

Perhaps we need to distinguish here between an intellectual and a practical subversion. There is reason to believe that ideas have power, and that in the long run they can move mountains and topple tyrannies. Elliott thus argues that "major satire" is ultimately a revolutionary force. Molière's satire against hypocrisy is "genuinely subversive" and "radically disruptive" (*Power of Satire*, pp. 272, 274), its power to disturb still felt centuries later. The moral force of the satire, Elliott says in an idealistic spirit, "subsumes" an attack on the "social structure." But one has the sense in reading him (and in reading most critics on satire) that changes in the "social structure" are viewed as unimportant, that the moral victory is more important than local political victory, that the satirist who writes for truth and honesty may lose some battles yet will eventually win the war. But in the short run (and politics is about the short run), Molière's comedies did not disturb the social structure; they constituted no practical threat to the established order. The Restoration "Poems on Affairs of State" may well (as George Lord argues) have "helped to introduce a fundamentally secular attitude toward monarchical government," but it is very unlikely (*pace* Lord) that the poems actually served "to expose and help thwart the designs of Charles II and James II to achieve arbitrary power."[104]

By the same token, Lucian's satire makes readers skeptical of every orthodoxy and pious convention he touches. But he is a revolutionary satirist only in a narrow sense: he is intellectually subversive. Despite the attacks on him as a dangerous scoffer, one doubts that he seriously undermined the traditional order anywhere in any era. It is more probable that, like Gibbon's Romans, the sophisticated readers of Lucian privately considered "the various modes of worship" exposed in his dialogues to be false but nonetheless determined to show public respect for their ceremonies and rituals in the interests of "civil government" (*Decline and Fall*, chap. 1). The social and political order, in other words, is more resistant to whatever power satire possesses than Elliott and others urged thirty years ago.

In making this argument I do not wish to appear merely cynical, or to discount the value of satire. I argue instead that we need to reconceive the relations between satire and the society of which it may make a radical or even subversive critique. Like all works of literature or art, satire is inescapably a product of and therefore implicated in the social, political, and economic culture that produced it. Certain conditions in the culture make it possible for writers to publish satire, find readers, and be compensated for their efforts (by material or moral rewards). Those conditions include on the one hand a system of patronage, a class of educated readers with leisure and a taste for wit, and a system of circulation or distribution whereby manuscripts or books reach readers; and on the other, a tradition of moral inquiry based on widely respected classical authors. We mistake satire's power if we see it simply as an attack from outside.

Any critique so constructed within the walls of the dominant culture is, one could argue, easily absorbed or accommodated by that culture.[105] The "subversive" force of satire is "contained."[106]

This is not to say that satire has no political power. I would argue rather that claims about that power have been overstated or (perhaps better) misplaced. We need to value satire for what it is and does. Its effects can rarely be measured in terms of political change or even personal conduct. Except in mythical Ireland, satire does not cause the fall of princes or bring on revolutions. One doubts too that satire ever brought the wicked to repentance. Perhaps (as satirists like to think) it at least has the power to deter, or to intimidate. Thus Dryden could warn Tonson off with a sneering epigram. This is "political power" at the very local level. "The very Name of Satire," said Dryden, "is formidable to those Persons, who wou'd appear to the World, what they are not in themselves."[107] Rochester, it is said, maintained his own power and authority at court by instilling a "general dread of a Pen so severe and impartial."[108] Aretino had such power, so the familiar story goes, that the "Princes of Europe" bought his silence by paying blackmail when they had "committed a Folly that laid them open to his Censure."[109] But satire's real subversiveness operates more stealthily by means of the inquiry and paradox described in Chapter 2. By conducting open-ended speculative inquiry, by provoking and challenging comfortable and received ideas, by unsettling our convictions and occasionally shattering our illusions, by asking questions and raising doubts but not providing answers, satire ultimately has political consequences. Montesquieu worried about the tendency of political satire to cool our ardor and loosen our attachments (to an idea, a leader, a government), so that we cannot be mobilized in support of some public goal.[110] What government, except one that rules by fear, would want such moody, murmuring subjects?

7

The Pleasures of Satire

In the well-known comparison between the merits of Horace and Juvenal in his "Discourse" on satire, Dryden at one point winningly observes that Juvenal "gives me as much Pleasure as I can bear" (*Works*, 4:63). The remark is a salutary reminder that satire, like all other forms of literature, is designed to please. No matter how instructive, the work that does not please will be thrown away unread. Pleasure, Dryden later insists, is fully "one half of the Merits" of satire, not simply a means of attaining a moral end but itself one of the "Ends of Poetry" (4:73, 88). If the reader is pleased, so is the satirist. Dryden's contemporary John Oldham declares that "Satyr's my only Province, and Delight, / For whose dear sake alone I've vow'd to write."[1] His Elizabethan predecessors Hall and Marston take "pleasure" in "displeasing."[2]

But what is *pleasing* about a form that has often been regarded as displeasing, harsh, obscure, splenetic, malignant, too mired in historical particulars, or even unpoetic? Why do we continue to read and enjoy satire? The conventional answer is that the pleasure we take in satire derives from its wit.[3] But just how does wit do its work? By diverting our attention from the fact that satire is often abusive personal attack? By assuring us that the attack is in some way not wholly "serious"? Or does our pleasure in fact derive not only from the wit but from the pain of the attack, too? Modern commentators on satire have written much about the form and the end of satire but, with very few exceptions, have said too little about the special pleasures it offers to the writer or the reader, perhaps because they don't quite know what to say. As Elliott observed, "It is as difficult to account for our pleasure in vituperation as for our pleasure in tragedy. But it is there" (*Power of Satire*, p. 209n). Most critics, if they comment at all, are content with a brief acknowledgment, like Frye's: "Almost any denunciation, if vigorous enough, is followed by a reader with the kind of pleasure that soon breaks into a smile."[4] Most readers, I suspect, would implicitly trace their pleasure back to Hobbist "sudden glory" or even to a Christian view of fallen human nature.[5]

The few modern ciritics who have speculated at any length on satiric pleasures have largely depended upon Freud's account of jokes, and in particular his notion that what he calls "tendentious jokes" are an expression of repressed hostility. Thus one critic suggests that satire is a form of witty sadism. Both satirist and reader derive pleasure from participation in an act of rhetorical violence.[6] Another finds that the pleasure derives not only from the release of aggression but also from the reassurance that such release, normally unacceptable, is under the control of the conscious mind.[7] Such accounts sound plausible, especially to those raised in a culture that has absorbed Freud, or for that matter to those inclined to take a Hobbist view of human nature. And they remind us that satire produces pleasure for both the satirist and the reader who in some way—as observer, as accomplice, or as re-creator—participates in the event. Since Freud's is the best extensive discussion of the relationship between wit (*der Witz*) and hostility, it is perhaps well to inquire how useful his analysis is to our purposes.[8]

Freud's major discussion is found in his *Jokes and their Relation to the Unconscious* (1905).[9] He there argues that tendentious jokes (jokes with a "purpose," as opposed to "innocent," merely verbal, jokes) bring pleasure by enabling us to evade obstacles to our expression of hostility. Those obstacles may be either external, a powerful person whom we cannot safely attack, or internal—the prohibitions produced in us by a "highly developed aesthetic culture" (p. 119). Our pleasure lies, however, not simply in the expression of hostility itself but in a reduction of the effort required to prohibit hostility. Since "psychical expenditure" is required to erect or maintain prohibitions against aggression, the "secret" source of the pleasure of jokes lies in what Freud calls an "economy" of psychical expenditure.

Freud grants that his concepts of "economy" and "psychical expenditure" are "obscure," requiring considerable elaboration and ultimately some modification. By the end of his discussion he finds that the energy "saved" by the joke must go somewhere, and that there is a kind of pleasure (or "general relief") realized when that energy is discharged (p. 158). So the ultimate pleasure is not in saving but in spending. Elsewhere, Freud complicates his account of "economy" by suggesting that we derive pleasure from the "satisfaction of an instinct (whether lustful or hostile)," which seems like a kind of spending rather than saving. But we should not loosely call this instinct sadistic. It is striking that throughout his discussion Freud only once refers to the idea of sadism, and then to note that "aggressive tendentious jokes succeed best in people in whose sexuality a powerful sadistic component is demonstrable" (p. 143). Perhaps he prefers to restrict the term "sadism" to a species of sexuality: the joker, strictly speaking, is not intent on sexual pleasure through cruelty.

Even if Freud is right about psychic energy and about jokes, it remains to ask whether what he says about *der Witz* can be readily and equally applied to literary satire. Freud himself does not make the application. He only once uses the word satire: a hostile joke, he says, can serve "the purposes of aggressiveness, satire, or defence" (p. 97). In many respects, furthermore, a joke as Freud describes it is quite unlike what we usually mean by satire. The joke must be concise, not only brief but characterized by an economy of means. Much satire, by contrast, is extended in length and rich in elaboration. Jokes must also be clear and obvious, without "difficult allusions," and readily apprehensible; as Freud says, "an awakening of conscious intellectual interest usually makes the effect of the joke impossible" (p. 150). But satire, though it sometimes hits its target squarely and cleanly, is often obscurely allusive and "difficult"; in some forms it even cultivates difficulty. As for "conscious intellectual interest," satire that does not awaken it will be brutal or insipid. Satire can make use of jokes, but a joke displays few of the elements of satire. A good joke comes to a point; its inventive must not be too strong; it will tend to be spoiled by the intrusion of moral elements. By the same token, somebody who can tell a good joke does not necessarily have the disposition or the full range of literary equipment that a satirist needs. Finally, a joke requires an audience for its completion. The pleasure of joking at the expense of another person is realized, Freud argues, only in the presence of the "third party." To be sure, the publication of a satire assumes an "audience" of readers. But satire does not always appear to require an impartial audience for its effect: Archilochus's satire is directed *at* his enemy and addressed *to* him; Lord Rochester writes *to* his enemies or rivals at the Restoration court.

Freud, then, can probably tell us *something* about the pleasure we take in reading Dryden and Juvenal. When Freud says that "by making our enemy small, inferior, despicable, or comic, we achieve in a roundabout way the enjoyment of overcoming him" (p. 103), we can recognize Pope's triumph over the dunces. When he speaks of jokes as a kind of rebellion against powerful authority, we can recognize Pope's satirical jibes against Walpole. And when we simplify Freud's complex description of the way wit overcomes our inhibitions against aggression, we recognize that there is probably something very satisfying to most of us in satire's power to hurt.

But the Freud-inspired accounts of the pleasures of satire are unsatisfyingly reductive, oversimplifying what looks like a much more complex business than his jokes. To begin with, satirists do not conceal their hostility from themselves or their readers. Satirists know full well that satire can hurt, sting, wound; indeed, if they are like Pope, they glory in the power. The fantasies that satire gratifies are not limited to those of simple aggression. When we read satire, we sometimes are encouraged to indulge in fantasies with grandiose scenarios, from retaliation against oppression to the extermination of all our enemies, the Godlike purging or cleansing of muck and sin (as in Marston's *Scourge of Villainie*),[11] or the special and exquisite delight of standing alone and defiant against a cruel, dull, or corrupt world (a fantasy that Pope notably gratifies). Sometimes satirists are motivated by straightforward anger or hatred (with or without moral justification or pretext); sometimes their motives may be more complex. They can through satire define themselves against some *other* or against a wicked world, but they can also project onto that world those failings they may sense in themselves. As Kenneth Burke once wrote, "The satirist attacks in others the weaknesses and temptation that are really within himself"; the gains are paradoxical: in punishing the Other, he at once "gratifies and punishes the vice within himself."[11] Pope's satire might well be interpreted along these lines.

Freud's theory, furthermore, does not explain why we are able to enjoy witty remarks directed against ourselves. Perhaps it is because we are able to focus on the wit rather than the victim. Erasmus once noted that "such is the power of wit and liveliness that we can take pleasure in a witty remark even when it is aimed at us."[12] But as the notion in Erasmus of wit's "power" suggests, it is unclear whether pleasure is spontaneously produced or is extorted from us. Perhaps we can enjoy a joke on ourselves because the joke substitutes for direct censure. We prefer to take a glancing blow rather than absorb a direct hit, particularly if it will satisfy the adversary's need to attack.

Freud's ideas may also focus too much on the abasement of the victim of wit. Despite its attention to the way jokers overcome their own inhibitions, a Freudian account does not say enough about the satirist's self-consciousness and self-delighting activity. One cause of laughter in men, said Thomas Hobbes in *The Leviathan* (chap. 6) is "some sudden act of their own that pleaseth them." To be aware of one's own "power and ability" produces an "exaltation of the mind." [13] But there has been no comprehensive discussion of such pleasure in satire. We have only the isolated insights of a few modern critics, especially when they try to tackle Swift. [14] A.E. Dyson, for example, thought Swift "enjoyed his control of irony: enjoyed its flexibility, the complex destructiveness, his own easy mastery of it." And Swift, Dyson goes on, "expects his readers to enjoy it." [15] This suggests that the victim is almost incidental. The ironic satirist and the reader revel in the technical operation of the irony. Such suggestions might also explain some of our pleasure in a satirist like Pope, particularly in *The Dunciad*, of which Johnson said Pope delighted to vex the dunces "but he had more delight in seeing how well he could vex them." [16] But for an emphatically moralized poem such as the *Epistle to Arbuthnot*, we might have to seek other explanations: are we perhaps pleased to be included among Pope's small circle, or gratified by the warm glow of conscious virtue that we too can feel? And insofar as satire provokes or perplexes, unsettling or complacency, can we find some corresponding gratification?

The pleasures of satire, then, are probably more various than a Freudian analysis would suggest. We need to look more closely and more systematically at the several sources of pleasure. For some guidance, we might turn to those writers and critics in the great age of English satire—from about 1590 to about 1800—who commented more often than we realize on why satire pleases us, whether we are readers or writers. When Susan Sontag in her manifesto *Against Interpretation* (1964) called for an "erotics of art," and when Roland Barthes used as a title *The Pleasure of the Text* (1973), their ideas seemed novel. [17] But that may be because we have forgotten that eighteenth-century equivalents of our modern cultural commentators were once preoccupied with inquiring into what Francis Hutcheson called "the various Pleasures which *human Nature* is capable of receiving." [18] Writers of all kinds took a keen interest in the topic, since pleasure is, as Pope put it, "or wrong or rightly understood, / Our greatest evil, or our greatest good" (*Essay on Man* 2.91-92). "Pleasure" was a crucial critical term for Johnson, for whom poetry itself was "the art of uniting pleasure with truth" (*Rambler* 92). [19] Eighteenth-century philosophers distinguished between the claims of Aristippus and Epicurus, the pleasures of stimulation and the pleasures of repose. Joseph Addison and Mark Akenside wrote of "pleasures of the imagination," Thomas Warton of "the pleasures of melancholy." Hume tried to account for our pleasure in tragedy, and Edmund Burke for our pleasure in the sublime. Corbyn Morris, in his quixotic *Essay towards Fixing the True Standards of Wit, Humour, Raillery, Satire, and Ridicule* (1744), tried to distinguish between our pleasure in raillery (traced to the embarrassment of the victim) and the fuller pleasure in ridicule.[20] Their collective discussion of literary pleasure suggests lines along which we might discriminate among a variety of satiric pleasures, from the simple to the complex, from the mental to the bodily.

We may begin with the Aristotelian idea that we take pleasure in representation for its own sake, whether the object represented be beautiful or ugly. Dryden suggests that we are moved to pleasing laughter by "the representation of deformity."[21] As Addition puts it, even something "Disagreeable" to look at "pleases us in an apt Description." We compare the "ideas that arise from Words, with the Ideas that arise from Objects themselves" and are "delighted . . . with the Aptness of the Description to excite the Image."[22] It is not the deformity that pleases but the satirist's skill in representing that deformity. Ordinarily, contemplation of absurdity, shame, vice, or inconsistency produces what David Hartley called "intellectual pain."[23] But representations of these evils will please, if they surprise us "by some more than ordinary Degree of Contrast or Coincidence." However, if the representation is "too glaring" or "too faint," it "raises Dislike and Abhorrence" or "becomes insipid."

Such pleasures in what Freud later called "the rediscovery of what is familiar"[24] do not significantly distinguish satire from many representational forms—comedy, even tragedy. Perhaps, however, the representation of the ridiculous produces what one might call a special satirical pleasure. Francis Hutcheson argued that we have an innate "sense of the ridiculous." But his interest is not so much to define the source of pleasure in ridicule as to account for its purpose: God's "implanting" of this sense gives us "an avenue to pleasure, and an easy remedy for discontent and sorrow." Our "sense of the ridiculous" serves also to check foolish enthusiasm and excessive admiration.[25] In our own day it is difficult to accept Hutcheson's notion, not simply because of his providential argument but because explaining the pleasures of satire by appealing to an innate "sense" simply begs the question.[26] Perhaps we should historicize his inborn "*Sense* of the

Ridiculous" as an attempt to deny the Hobbist claim that laughter is nothing but "Sudden Glory." People laugh, said Hobbes, at the "apprehension of some deformed thing in another" because the comparison with their own case makes them "suddenly applaud themselves" (*Leviathan*, chap. 6). Indeed, the reflections on laughter and ridicule in the eighteenth century may be seen as a continuing attempt to refute the bracing and cynical simplicity of Hobbes.[27]

The practice of satirists suggests another way in which the representation of deformity might please a reader. The ugly or ridiculous object need not remain merely ugly in its representation. No less than the beautiful, it can be transformed by the poet, given an ideal form. One of the special features of satire is to give *form* to *deformity*, to turn a mere Shadwell into the swelling bulk of "MacFlecknoe," to make stolid Lewis Theobald into the "piddling Tibbald" of *The Dunciad*. We take pleasure in the witty re-creation of the satiric victim. Pushed a little further, this pleasure is simply the pleasure we take in all poetic creation. T.S. Eliot praises Dryden for his "transformation of the ridiculous into poetry." Dryden's merit "consists in his ability to make the small into the great, the prosaic into the poetic, the trivial into the magnificent." The risk here is to pay less attention to the process of satiric transformation—with its attendant delights—than to the end product, "what he made of his materials": "In the end the result *is* poetry." But after all, the purpose of Eliot's essay is not to praise Dryden as a satirist. He writes at a time (1921) when satire is understood narrowly. Eliot wants to make a case for Dryden as a "poet."[28]

Another kind of relatively simple pleasure for readers might be called the delight of decoding. Satire, says Dryden, is "a Poem of a difficult Nature in itself, and is not written to Vulgar Readers" (*Works*, 4:54). There is a pleasure in its difficulty because our wits are occupied (and flattered) in making sense of satiric obscurity.[29] Addison points to a related pleasure deriving from satire's habit of innuendo and veiled topical allusion. We take pleasure, Addison says, in reading a poem such as *Absalom and Achitophel* because the mind, "applying Characters and Circumstances," is "pleased with it self, and amused with its own Discoveries."[30] In like manner, one of Addison's contemporaries said that we enjoy reading poems in which teasing gaps (for example, Pope's references to "Y—ng" or "H—v—y") are left in the middle of proper names: "Most people love to meet with such gaps, in order to fill them up."[31] We also assure ourselves that we are as witty as the satirist, and smirk in our sleeves at the fools who do not see the point of the attack. Dryden speaks of those readers of Horace who "value themselves on the quickness of their own Understandings, that they can see a Jest farther off than other men" (4:72). Smugness is an implicit danger in this apparently innocent pleasure. Swift claims in *A Tale of a Tub* to write "only to the Men of Wit and Tast" ("Apology"). Much of his traffic with his audience involves ironically flattering (and teasing) his "judicious" readers that they stand among a select elite. "The Men of Tast," he says (but not the common, the *"Superficial,"* or the *"Ignorant"*) will be able to "observe and distinguish" the thread of irony that runs through Swift's book and to penetrate its dazzling surfaces. In the hands of a satirist like Swift, the flattered readers may well begin to suspect that their pleasure only makes them victims too.

We might combine the ideas of intellectual satisfaction (our pleasure in understanding a difficult matter) and the Hobbist idea of gratified superiority to suggest that another simple form of satiric pleasure lies in its reductiveness. Satire reduces complex institutions to simple caricatures, like Marvell's monster, the Excise ("Last Instructions to a Painter"). It simplifies Sir Robert Walpole, a cunning and adept administrator whose character and achievement have divided generations of historians, flattening them to surfaces: a "bold Front," a "Wall of Brass," a "Great Man." It discerns in a welter of sociological, military, political, and economic factors the clear decline of republican virtue in imperial Rome. Such reductions enable both satirist and reader to grasp a complex matter, to arrive at a judgment of it, and thereby to master it.[32] This sense of mastery (while it lasts) brings with it some relief from the burdens of complexity, a pleasure that we have proved ourselves more than equal to a difficult task of understanding and assessment. We have extended our imagined control of the world and in the process elevated our own status in relation to it.

Such pleasures, I suspect, are short-lived and never enjoyed without some partial consciousness that they are delusions. For the complexity of the world soon presses in on us again, or a contradictory reduction solicits our attention. It is rare, I think, that satirists (or their readers) attain a secure eminence from which their enemies can be seen in their petty simplicity. It has been suggested that the satirist attains, and enables us to attain, to a kind of divine laughter, a serene God's-eye view of the fretful stir of puny man.[33] True, a satirist like Pope sometimes imagines a divine perspective on man as corroboration and validation of his satiric conclusions. When we read his

Essay on Man, we are sometimes encouraged to think we see as God sees, but Pope does not allow us to remain long on such an eminence. We are always thrust back into the maze from which everything seems a riddle. Satirists rarely seem as serenely mirthful as Jove (such pleasures may be more proper to comedy).[34] The satirist *can* attain to the detached amusement of the wide "philosophic eye" but more commonly and more characteristically looks on from close quarters, angry, engaged, partial.

A divine laughter belongs to the gods, but words (as Johnson says) are the "daughters of men." And words are the source of another of the satirist's pleasures, especially for a satirist such as Rabelais. When in Book I of *Gargantua and Pantagruel*, that great feast of words, the cake-bakers of Lerné quarrel with the local shepherds, they "heap insults on them," calling them "babblers, snaggle-teeth, crazy carrot-heads, scabs, shit-a-beds, boors, sly cheats, lazy louts, fancy fellows, drunkards, braggarts, good-for-nothings, dunderheads, nut-shellers, beggars, sneak-thieves, mincing milksops, apers of their betters, idlers, half-wits, gapers, hovel-dwellers, poor fish, cacklers, conceited mon-keys, teeth-clatterers, dung-drovers, shitten shepherds, and other such abusive epithets."[35] These delights, one might say, are properly those of the demotic lexicographer, in love with the richness and variety of the language of insult. Marston half a century later shares such plea-sures. He rails at "*Castilios, Cyprians*, court-boyes, spanish blocks, / Ribanded eares, grando-netherstocks, / Fidlers, Scriveners, pedlers, tynkering knaves, / Base blew-coats, tapsters, broad-clothminded slaves." He takes special delight in unusual words and neologism: *jobernole, barmy froth, guzzel dogs*.[36] It was perhaps the exuberant riot of words as much as anything else that attracted Sir Thomas Urquhart to elaborate Rabelais's lists from his own lexical stores, de-lighting (as F.C. Roe put it) "to release in wild spate a flow of original and high-sounding words." His sentences tumble along "with a sav-oury or pungent raciness." He feels and he offers a "joy in loquacity.'[37]

But satirists do not delight simply in *words*; they are connoisseurs of *abuse*, taking pleasure (and giving it) in the unrestrained flow of invective. William Anderson finds in Lucilius a licentious and exuber-ant (and Rabelaisian) flow of "obscenity, sheer bombast, and delight-ful inventiveness" (*Essays on Roman Satire*, p. 21). Perhaps even Mil-ton offers such delights in his sardonic attacks on prelatical opponents where one critic finds a Falstaffian "fertility in epithets."[38] The satirist seems almost to forget the target and to delight instead in the range, inventiveness, and even the euphony of abusive vocabulary ("mincing milk-sops," "shitten shepherds"). It was probably from Rabelais that Swift learned his love for the satirical catalogue, though his lists disturb the simple delights in sheer abundance and energy with a calculated mixing of categories: "a Lawyer, a Pick-Pocket, a Colonel, A Fool, a Lord, a Gamester, a Politician, a Whoremunger, a Physician, an Evidence, a Suborner, an Attorney, a Traytor, or the like" (*Gulliver's Travels* 4.12). In Swift, our pleasure in the catalogue must often compete with the nearly overpowering pain of the subject matter, as in the lines from *A Modest Proposal* quoted earlier: "the *Oppression of Landlords*; the Impossibility of paying Rent, without Money or Trade; the Want of common Sustenance, with neither House nor Cloaths, to cover them from the Inclemencies of Weather, and the most inevitable Prospect of intailing the like, or greater Miseries upon their Breed for ever." The Rabelaisian belly laugh shrinks to a shudder.[39]

The representation of deformity, the delights of decoding and reductiveness, the relish in abusive language—these are all relatively simple satirical pleasures. But satire probably pleases us in more complex ways, too, both in body and in mind. We can again turn to Dryden and his contemporaries, who had available a vocabulary (which we largely lack) to describe the *physiological* pleasures of reading. The "poignant sauce" of Juvenal, Dryden says, raises in us "an appetite of reading him." The metaphor of appetite perhaps seems to us merely that: a dead metaphor, or a word like "taste," used in a transferred sense, for a purely mental operation. But "poignant" ("sharp, stimulating the palate," according to Johnson's *Dictionary*) suggests that Dryden wants to invoke the physical sense of the word.[40] Most critics after A.E. Housman (who reported that his skin bristled) have been reluctant or embarrassed to describe our responses to poetry in physiological terms. But earlier writers had no such embarrassment. Juvenal, Dryden goes on to say, "fully satisfies my Expectation, he treats his Subject home: His Spleen is rais'd, and he raises mine: I have the Pleasure of Concernment in all he says" (*Works*, 4:63).[41] A raised spleen is not simply a metaphor for strong feeling; the spleen was as late as the mid-eighteenth century supposed to be the visceral seat of anger, melancholy, and mirth. "My Spleen's afire in the heat of hate," says Marston's satirist in his play *What You Will*.[42] "Fierce Indignation boils within my Veins," declares an imitator of Juvenal.[43] The satirist's heat stirs more than the blood. As a later eighteenth-century commentator put it, Juvenal's "fire and spirit is . . . delightfully striking to an English ear."[44] It is not easy to read and understand Persius, says Vicesimus Knox, "without catching the glow with which he evidently wrote."[45] The gall of the satirist is released in his own body in such a way as to affect the reader's body sympathetically. "Glow, glow, my muse," says another eighteenth-century imitator of Juvenal, "th'enflaming theme to fit," so that the dullest reader will "kindle into wit."[46] These critics imply a kind of carnal pleasure in the very exercise of our capacity for indignation, in both the arousal and the discharge. Their terms—raising the spleen, catching the glow, sharpening the appetite—also imply that the seat of indignation or distemper is in the blood or the passions rather than the mind or moral faculty. Even Pierre Bayle, though hostile to satire, thought that it could produce (prior to the operation of any "reason and reflexion") "an agreeable sensation" no more under our control than our tongues are when touched by sugar or honey.[47]

Physiologists and critics have since the eighteenth century become reluctant to link specific emotions with specific parts of the body, but physiological explanations have persisted in our attempts to describe the pleasure of satire. Blake put it concisely—"Damn braces: Bless relaxes"—in one of the "Proverbs of Hell."[48] A Victorian clergyman confessed that the "hearty cursing" in A Tale of a Tub "goes straight to my midriff—so satisfying, the best of tonics."[49] Even for a mid-twentieth-century critic, satire provides "a kind of astringent pleasure like an acid drop or a dash of bitters."[50] Another suspected that the "exhilaration" produced by satire came from the "tone-restoring exercise of our sluggish moral muscles."[51] Such remarks make no claim to critical precision and would probably not be heard today. But even now the best Swift critics speak of his "astringent" tone, or the "exhilarating" or "euphoric" effects of reading A Tale of a Tub, perhaps betraying their unarticulated sense that satire makes itself felt in the body of the reader.

For one explanation of satire's power to produce a pleasure almost physical, we can look to eighteenth-century observers such as Hutcheson and Hartley, who sought to trace the source of the pleasures of mind to those of sense. Indolence, for example, is a melancholic condition of body and of mind. It is a malady that preoccupies both poets and physicians, each of whom prescribes vigorous exercise. In the older physiology, melancholy is "an indisposition of the Animal Spirits." As the famous Restoration medical man Thomas Willis put it, when the animal spirits ought to be "transparent, subtle, and lucid," they become in melancholy "obscure, thick, and dark."[52] For this and other similar distempers one well-known medical writer prescribed riding, cold baths, chafing with a "Flesh-Brush."[53] The goal is to heat the blood, so that the "Animal Spirits flowing forth from the inkindled Blood, go forth after a manner as the ray of light from a flame."[54] Though the medical writers do not actually go on to recommend the reading (or writing) of satire, it appears that the writers on satire, drawing on contemporary physiological models and principles, were implicitly filling the prescription. Juvenal's swift pace, notes Dryden, "adds a lively agitation to the Spirits" (*Works*, 4:64). "Spirits" (apparently Willis's animal spirits) seems a merely quaint term to today's critics (and physiologists), but it has the advantage—which today's critical and medical vocabulary lack—of suggesting a continuum between mind and body. In Johnson's *Dictionary*, spirits are "the purest part of the body bordering, says *Sydenham* [a famous medical writer], on immateriality." Thus, to agitate the spirits, to heat the blood, and to "kindle" the soul—as Walter Harte says Juvenal does[55]—come to the same thing. Perhaps the critic of today who wants to account fully for satire's effects on body and mind will need to develop a comparable vocabulary.

In the newer, more rationalistic eighteenth-century physiology that succeeded the older physiology, the recommended cure for melancholy could take the form of mental stimulation. The mind dislikes indolence, wrote the Abbé Du Bos in 1719. Mirth, or course, is a sovereign remedy against melancholy, as Sterne often reminded his readers. But according to Du Bos, the mind prefers *any* passion to insipid languour. Man wants "to have his mind incessantly occupied." He seeks to avoid that "heaviness" which "quickly attends the inactivity of the mind." He finds "in the bustle of business, and in the tumult of his passions, a motion that amuses him." Poetry and painting, Du Bos explains, have the power to exercise the mind. He reminds us that Nicolas Poussin's picture of the death of Germanicus caused the spectators to be "seized with indignation against Tiberius." And he repeats Quintilian's story of accusers who displayed the painting of a crime "in order to excite more effectually the judge's indignation against the criminal." So great is our dread of "heaviness" that we even prefer those passions that produce pain to a state of inactivity and indolence. Thus, we find a kind of "natural" pleasure "upon feeling our fellow creatures in any great misfortune or danger," not because we ourselves are safe (the Lucretian argument) but because the "attractive" emotion is a passion "the motions whereof rouse and occupy the soul."[56]

Du Bos's ideas had an eager reception in England, where Hume drew on them to account for our pleasure in tragedy and in sublime terror,[57] and Boswell found in them an explanation for our pleasure in seeing "spectacles of cruelty" such as public executions.[58] Though neither Du Bos himself nor his commentators explicitly apply his remarks to the amusements of satire, one can see that his psychological theory points to an explanation of why, in the eighteenth-century mind, the power of satire to "kindle" the soul or the blood might produce delight.[59] And when we recognize that like Du Bos we still think of mental life in physical terms (we speak of being roused, stirred, stimulated), we might want to pursue a physiological reading.

The old idea that satire could heat the blood suggests a link between sexual and satirical pleasure. It is perhaps only coincidental that *satyricus* is an old medical term meaning "having the power of heating" or even "aphrodisiacal"; *satyriasis*, likewise, derived no doubt from the lusty satyrs, in the eighteenth century still meant "a vehement appetite for venery";[60] and Petronius in the *Satyricon* refers to the ancient aphrodisiac satyrion (derived from a plant of that name). One modern critic of Swift wonders if there may be "a vaguely erotic effect in at least some satire," but he leaves the matter there.[61] Perhaps satire is erotic because it exposes what lies hidden, metaphorically stripping away clothes and veils. Perhaps because it often reveals a sexual motive at the base of actions in other realms, as when Swift discovers that Henry IV of France "raised a mighty Army" and alarmed the whole world only because of "an absent *Female*, whose eyes had raised a Protuberancy, and before Emission, she was removed into an Enemy's Country" (*A Tale of a Tub*, sec. ix). A long tradition of misogynist satirists, from Juvenal to Swift, claims to reveal the dirty truth about the sexual nature of women. This makes the satirist a kind of Peeping Tom, like the man who sneaks into the orgiastic women-only Bona Dea festival in Plutarch's *Life of Caesar* and Juvenal's sixth satire, or a pornographer who degrades women even as he exhibits their naked bodies and insatiable lust. One may object that the pleasures of such satire are hardly erotic. Indeed, it would seem that the misogynist satirist seeks primarily to arouse male disgust and even to suppress or kill desire.

The metaphor of stripping away, then, leads not to the erotic but to its antidote. Other metaphors favored by satirists—whipping, easing, and tickling—suggest pleasures that we might call quasi-erotic. The satiric whip or lash is often wielded with such gusto as to arouse suspicion about the wielder's motives. The charge that the satirist is a kind of sadist is so common that satirists themselves have taken it up. Some, Swift says in the *Tale*, "use the Publick much at the Rate that Pedants do a naughty Boy ready Hors'd for Discipline [that is, mounted on a rack or "horse" or flogging]: First expostulate the Case, then plead the Necessity of the Rod, from great Provocations, and conclude every Period with a Lash" ("The Preface"). In a late poem Swift half jokingly suggests that he too hangs with sadistic glee over his own victims "Hors'd for Discipline": "Let me, tho' the Smell be Noisom, / Strip their Bums; let CALEB hoyse 'em; / Then apply ALECTO's Whip, / 'Till they wriggle, howl, and skip." [62] Inflicting pain on another body produces relief in the body of the punisher, like Butler's pedants who whip dull schoolboys in order to "claw and curry their own itches." [63] Swift suspects that satire derives from a "Satyrical Itch"—a crude physical compulsion—that requires to be scratched. [64]

Always the most self-scrutinizing of satirists, Swift goes so far as to suggest that if the satirist is a kind of sadist, then his audience complements him, "the World being soonest provoked to *Praise* by *Lashes*, as Men are to *Love*" (*A Tale of a Tub*). Our pleasure in being the target of satire is analogous to the masochist's pleasure in being whipped—unless we derive a kind of perverse delight from a tongue-lashing, in which case the pleasures are identical. In the dark world of Otway's *Venice Preserved* (1682) the lecherous and fumbling Antonio appears to derive sexual stimulation from being verbally abused by the prostitute Aquilina (3.1). [65] By the same token, perhaps we love to hear the satirist talk dirty.

But satirical whipping is usually conducted in public, suggesting that we need to look for a social dimension. Hall compares his satire to bear-baiting (a sanctioned public taunting, associated with holidays and street fairs). We need to remember that Hall's society was accustomed to frequent public displays of cruelty, from legally administered punishments to the self-flagellation of fanatics. God himself might deliberately seek to "scourge" the world, and his angels, in *Paradise Lost*, take pleasure in contemplating the destruction of a sinful world by his "Hell-hounds." For the Renaissance sensibility, physical punishment is mixed up with ideas of entertainment, festivity, and justice both human and divine. In wielding a verbal whip, the satirist works in both spheres. By setting Hudibras in the stocks, Butler administers public punishment to the killjoy Puritan who would break up bear-baiting; Butler's satire itself baits the defeated Puritans, harassing them with ridicule from all sides without fear of reprisal. Associating pleasure with violence and pain did not disappear with the Enlightenment. Until well into the eighteenth century, English crowds gathered at "Tyburn Fairs" to be entertained by the witty farewell speeches of the condemned and to witness their last end. Like Horace before them (*Sat.* 1.4.78-79), most eighteenth-century satirists denied that they liked to give pain, but it would appear that their audiences did not mind watching.

The metaphor of "easing" suggests that what the satirist seeks is not to be aroused but to be relieved from some internal tension. Dryden is said by Johnson to "ease his pain by venting his malice [at his rival Elkanah Settle] in a parody." [66] For La Bruyère, the satirist writes "to ease him of his resentments." [67] Edward Young says that "laughing at the misconduct of the world will, in a great measure, ease us of any more disagreeable passion about it." [68] Easing oneself by some kind of release or relief suggests both sexual tension—in Rochester, "nature" is "eas'd" by orgasm—and scatalogical pleasures in the "house of ease" (i.e., privy).[69] In either case we are not far from the pleasures of writing, as the impudent Rochester brings out: "Whilst your rich head eases itself of wit," "I'd fart, just as I write, for my own ease." [70] Giving "birth" to satire produces the same relief: Marston's "pate" is "great with child" and "here [in satire] 'tis eas'd." [71] The underlying idea would seem to be that of the venting of some pressure, symbolically located in the "spleen," an organ whose dangerous swelling (in premodern medicine) needed to be relieved by purgatives, vomitives, or bloodletting.[72] As I have suggested, venting the spleen may, from the point of view of public order, harmlessly release pent-up steam; from the point of view of the private comfort of the satirist, it brings relief. "Malice," says Butler, "is Restles, and never finde's ease untill it has vented it self." [73] Pope's familiar claim that having told a fool he's an ass, "the Queen of Midas slept, and so may I" (*Epistle to Arbuthnot*), emerges as a variant on an old satiric theme.

If satire produces ease, it also produces dis-ease and discomfort: in the reader it can produce a blend of pleasure and pain that satirists have often compared to tickling. Of "fine raillery" Dryden says: "A witty Man is tick'ld while he is hurt in this manner" (*Works*, 4:71).[74] Elsewhere Dryden says that Butler's burlesque rhymes "give us a Boyish kind of Pleasure. It tickles aukwardly with a kind of pain. . . . We are pleas'd ungratefully, and, if I may say so, against our liking" (4:81). Horace, so Dryden translates Persius as saying, "tickles" when he probes a wound (*tangit*, "touches").[75] That there is something quasi-sexual in satiric tickling comes out in Dryden's comparison between his pleasures in Horace and Juvenal. Horace, he says, gives only a "*languishing*" delight: "He may *Ravish* other

Men; but I am too stupid and insensible to be tickl'd." By comparison, Juvenal is "of a more *vigorous* and *Masculine* Wit" (4:63). To
be tickled is to be both provoked and gratified. "I cannot rule my
Spleen," says Dryden's Persius. "My scorn Rebels, and tickles me
within" (*Sat.* 1.27-28). Pope picked up Dryden's metaphor in describing his own *Rape of the Lock*, "at once the most a satire, and
the most inoffensive, of anything of mine. . . . 'Tis a sort of writing
very like tickling."[76]

The comparison may strike us as an undignified one until we
note that tickling has attracted the attention of serious critics concerned to discern the relations, and the border, between pleasure and
pain. Bacon associated tickling with a stirring of the animal spirits.[77]
In his essay "Of Tragedy" Hume cites Fontenelle, who in his *Refléc-
tions sur la Poétique* notes that "the movement of pleasure, pushed a
little too far, becomes pain," and offers as an example "the instance
of tickling."[78] And Hartley, in his *Observations on Man*, locates the
sensation of tickling "as it were, between Pleasure and Pain" (1.252),
and links it with a whole range of in-between "mental Emotion."

What Dryden and Pope precisely meant by their comparison between satire and tickling is not clear. Physical pleasure with moral
pain? Or the contrary, painful wit and healing morals? Delight at form
or technique, with distress at the subject or the substance? Or even
that vexation at which Swift aimed? One of the pertinent eighteenth-
century meanings of "tickle" is "to vex or provoke"; another is "to
irritate lightly, so as cause a peculiar uneasy sensation."[79] Tickling is
the physical equivalent of mental perplexity, which (as David Hartley
notes), gives us "a limited Degree of Pain" but also has "some good
Effects" (*Observations on Man* 1.442). Perhaps the "Perplexity, Confusion, and Uneasiness which we labour under in abstruse Inquiries,
philosophical, moral, and religious" (1.441) are akin to the perplexity
induced in us by satire. We laugh, but we laugh uneasily.[80] Very like
our reaction to tickling.

The complex pleasures of satire are not limited to the physiological. Indignation may fire the blood, but it is also the sign of a deeply
moral response. Once again, we in the late twentieth century have lost
touch with an older way of describing our response to satire and might
profit from remembering eighteenth-century accounts of "the pleasure of doing good." "There is a pleasure," Pope wrote, "in bearing
Testimony to Truth."[81] Particularly in the middle third of the eighteenth century, as satire increasingly came under attack for its malice
and ill-nature, practitioners and defenders of satire alike seemed to

turn away from the moral delights of sudden glory and ridicule to the pleasures of righteousness. In 1729 "William Cleland" (under Pope's supervision) denies that Pope's dunces are ridiculed simply "because Ridicule in itself is or ought to be a pleasure." [82] In the poems of the later 1730s Pope feels an evident pleasure in branding "the bold Front of shameless, Guilty Men," though the directness and gusto of the attack suggests that for Pope the moralist is by no means a passive or harmless observer of evil. The reader feels a corresponding delight: "What a pleasure it must be," says Cleland, "to every reader of humanity, to see all along, that our Author, in his very laughter, is not indulging his own Ill nature, but only punishing that of others." [83]

Satirists who claimed to offer such moral pleasures were of course not disinterested parties. But their promises would have met a ready reception in those who read contemporary moral theory. For moralists in the Shaftesburian tradition, the innate "moral sense" was even more important than the "sense of the Ridiculous." For most modern criticism and philosophy the "moral sense" is an exploded universalist fiction, but for Hutcheson it was "the Foundation of the chief Pleasures of POETRY." The moral sense, he wrote in explication of his predecessor Shaftesbury, is "that Determination to be pleas'd with the Contemplation of those Affections, Actions, or Characters of rational Agents, which we call virtuous." [84] Hutcheson and his followers were reacting against the Hobbist assertion of man's natural and prevailing egoism and against Lockean denials of "innate ideas," even in the moral realm. In arguing for an innate moral consciousness, they were building on the venerable idea, found in both classical and Christian tradition, that virtue rewards us by bringing pleasure. As Pope summed up the tradition, "Virtue alone is Happiness below" (*Essay on Man* 4.309-26). [85] Or as Addison put it in the nearly contemporary *Spectator* 172, there is an "exquisite delight" in being able to say to yourself that "you have done well."

Hutcheson's system remained a powerful counter to Hobbist cynicism throughout the eighteenth century and continued to provide both a philosophical explanation of and an inducement to virtuous thoughts and deeds. Some Lockean skeptics doubted his claims of an innate moral sense, and partly in response to their doublts Hartley at midcentury modified Hutcheson's theory by arguing that one can explain our pleasure in virtue by means of the Lockean doctrine of the assocation of ideas. We need not assume an implanted "moral Instinct," he argues, or that our moral judgments are based on "Determinations of the Mind, grounded on the eternal Reasons and Relations of Things." We can instead deduce "all our moral Judgments, Approbations, and Disapprobations, from Association alone." Such associations, among virtue, praise, reward, and pleasure, for example, are "formed so early, repeated so often, riveted so strong, and have so close a Connexion with the common Nature of Man, and the Events of Life which happen to all" that they might appear to be "original and natural Dispositions," but they are in fact "the mere Result of Association" (*Observations on Man* 1:498-99).

Hartley distinguishes between the "sensible pleasures" and the derived "intellectual Pleasures" (that is, those felt in the mind). Among the six classes of intellectual pleasures are the "Pleasures of Imagination," those of "Sympathy" and the "Moral Sense," now understood not as implanted but derived. But as with Hutcheson, the moral sense is the source of pleasure:

> There are certain Tempers of Mind, with the Actions flowing from them, as of Piety, Humility, Resignation, Gratitude, &c. towards God; of Benevolence, Charity, Generosity, Compassion, Humility, Gratitude &c. towards Men; of Temperance, Patience, Contentmant, &c. in respect of a Person's own private Enjoyments or Sufferings; which when he believes himself to be possessed of, and reflects upon, a pleasing Consciousness and Self-approbation rise up in his Mind, exlusively of any direct explicit Consideration of Advantage likely to accrue to himself, from his Possession of these good Qualities. [1.493]

Between the pleasure of being virtuous and the pleasure of "disapprobation" (or of punishing the vicious), Hartley's emphasis falls on the "Pleasures of Self-approbation" (2.337), on the "Pleasures of moral Beauty and Rectitude" (1.498). He does not explicitly say that we derive pleasure from condemning the wicked, but by his own key principle of association, hatred of vice is linked with the love of virtue.[86] A Hartleian theory would explain why denouncing a wicked (or a merely foolish) world adds to one's self-esteem, vouches for one's "humanity" (that is, benevolence and tenderness), and confirms one's moral superiority.

Hartley's major work acquired a solid reputation that endured for the remainder of the eighteenth century (Joseph Priestley, J.S. Mill, and the early Coleridge were great admirers). Its significance for the reader of satire is in its showing how the idea that our moral judgments produce pleasure was by no means original in 1750— Hartley credits the Reverend John Gay's work twenty years earlier as a predecessor—and was so widespread as to be ready for a systematic treatment on a Lockean foundation. Hartley's work has some bearing too on the moral fiction being produced at midcentury. Indeed, its printer was none other than Samuel Richardson, whose *Clarissa* appeared in the same year as the *Observations on Man*, and whose Pamela takes a conscious "Pleasure" in her innocence (*Pamela*, Letter 24).

If we think of the angry satirist's pleasing emotional arousal and satisfied conscience, we can perhaps discover secret links with two apparently quite different eighteenth-century figures: the man of sentiment, and the Richardsonian heroine. The softer sort of sentimentalist likewise enjoys tears and the exercise of the tender emotions, and sympathizes (so critics say) not so much to aid the distressed as to indulge personal sensibilities. We should not be surprised to find that satire and sentiment meet in Sterne. Richardson's Clarissa enjoys the pleasures of conscious rectitude: "It gives a worthy mind some satisfaction in having borne its testimony against a bad one." [87] "To Virtue only and her Friends a Friend" is Pope's motto, but it might serve too as Clarissa's. In her haughty disdain of her family and her contemptuous disapprobation of Lovelace (as well as her fascination with his evil), she is something of a satirist herself. But righteous denunciation of vice is perhaps a dangerous sort of pleasure, since it readily slides into smugness and Pharisaism. As Swift notes, satire is a mirror in which the viewer sees everybody's face but his own. Clarissa, no less than Pope, was attacked for pride.

Today we are hesitant to proclaim that doing good makes us feel good, perhaps too ready to suspect that conscious rectitude is only paraded righteousness. We suspect that the satirist who urges us to denounce evil is offering a moral cover for anger. Though moralists since Seneca (especially Stoics) have considered anger an irrational passion that must be controlled, satire encourages us to think that anger is the appropriate and even rational response to evil. (We could find support from Milton, a potent satirist in his controversial prose, who goes so far as to declare that "anger and laughter" are "the two most rational faculties of humane intellect." [88] Such a satirist, in his "grim laughter," assures himself that he acts as the servant, the agent, and the imitator of a justly angry God.) What Hartley would regard as confirmation of our moral sense, we would now see as self-pleasing fantasies, whether one triumphs as a Warrior for Truth, rescues the fair Virtue from the last dishonor, or dies a martyr's death in the cause. To the extent that we cannot imagine such moral pleasures, we are unable to enjoy unguardedly some of the later satires of Pope. Most readers today, I imagine, are ready to assume that what pleasures satire offers are of a lower kind. This is not to suggest that we are less naive, or better judges of human posing, than our eighteenth-century forebears but only that we are less disposed to moral idealism. They could in fact be just as skeptical about human nature as we are.

For every defender of the moral pleasures of satire in the mid-eighteenth century, when such a defense was most commonly offered, there were two who were troubled that the real pleasures were lower. Perhaps, as Vicesimus Knox suspected, there is an innate "love of censure" in readers that ensured satire an eager and a gratified audience.[89] Just as satirists delight in giving pain, so readers enjoy watching others being corrected (at least one eighteenth-century commentator compared this enjoyment with the delight of Britons in "cruel Sports, and bloody Sights").[90] Addison and Steele were particularly troubled by "the strange Delight Men take in reading Lampoons and Scandal" on eminent figures: "The low Race of Men take a secret Pleasure in finding an eminent Character levelled to their Condition by a Report of its Defects, and keep themselves in Countenance, though they are excelled in a thousand Virtues, if they believe they have in common with a great Person any one Fault."[91] The satirist shares some of the blame, however, since he "gratifies this baseness of Temper."[92]

Satire's ability to feed or *gratify* base appetites becomes of increasing concern in the later eighteenth century. For a time, however, especially around 1700, satirists seemed to think their pleasure in writing satire was innocent (or at least a private matter). Boileau, remembering Horace, explains why he writes satire: "Enfin, c'est mon plaisir. . . . je me veux satisfaire" ("In the end, it's my own pleasure . . . I want to gratify myself," Satire 7).[93] (Is there a hint here of feeding to satiety?) Pope imitates (and softens) the same original in noting that just as "every mortal has his pleasure," so he writes satire because he loves "to pour out all myself" (Imitation of Horace *Sat.* 2.45-50). Swift once noted that satire was written with two ends in mind, "one of them less noble than the other [though not positively wicked], as regarding nothing further than the private Satisfaction, and Pleasure of the Writer."[94] As late as 1752 Fielding could praise Lucian's ability to gratify those readers "who have a true Taste of Humour" with "the most exquisite Pleasure."[95] To feed on satire still seemed to Fielding—despite Plato's disapproval—a keen and delicate pleasure.

But even Dryden, though not tenderhearted, thought that Persius occasionally took a criminal "pleasure" in "insulting over Vice and Folly" rather than simply exposing it (*Works*, 4:52). And after 1750 one hears little about the satirist's innocent pleasures. Lord Kames in 1762 regretted that satirists gratify their own ill nature: "Those who have a talent for ridicule . . . are quick-sighted in improprieties; and these they eagerly lay hold of, in order to gratify their favourite propensity."[96] Henry MacKenzie's *Man of Feeling* (1771) worried about our "selfish pleasure" in conveying "tidings of Ill" (and a satirist is among other things a bringer of bad news).[97] And Knox argued in 1782 that satire derives its "power of pleasing" by appealing to "some dispositions in human nature not the most amiable." By arousing a "spirit of indignation" in the reader, it "gently gratifies the irascible passions."[98] Johnson, ever suspicious of Pope's claims to high moral purpose or to harmless diversion, saw rather that Pope "pleased himself with being important and formidable, and gratified sometimes his pride and sometimes his resentment."[99] Speaking for many skeptics in 1764, William Shenstone said quite simply that "SATYR gratifies self-love."[100]

But how can satire gratify our self-love if its target is general rather than particular, if it attacks faults common to the entire species, if it attacks us too? Swift knew well that general satire, "levelled at all, is never resented for an offence by any, since every individual Person makes bold to understand it of others, and very wisely removes his particular Part of the Burthen upon the shoulders of the World, which are broad enough, and able to bear it."[101] But Swift went further, as I've noted, and proposed that in some perverse way we enjoy being the target of satirical abuse. Does this perhaps in part explain why readers take pleasure in works such as Rochester's *Satyr against Reason and Mankind*, or Swift's own *Tale of a Tub* and *Gulliver's Travels*, which level discomfiting charges against our self-esteem, our pride in species, our hypocrisy? In the conventional view, our pleasure in the *Tale* derives simply from the "vehemence and rapidity of mind" that Johnson praised, an intellectual power and activity that stimulates exhilarating mental activity in us. It is Swift's wit, we say, that accounts for our enjoyment and in some way enables us to bear Swift's burden—a vision of a world in which all forms of spirit have a base material origin.

But perhaps it is that very *knowledge* that we most delight in. Is there something in human nature that attracts us to contemplate the worst we can imagine? Our own sour delight in reading about the latest political scandal, or in watching the day's disasters on the eleven o'clock news may suggest as much. Such perverse pleasures are not delights of our age only. Gulliver blithely tells the Houyhnhnm master of the mass destruction made possible by modern warfare; he himself has seen his countrymen "blow up a Hundred Enemies at once in a Siege, and as many in a Ship; and beheld the dead bodies drop down in Pieces from the Clouds, to the great Diversion of the Spectators" (4.5). MacKenzie was troubled by the philosophical spectators at Tyburn who delighted in "observing the effects of the stronger passions." [102] Addison lamented on the pleasure we take in reading of "Torments, Wounds, Deaths, and the like dismal Accidents." He thought that our pleasure derived from the "secret Comparison which we make between our selves and the Person who suffers." [103] That is, our self-love explains our delight in the adversity of our best friends, or the Lucretian joys of contemplating a shipwreck from the safety of land.

But Addison may not have seen far enough. Perhaps we are secretly pleased to think ill of human nature itself. This only confirms our cynicism. If we susect that we live in a Hobbist state of nature, there is some grim satisfaction in hearing and believing the worst. [104] Compare a modern satirist, the painter Tod Hackett in Nathanael West's *The Day of the Locust* (1939), contemplating his canvas of the apocalyptic "Burning of Los Angeles." Hackett is "amused by the strong feeling of satisfaction this dire conclusion gave him. Were all prophets of doom and destruction such happy men?" [105] Even Gulliver, that "Lover of Mankind," when he reviewed the ghosts of the modern dead in Glubbdubdribb, found that "it was not without some Pleasure" that he was able to trace the origins of a long chin or of "Cruelty, Falshood, and Cowardice" in the ancestors of "old Illustrious Families" (3.8). Orwell saw this element in Swift; there is, he said, "a sort of inner self which at least intermittently stands aghast at the horror of existence"—stands aghast in a kind of detached wonder, rather than censure and horror. "In the queerest way," Orwell continues, "pleasure and disgust are linked together." [106] What can be the cause of this perverse pleasure? Perhaps thinking and declaring the worst about humanity offers a kind of self-protection, the kind Edgar sought in *King Lear* when he assured himself that "this is the worst." If you have seen the worst then you will avoid future disappointment; you will avoid the fate of Gulliver, whose faith in the dignity of human nature, when shattered, left him crazed in a stable. Freud commented briefly on a rare class of tendentious jokes that may be analogous to this kind of satire: the "skeptical" joke that attacks not persons or even institutions but "the certainty of our knowledge itself, one of our speculative possessions."[107] Perhaps too there is a "skeptical" satire that allows us to express our deepest doubts and fears about the foundations of human culture and, by expressing them in satiric fiction, to protect ourselves from their full force.[108]

It troubled Johnson that Swift "took delight in revolving" ideas of "disease, deformity, and filth" and that both Swift and Pope "had an unnatural delight in ideas physically impure." For a moralist like Johnson, who insisted that the writer has a responsibility to make the world better or at least more tolerable, Swift's delight was not only singular and unnatural; it was evidence of some "depravity of intellect." But were Swift and Pope perhaps following in a great satirical tradition—like Dryden taking pleasure in the representation of deformity, or Marston reveling in the "dungy slime" and "reeching streames" of the world or the "snottery of our slimie time"?[109] And is satire ultimately perhaps not a call for reformation or even punishment but a form of meditation—of "revolving" (that is to say, turning over in the mind) ideas "from which almost every other mind shrinks with disgust"?[110]

The traditional purpose of meditation on death, for example, is to understand death, prepare for it, and familiarize ourselves with it and thereby rob it of its power over us. Can we say the same of satiric meditation? Satirists "revolve—explore, play with, manipulate, try out—ideas of uncleanness and deformity, vice and corruption, not only (as hostile critics have charged) because this permits them to indulge dirty minds and malevolent natures, or to familiarize deformity so as to rob it of half its ugliness, and not just (as Emrys Jones has suggested of Pope) to revert to a kind of pre-moral childhood state, and to find imaginative stimulation and excitement in filth and ugliness.[111] We can speculate even further. Meditating on deformity means measuring its depth and its allure, acknowledging its power, cultivating what Pope would call a "taste" for it, appropriating it. The point of satire is not to banish deformity but to call it by its right name and only in that sense to rob it of its power over us.

But if Swift invites his reader to meditate on deformity, does he not defeat what we have ususally assumed to be his satiric purpose—to shock and vex his readers and to mortify their pride—particularly since to declare that we have seen "the Flaws and Imperfections of [our own] Nature" affords a kind of perverse complacency? We peel the scales from our eyes only to wear them as a badge of the proudly unillusioned. If we thereby seem to outwit the satirists, they may yet have a final trap in store. By reveling in the horror that Swift exposes, do we in effect divert ourselves, and thereby defuse or dilute the dangerous powers of our corrosive skepticism? "The Reader truly *Learned*, chiefly for whose Benefit I wake, when others sleep, and sleep when others wake, will here find sufficient Matter to employ his Speculations for the rest of his Life" (*Tale*, sec. 10). Swift here implies what may be the ultimate pleasure of his satire: it provides matter for speculation, occupying and stimulating our wits.

Swift's hints and implications about the pleasures of satire considerably complicate the picture we gain from its usual apologists, Augustan or modern. The greatest of those apologies is itself enriched—more than we have noticed—by Dryden's characteristically frank acknowledgment of delight in reading and writing satire. The various pleasures of satire that he and his contemporaries discern—intellectual, moral, psychological, and even physiological: high-minded and low-minded—make modern Freudian accounts seem reductive. Any full account of satire as a form and as a social transaction is going to have to pay more attention to the pleasure-seeking satyr in the writer—and in the reader—of satire.

Conclusion:
Prospects and
Further Investigations

The preceding chapters have been designed in large part to vex the calm surface of contemporary theory of satire. Upon close scrutiny, so I argue, the consensus established about 1960—and not significantly questioned since then—no longer seems valid. At a distance of a generation the old consensus seems now to reflect essentially New Critical concerns about the moral purpose and rhetorical nature of literature. Those concerns, in today's critical climate, have been sharply challenged. Indeed, a review of the dominant theories of satire from the time of Horace to the twentieth century suggests that we should view with suspicion or skepticism any universalizing claim about the nature of satire, since most theories can be shown to have a polemical base or to derive from a partial view of the genre (this is probably true about most literary theory). More specifically, I have sought to decenter the moral theories of satire and to acknowledge that good satire (as Wyndham Lewis says) is often "nonmoral."[1] I have challenged the prominence, in theoretical accounts, of formal verse satire—always a slender tradition at best—and urged that our sense of the form be broadened to include the diverse Menippean range as well as the lampoon. If we shift our gaze from the *Epistle to Arbuthnot* to *A Tale of a Tub* or *The Praise of Folly*, features other than a bipolar pattern come to seem prominent. I have likewise sought to raise doubts about the claims for satire's "power" in the world of politics. And I have questioned confident arguments about the relationship between the literary world of satire and the external world to which it allegedly "refers."

If my effort has largely been to provide a strong critique of the existing consensus, to what extent does my argument have a reconstructive thrust? To what extent do I aim toward a new and more adequate comprehensive theory? In some respects, the separate inquiries into satiric rhetoric, satiric closure, satiric pleasure, and the historical satirist can be said to converge. Satire is in my view rather an "open" than a "closed" form, both in its formal features (particularly in its reluctance to conclude) and in its more general rhetorical and moral features, in its frequent preference for inquiry, provocation, or playfulness rather than assertion and conclusiveness. My argument about satire-as-inquiry accords with the claim that one of satire's pleasures is the speculation into which its readers are led. And satire-as-display provides the pleasures of competition, whether we participate or merely look on. If we stop insisting on the centrality of the moral in satire, then we are readier to see the satirist as a figure struggling for notice in a particular kind of sociopolitical context.

But in some other respects, my separate inquiries do not converge. Some satirists (like Horace) put their emphasis on inquiry or provocation, and others (like Juvenal) on display or play. And there are still others (such as Persius and Pope) for whom satire is often a sharply focused and highly moralized form. The argument that satiric pleasures often take the form of gratifying our aggressiveness or our sense of righteousness is based on satire that is itself aggressive and moralizing rather than inquiring or provocative. And if satiric inquiry seems to open up an ethical or a political question and to disturb complacency, I have also argued that such satiric speculations can ironically have the effect of promoting sociopolitical equilibrium (on the assumption that a reader who is lost in speculation is not likely to take action). Divergent arguments such as these make it difficult to achieve a comprehensive theory of satire.

But this should not be cause for despair. The goal of the theorist of satire (as I see it) is not to arrive at elegant and irrefutable definitions of satire as a genre but to enable readers of satire to become more attentive, to enable them to see an interplay of impulses and effects in a text that—whether written now or five hundred years ago—may or may not have been called a "satire" on its title page, in its "preface to the reader," or in the classifications of literary historians and editors. Even if a comprehensive theory is beyond us, much remains to be done by more limited theoretical investigations. Here I can only suggest a few avenues.

We need first to acknowledge the historicity of interpretation. Our century's questions about satire are not the only questions to ask. They reflect our own concerns about art. Topical versus universal, timeless versus timebound, factual versus imaginative, art versus non-art (a crucial New Critical concern)—these are not the distinctions that earlier ages would have cared about. Until recently, much that we exclude from art was included in its sphere: historical and biographical narrative, character sketch, essay, philosophical inquiry (it is noteworthy that all these forms have strongly "satirical" coloration). The eighteenth century made no sharp distinction between factual and fictional genres, between the techniques used in the *History of Tom Jones* and the *History of Great Britain*. Such a distinction is a reflection of the rise of our idea of "literature" and the appearance of the aesthetic as a distinct category at the end of the eighteenth century.[2] In our minds art is both superior to fact—transcendent, universal—and yet also marginalized, since it has been segregated from ethics and politics. Satire is now discussed not in coffee houses but in seminar rooms. Theorists of satire are professors, not practicing satirists like Dryden and Pope.

Critics in earlier ages did not care about the distinction between art and non-art, fictive and factual. They asked whether satire was moral and whether it was effective. They wrote at a time when satire was being produced and avidly read. Satire was once much closer to contemporary history than it is now (in the West, anyway). Because it might touch individuals, there was once considerable interest in the differences between general and particular satire. Which was more lawful? Which was more dangerous? (This is not simply a version of our "Yale" vs. "Chicago" debate.) And so long as satire was a continuous living tradition, theorists and practitioners were concerned with the imitation and emulation of their predecessors, and the appropriate deviations from them. This is not to say that their questions were better than our questions. There was a lot of sterile, repetitive debate in the eighteenth century about the difference between vice and folly, or the relative merits of "Juvenalian" and "Horatian" satire; narrow obsession with the proper character of the satyr-satirist and his "cankered muse" in the English Renaissance; and pedantic concern with satire's generic status and proper style on the Continent in the sixteenth century.

Some of the questions that we now want to ask of satire derive from our increasing sense—over the last ten years or so—that works of satire, like all literature, reflect and in some ways constitute the system of relationships (political, economic, legal) that governs a culture, distributes its rewards, and controls access to power. An intenser historicist understanding of satire—and not just better or more complete annotation—would help us recognize the ways in which satirists and readers are always embedded in an ideological matrix. The rhetorical function of the "particulars" that satirists employ must be defined in terms of historical context. To assess the satirist's purpose and strategy, we need to know for whom and against whom the satire is written. And historical context must be understood not just as inert background but as that milieu which produced the satire, the historical world it conjures up, and (rhetorically speaking) the various historical audiences for which it was originally intended. For a satire's audience is never unitary or homogeneous: its audience comprehends those readers with whom it seeks to ingratiate itself, those it expects to antagonize, those whose prejudices it flatters, those whose attitudes it may actually hope to alter. Satirists—unless they seek revenge against a private enemy—implicitly address both the enemies of society (as they define them) and the custodians of the society's laws. The former must be attacked because the latter are unable or unwilling to discharge their responsibilities. If the custodians are unable to act, the moral satirist offers to act in their stead. "Law can pronounce judgment only on open Facts," says Pope's "Letter to the Publisher" (of the *Dunciad*): "Morality alone can pass censure on Intentions of mischief; so that for secret calumny or the arrow flying in the dark, there is no publick punishment left, but what a good writer inflicts."[3] If they are unwilling to act, then an attack on the wicked can be, more dangerously, an attack on the custodians themselves.

But the custodians of the law are of course not simply passive onlookers. Usurping the functions of the judge renders the satirist subject to legal reprisal. Thus the satirist must accept the risks of the vigilante, often offending against the law in order to enforce it. Defining himself as a dispenser of justice is one of Pope's favorite satiric strategies, and his satires are often sprinkled with the language of the courtroom. To understand the social function of his work or the work of any satirist, we need to situate it more fully in the particular context of whatever legal and quasi-legal procedures and penalties—ritual scapegoating, shame, banishment, excommunication, branding, display in the stocks, show trials, public execution at Tyburn—a society establishes to enforce its norms.

To think of readers as a juridical audience—onlookers or participants as the satirist conducts a trial or an execution—assumes that they perceive a work *as a satire*, and as a satire of a punitive sort. But on what principles and under what conditions do readers consider a work to *be* a satire? *The Shepherd's Week* began as satire, but as

Johnson noted, Gay's poem was later "read with delight, as just representations of rural manners and occupations." For some readers *Utopia* is a learned Menippean fantasy; for Marxists it embodies a proto-socialistic critique of incipient capitalism. It has been suggested that as historical particulars become obscured by time, what began as "satire" may become "comedy." Conversely, under charged political conditions, works created as "history" are subsequently understood as "parallel history" and thus implicitly as satire. *The Praise of Folly* has moved in and out of the satiric genre. What has been the generic status of (and the consequent reader expectations of) such works as *Gargantua and Pantagruel, The Anatomy of Melancholy, The Marriage of Heaven and Hell,* or *Sartor Resartus?* May a work not be both satire and something else at the same time? Are generic categories exclusive or overlapping? To answer such questions will require that an interpreter of satire pay more attention to the history of reception and draw on the insights of contemporary reception theory. What can be learned from the generic classifications imposed by editors, anthologists, literary historians, or authors themselves? To include *Gulliver's Travels* as "prose fiction" in the Oxford English Novels series is to adopt a flexible and inclusive (or unrigorous?) sense of that genre against the rigorous discriminations of such theorists as Sheldon Sacks. To call *Don Juan* a "romantic long poem" is probably to privilege "narrative" over "satire" and to enable critics to discuss Byron *as Romantic.* Notwithstanding disagreements on individual cases, I take it that there is a core of works at a given time that, for most readers, implicitly constitutes the canon of satire. Judging from anthologies and from published criticism and theory, in the 1960s "satire" implicitly meant the work of Horace and Juvenal, the English "Augustan satirists" (from Dryden to Johnson), and (secondarily) the Elizabethans, with a nod to Byron. "Modern satire" largely meant Waugh, Orwell, Aldous Huxley, and Nathanael West, with nods to Mark Twain, Auden, and the South African poet Roy Campbell. Today our sense of the canon is wider, and my own range of reference has tried to encourage this broader—though still rather circumscribed—sense of what counts as central to satire in English.

Conceptions of satire, before they can be applied to works on the margins, need to be tested against those in the central core. Such investigations all require a better literary history, and ultimately a better and an enlarged analysis of how cultures constitute and govern themselves. Why, for example, have women writers been excluded from the canon of satire? Have they (like women elsewhere) been excluded by male readers, or have they excluded themselves? Whichever the case, the organization of culture has made it difficult for women to write and publish satire. Tentatively, one might assign several reasons: because women historically lacked access to a classical education (and thus to the conventions and traditions of satire); because women were long permitted little knowledge of the world outside their own domestic domain; because until recently women have been trained not to develop or display aggressiveness; because hostile images of gossip, nag, complainer, termagant, and virago may have discouraged women from cultivating in public a form that deals in grumbling and railing. To discover how women writers sought to evade or overcome such discouragements might not only expand our sense of the range of satire from Aphra Behn to Jane Austen but might also enhance our sense of how satire functions within a culture.

One example of a problem in cultural interpretation might be presented at some greater length. How are we to understand the enduring association between satire and the offering or consuming of food? As etymology suggests, the links are ancient. The *lanx satura* is a platter of mixed fruits;[4] the *farrago* (or "mishmash"), originally a term for the mash or fodder fed to cattle; the *symposium*, a drinking or dinner party; the *lampoon* (from French *lampons*, "let us drink"), a drinking song. Satire is sometimes compared to cookery by its practitioners: Dryden speaks of Horace's "nourishing" meat and Juvenal's "exquisite cookery," and Pope of a "Satyrical Cooke" who can make a hash even out of a "stale cold Fool."[5]

Satirists themselves like to write about eating. Three of Juvenal's sixteen satires focus centrally on food: the giant turbot in the fourth, the pains of sitting below the salt at Virro's table in the fifth, the invitation to dinner in the eleventh. Horace has Ofellus lecture on the superiority of plain food (*Sat.* 2.2) and (in *Sat.* 2.8) describes an extravagant Roman dinner that became the model for a series of *repas ridicule* poems by Regnier, Boileau, and Rochester. The central set piece in Petronius's *Satyricon* is the great feast of Trimalchio. *Gargantua and Pantagruel* begins with a banquet of tripe and breaks off with a call for more drink. The knight in Butler's *Hudibras* is equally equipped for breaking heads and cutting bread.[6] Pope's satires touch repeatedly on grotesque scenes of eating—at Sir Balaam's table, at Timon's villa, and in the fourth book of the *Dunciad*, or with the Westphalian hogs, feeding head to tail on excrement.[7] Swift's Gulliver sits at table in Brobdingnag and in Houyhnhnmland. In Thomas Carlyle's Menippean *Sartor Resartus*, Teufelsdrockh's book is said to be like a "mad banquet, wherein all courses have been confounded, and fish and flesh, soup and solid, oyster-sauce, lettuces, Rine-wine and French mustard, were hurled into one huge tureen or trough" (1.4).

Critics commenting on food in satire have for the most part dealt with it in one of two ways. The first is to regard it as a sign of fertility, of life, of festivity. In Aristophanes' *Acharnians* Lamachas prepares for war, but Dicaepolis delights in peace, food, and sex. In *The Clouds* Socrates is lost in speculation, and the earthbound Strepsiades wonders whether the philosopher's teachings will supply him with something to eat. Eating in Rabelais is said to be part of his celebration of the life of the body and an affirmation of nature and physical pleasures; hearty eating in *Tom Jones*, a way of showing that Tom and Mrs. Waters have hearty appetites for each other.[8] The satirist who deals with food, or metaphorically offers food to the readers, welcomes them to the feast.

The second typical way to discuss eating in satire is to invoke the old binary model and argue that satirists contrast good eating and bad eating. Thus Timon's inhospitable meal, a feast of pride, is contrasted with the simple meal that Pope serves at home (local chicken and mutton from nearby Banstead Down), or—shifting into metaphor—the "Feast of Reason, and Flow of Soul." By contrast, the proud or uncivil host offers too much or too little ("Cool was his kitchen, though his brains were hot," says Dryden of Shimei),[9] or offers food for the wrong reasons—to impress his guests or to display his wealth, as in a series of grotesquely extravagant dinners from Horace onward.[10] In Juvenal the plain meal is associated with the virtues of the long-lost Roman Republic, and the overlavish feast with the gross corruption of the Roman Empire. In English satire plain honest beef embodies the plaindealing virtues of John Bull, while fricassees and ragouts suggest the moral dubiousness and excessive refinement of slippery Frenchmen, who will even eat frogs. In Horace the wise man is satisfied with little, happier to boil herbs over the fire in the country than to dine on Epicurean dainties at court in Rome. The story of the town mouse and country mouse depends largely on the central symbol of food.

Both ways of thinking about food in satire—as a sign of festivity and as an index of character (by a man's meals you shall know him)—seem to me legitimate. But they don't tell us enough. As in much of the existing discussion about moral wisdom in satire, commentators focus on such themes as if they were the figure rather than the ground, the endpoint rather than the starting point. Eating in satire seems more problematic if we focus on the ambiguous character of the satirist's invitation to the feast, and the persistent associations among feasting, violence, and mortality.

The traditional Roman feast was presided over by the *magister bibendi*—literally, the "master of drinking"—who invited the guests, set the rules of the house, and established the order of the courses.[11] In the literary feast of satire, it is said, this role is played by the satirist. The good master of the feast, or host, makes his guests feel comfortable, sustains an atmosphere of freedom and contentment (nobody to spy on you, nobody to count your cups, or the spoons), and gratifies the palates of his companions at table. This is a figure familiar to us from many poems, both classical and modern, "inviting a friend to dinner." But he is in fact not a familiar figue in satire. The satirist may *pretend* to offer plain fare in simple, unadorned style, acting as our genial host, putting us at our ease, fostering easy conversation. But this is often just a pose.

In the second satire of his second book, Horace invites us to listen to a little plain talk about plain living, not from Horace himself but from Ofellus (and Horace may or may not agree with him). As for the reader's reaction, it is significant that Horace includes two images of readerly befuddlement, both of them associated with food. Let's talk before we eat, says Horace, because "amid the tables' shining dishes, . . . the eye is dazed by senseless splendor, and the mind, turning to vanities, rejects the better part." We note first that Horace seems to set a fancier table than Ofellus, and second that (so he himself warns us) a meal with Horace may leave us a little puzzled. He later comes back to this idea when he contrasts Ofellus's *simplex* ("plain fare") with a *cena dubia* (not "mystery meat" but an "uncertain meal" with a great variety of dishes, *variae res*, mixing "boiled and roast, shellfish and thrushes") which leaves you puzzled—perhaps because you don't know what to eat first, or because you don't feel so good after eating it. (Horace says the guests get up looking pale—*pallidus*.) The varied meal, then, is bad for you.[12] But what is the *satura lanx* if not a miscellany of bits and pieces served up in such a way that you're not always sure what to think? By the same token, Swift's *Tale* warns that "ollio's" (mixed stews) are for the "depraved and debauched Appetite," but by offering a mixed bag of tale, digression, and whatnot, Swift provides just such fare.

Petronius provides another example. Trimalchio's feast serves as a metaphor for Petronius's satire, and Trimalchio a figure for the sati-

rist. What is the feast but a display of ingenuity and wit, a series of
tricks, from the *trompe l'oeil* dog painted on the entrance wall to the
culinary cleverness that disguises cooks as hunters and pastry as pigs
or eggs? By means of a series of bizarre surprises and reversals, Trimalchio stimulates the jaded palates of his guests and compels their
admiration. So too Petronius himself, in a narrative satire constructed
like a series of separate courses, startles and astonishes, keeps his
readers off balance, makes them wonder what is coming next. He
offers tempting foods that we're not sure we should accept, just as he
has Eumolpus leave a legacy on condition that his heirs cut up and eat
his corpse.[13] Dining with Trimalchio, or reading Petronius, does not
gratify simple hunger or satisfy our basic needs, physical or ethical.
Petronius assumes sophisticated, even jaded, readers and finds a way
to sharpen and gratify their appetite by mixing high and low, dis-
guising himself as a vulgar buffoon and in a spirit of Saturnalia making the ex-slave into the Master of the Feast. For readers the whole
process is a little dizzying: we're glad to be invited, the fare is extraordinary, but it's all a bit too much, and we're finally glad to escape.

One could suggest the ambiguous character of the satirist's invitation with other examples: with Rabelais, who invites us to suck the
marrow out of his bone but who addresses us alternately as "my
dear" and "numbskull," in a pattern that Bakhtin calls "abusive
praise and praiseful abuse."[14] Or with Pope, who deliberately dis-
gusts his readers with images of foul eating: if his filthy similes turn
our stomach, he would rather that we be revolted by flattery and
courtly perfume (*Epilogue to the Satires* 1.171-84). Or with Fielding,
who invites us to sample his "Bill of Fare" not because we're his
friends but because he'll take anybody who pays. When we eat at
Swift's table, we must of course always "chuse with Judgment," lest
we break our teeth on his nut and find nothing but a worm. In Swift
the process of eating is often distinctly unsettling. Gulliver in Brobdingnag is kidnapped by the monkey and force-fed with some "filthy
Stuff the Monkey had crammed down my Throat" (2.5). The court
style in Luggnag requires anybody with a suit to crawl on his belly
and eat the dust off the throne-room floor: "I have seen a great Lord
with his Mouth so crammed, that when he had crept to the proper
Distance from the Throne, he was not able to speak a Word" (3.9).
In the Drapier's last letter, the Irish, so it is said, "must either take
these Half-pence or eat our Brogues." If we Irish won't take it willingly, says the Drapier, "Mr. Walpole will cram his Brass down our

Throats." Swift follows with a lurid fantasy in which 50,000 "Operators" administer an explosive "Dose" of the copper coins by mouth to a million and a half wretched Irish.

Here one might object that it is not Swift who does the force-feeding. We have no reason to think that as satirist Swift force-feeds his reader. Or do we? Swift's hostility to his reader is by now a critical commonplace. We are ready to say that Swift "rubs our noses" in filth. Should we perhaps say that Swift forces the unpalatable down our throats? Isn't this what goes on in Swift's great eating satire, *A Modest Proposal*? Think of the lip-smacking delight in culinary details: "the fore or hind Quarter will make a reasonable Dish; and seasoned with a little Pepper or Salt, will be very good Boiled on the fourth Day." Think of the way Swift metaphorically displays his dish early: "a young healthy Child, well nursed, is, at a Year old, a most delicious, nourishing, and wholesome Food; whether *Stewed, Roasted, Baked, or Boiled*." When we recoil in disgust, he relentlessly presses it upon us, dressed as "a *Fricasie*, or *Ragoust*," "excellent nutritive Meat," "a new Dish" at a Lord Mayor's feast. Swift forces such foul food on us not only to punish and mortify but to ask us how we like the taste of it, since as Englishmen we are already "eating up" the whole nation, and as landlords have already "devoured most of the Parents." [15]

Force-feeding, which perverts or at least distorts the primal act of nurturing by introducing the element of compulsion, is all the more effective as a trope for what the satirist does to us, since it is not easy to determine the motive of the one doing the force-feeding. In satire, force-feeding takes various forms, not easily distinguishable. It can be the importunate offer of a host, urging that guests continue to eat when they may well have had more than enough, as when the narrator of *A Tale of a Tub*, after his narrative reaches something of a climax in the "Digression concerning Madness," insists that his "Guests . . . shall have my whole Entertainment at a Meal" (sec. 10). But the administering of food in Swift is elsewhere conceived as punishment. Gulliver declares to his cousin Sympson (in the letter that opens the travels) his disappointment that "all Disgracers of the Press in Prose and Verse" have not been "condemned to eat nothing but their own Cotten, and quench their Thirst with their own Ink." As is often the case in Swift, the satiric fantasy is not far removed from real life. Swift no doubt knew that the disreputable bookseller Curll, a "Disgracer of the Press," had indeed been administered an emetic by Pope—who exulted over the victim and turned the event into literary satire in the *Full and True Account of a . . . Revenge by Poison on the Body of Mr. Edmund Curll* (1716).

But force-feeding in the traditional pharmacopeia is also a means to cure disease. Gulliver tells the Houyhnhnm master of the "abominable, nauseous and detestable "compounds" mixed from "Excrements, Barks of Trees, Serpents, Toads, Frogs, Spiders, dead Mens Flesh and Bones, Birds, Beasts and Fishes" that European doctors prescribe to cure "*Repletion*" (4.6). The Houyhnhnm master responds with a report of the "Mixture of *their own Dung and Urine*" that is "forcibly put down the *Yahoo's* Throat" to cure the disease known as "the *Yahoo's*-Evil" (4.7). Swift's own dressing-room poems are presented as a kind of violent remedy for the lovesick reader: "Who sees will spew." (Mrs. Pilkington's mother is said to have thrown up upon reading Swift.)[16] And in a letter to Swift, Pope recognized his friend's satiric strategy. He calls Swift an "Avenging Angel of wrath" who (like the angel in Revelation) has a book that the reader must "eat": "Nay [you] would make them [that is, "the wretched, pityful creatures of the World"] Eat your Book, which you have made as bitter a pill for them as possible." By donning the traditional mantle of satirist-as-physician, satirists such as Swift and Pope can claim— whatever their mixed motives—to be feeding us, and making us "spew," for our own good.[17]

As the idea of force-feeding suggests, eating in satire is often linked with violence. "To roast" is to make flesh ready for eating and also to torture by exposure to flames. As early at 1726 it could also mean to ridicule mercilessly, presumably by analogy with satire's mythical ability to make the victim redden and even blister with shame.[18] If the ambiguous character of the satirist's invitation should make us question easy assumptions about festivity and the celebration of our bodily nature, then the violence implicit in the eating of flesh might blur the apparent distinction between the grotesque meal we laugh at and the pleasant meal we partake of, and might remind us of satire's mythical murderous origins. Examples can be drawn from Petronius, Rabelais, and Swift.

Violent acts, threatened or performed, recur with such frequency at Trimalchio's feast in the *Satyricon* that any diner might well sit nervously on the edge of his couch. The violence directed toward the food itself is theatrical. The wild boar, ushered into the hall by real barking hounds, is attacked by the carving man with a hunting knife, and out flies a flock of real thrushes. A pig, allegedly not yet gutted, is cut open at the table—and out pours not blood and guts but sausages and blood puddings: another culinary trick. A calf is brought in wearing a helmet. Then comes a servant, dressed as Ajax, "slashing at the calf with a drawn sword like a madman." But the furious slashing turns out to be a carving performance, and the slices are passed around to the guests. Apparent death and destruction lead instead to the sustenance of life through the offering of food. As in Bakhtin's carnival, birth, life, and death are curiously intertwined.[19]

Trimalchio's servants are likewise under threat of violent reprisal, or so it seems. A boy has his ears boxed for picking up a dropped dish. A servant is beaten for bandaging his master's arm with white instead of purple wool. The chef who has apparently forgotten to gut the pig is stripped and held by guards. A slave who has neglected to look after some clothes is threatened with flogging. In some cases the violence is all a joke to excite the guests. But it serves also to remind us of Trimalchio's absolute power over his servants (at one point he tells a story of an emperor who cuts off the head of one of his craftsmen), which in turn becomes a metaphor for his power over his guests, who are prevented from leaving and escape only when the fire brigade breaks down the front door.

Rabelais's great feasts are likewise initiated by acts of violence. Gargantua's mother dies in childbirth from eating sixteen quarts of tripe—tripe produced by the mass slaughter of 367,014 oxen.[20] As Bakhtin has suggested, the trope of tripe—the lining of the second stomach or intestine—serves to unite high and low, life and death, food and filth.[21] Grandgousier's shepherds feast on cakes and fine grapes, but only after they have beaten up the cake-bakers of Lerné, who had refused to sell their wares. Gargantua consumes six pilgrims who had hidden among the lettuce he picks for a salad. But the real violence in Rabelais is verbal, as when the author repeatedly invites us to drink and believe, threatening us with disease, pain, and perdition if we fail to believe his stories. Like Trimalchio's threats of violence, Rabelais's curses are an index of his power over us, and of the satirist's power over the readers.

In Swift's Modest Proposal the association of birth, feeding, violence, and death is intimate: Irish children born from "breeding" mothers into poverty, if they are well fed, can themselves be converted into food. Their violent death can lead to new life. Familiar with Petronius and Rabelais, we can see that the nexus of horror in Swift's Proposal is neither simply his invention nor the consequence of a particular satiric situation. It is almost traditional in satire, where cutting, killing, cleaning, and eating form an unbroken sequence.

As Byron (another satirist drawn to the idea of cannibalism) says in *Don Juan*, there's something about "the act / Of eating" that "makes us feel our mortality" (5.32). Foul foods, force-feeding, cannibalism—the *lanx satura* does not always look inviting. If eating makes us feel our mortality and is at the same time essential to life, then it is not surprising that satirists have fastened on it as a central image of what makes us human, and as an image too of the relationship between satirist and reader. To understand more fully the way satire functions in culture, we would ultimately have to consider the ways in which the cooking, offering, and consuming of food can be socializing acts (building community or regulating appetite), symbolic acts (manifesting the difference between "raw" and "cooked," nature and culture), and ritual acts (appeasing gods and expiating sins).[22] But this must be the subject of another book.

In arguing for a more interdisciplinary understanding of satire,[23] I do not mean to suggest that we should turn away from the literary study of satiric language, conventions, and structure. Such matters received considerable attention in the 1960s, but we can still benefit from better theory of satiric rhetoric. Just as it would be naive to assume that a satirist uses objective "facts," so we must not ignore the fact that "facts" are put to the service of patterns, patterns that exert a shaping influence. Theorists have tended to call such patterns the "plot of satire." But what is a satiric plot? Northrop Frye found three different "phases" of satiric plot (which he calls "myth").[24] Kernan (*Plot of Satire*) sees crowding, purposeless activity, and stasis, but I have argued that satire always finds a way to keep moving.[25] Hayden White, who draws freely on Frye, converts plot to theme: he finds that the "archetypal theme" of satirical plots in history-writing is "the apprehension that man is a captive of the world rather than its master."[26] Michael Seidel argues that all narrative satire tells a story of degeneration, of subverted continuance, of entropy.[27] Clearly we don't yet agree about what constitutes a satiric plot. Furthermore, is a narrative model adequate to account for the full range of satiric forms? Dryden, we may recall, affirmed Heinsius's idea that satire lacks a plot, has no "Series of Action." Perhaps it would be better to speak not of satiric plot but of satiric discourse. This puts the focus not on the "events" within the satire but on the satirist, the satire's rhetorical purposes, and its audience.

In what is offered as a critical reintroduction to satire, I cannot follow out all my own suggestions. My purpose has been rather to open up than to close off, to clear away some false or limited understanding, to pose some new questions, and (reverting once more to a favorite metaphor of the satirists) to whet the appetite for renewed reading and renewed speculation.

Notes

Introduction

1. For a recent survey that aims to be comprehensive, see Test, *Satire*. Test broadens the field to include oral performance, ritual, and folk behavior.

2. See Kernan, *Cankered Muse* and *Plot of Satire*; Elliott, *Power of Satire*; Rosenheim, *Swift and the Satirist's Art*; Sacks, *Fiction and the Shape of Belief*.

3. See Bloom and Bloom, *Satire's Persuasive Voice*; Ingram, *Intricate Laughter*; Guilhamet, *Satire and the Transformation of Genre*; Nokes, *Raillery and Rage*; Weinbrot, *Eighteenth-Century Satire*. Even Test (*Satire*) remains within the old paradigm: satire, he says, combines aggression, laughter, play, and judgment.

4. *Satire Newsletter* 2 (1964): 2-25; 3 (1966): 89-153.

5. Robert C. Elliott, "Satire," in *New Encyclopaedia Britannica* (1984), *Macropaedia* 16.

6. For a general book that provokes fresh thought, see Seidel, *Satiric Inheritance*. See also Palmeri, *Satire in Narrative*.

7. Morton, "Introduction," in Browning, *Satire*, 2. Cf. Rawson, *English Satire*, p. v.

8. *Kinds of Literature*, p. 110.

9. Seidel, *Satiric Inheritance*, p. xii. Cf. Guilhamet, *Satire and the Transformation of Genre*.

10. Kernan calls *Troilus and Cressida* "an exploration . . . of the validity of certain attitudes and modes of conduct" but finds no "attack" on "any specific attitudes and modes of conduct" (*Cankered Muse*, p. 197). In his terms the play is not satiric; in mine (as will be seen) it is.

11. For a recent survey of satiric themes and stratagems in modern fiction, see Clark, *Modern Satiric Grotesque*.

1. Theories of Satire in Polemical Context

1. Horace's own satiric apology was probably in turn based on that of Lucilius, of which only fragments (especially from his Books 26 and 30) survive. See Van Rooy, *Studies in Classical Satire*, pp. 147, 173.

2. See Fraenkel, *Horace*, p. 152.

3. Horace declares (*Sat.* 2.1) that Lucilius was the "first" to write Roman satire, though he knew that Ennius and Pacuvius preceded. André Dacier (his French translator) and Dryden (*Works*, 4:44; hereafter cited in text by volume and page number) assume that Horace here means not that Lucilius invented a new form but that he polished an old one.

4. Van Rooy, *Studies in Classical Satire*, p. 149.

5. See ibid., pp. 66-71, 79, on Horace's use of the term *satura*. Knoche suggests that Horace avoided the term because it carried "connotations of personal abuse" (*Roman Satire*, p. 78).

6. *Satire Newsletter* 1 (1963): 4-5. See also *Essays on Roman Satire*, p. 15.

7. Casaubon, "Prolegomenon" to his edition of Persius (1608), quoted in Dryden, *Works*, 4:578.

8. See Fiske, *Lucilius and Horace.*

9. Whether or not satire and epistle can be distinguished in Horace (and in Pope) is a question that continues to vex and divide critics.

10. Unless the commentator, like the fourth-century Diomedes in his *Ars Grammatica*, resolutely declined to choose among rival claims. The Diomedes passage is reprinted in Van Rooy, *Studies in Classical Satire*, pp. xii-xiii.

11. See the summary in Van Rooy, *Studies in Classical Satire*, pp. 137-39.

12. Ibid., p. 117.

13. Williams, *Tradition and Originality*, p. 445.

14. For a full text, see Van Rooy, *Studies in Classical Satire*, pp. xii-xiii.

15. For a suggestive discussion of the metaphorical implications of Diomedes' etymologies, see Knight, "Imagination's Cerberus."

16. G.L. Hendrickson, "Satura Tota Nostra Est," *Classical Philology* 22 (1927): 46-60; reprinted in Paulson, *Satire*, p. 40.

17. Peter's term in *Complaint and Satire.*

18. See Mary Claire Randolph, "Thomas Drant's Definition of Satire, 1566," *N&Q* 180 (1941): 416-18. Drant's definition, which appeared in his edition of Horace, is reprinted in Peter, *Complaint and Satire*, 301-3.

19. In Smith, *Elizabethan Critical Essays*, 1:80.

20. Ibid., 2:27, 32.

21. Dryden, *Works*, 4:34.

22. See Patterson, *Hermogenes and the Renaissance*, p. 110. At other moments Marston rejects "Grim Reproofe" (see Patterson, 98).

23. M. Thomas Hester has recently argued (to my mind unconvincingly) that Donne's satiric model is Jeremiah (*Kinde Pitty and Brave Scorn*).

24. Brower, *The Poetry of Allusion*, pp. 181-82.

25. As *Ariosto's Satyres, in Seven Famous Discourses*, reprinted as *Ariosto's Seven Planets Governing Italie* (1611). The translation apparently never became popular. England did not require a new one until 1759.

26. See M.C. Randolph, "The Medical Concept in English Renaissance Satiric Theory," *Studies in Philology* 38 (1941): 125-57; reprinted in Paulson, *Satire.*

27. For the sixteenth-century tradition of satirist as zealous rebuker, see Hester, *Kinde Pitty.*

28. Peter, *Complaint and Satire*, p. 109.

29. I quote here from Casaubon's "Prolegomenon" to Persius, trans. P. Medine, in *ELR* 6, no. 2 (1976): 271-87. Medine notes that Casaubon builds on the standard sixteenth-century view of Persius found in editions by Murmellius and Britannicus.

30. Casaubon's *De satyrica* has been fully translated only once, into Italian, and only selectively into English. Dacier's 1687 edition of Horace translated much of Casaubon's commentary.

31. Dryden, *Works*, 4:52, 53.

32. Preface to Holyday's 1673 edition of Persius (first published in 1616), sig. A2.

33. Heinsius, *De Satyra Horatiana* (1629), 2:54; Dryden's California editors (*Works*, 4:573) say page 83.

34. Rapin, *Whole Critical Works*, 2 vols., trans. "by several hands" (London, 1706), 2:227.

35. Dacier's *Oeuvres d'Horace* (1681-89), cited in Weinbrot, *Alexander Pope*, 16. Dacier's work was first translated into English in 1692.

36. Weinbrot, *Alexander Pope*, 22-26.

37. John Dennis in *Critical Works*, ed. Hooker, 2:218.

38. See the summary of critical disagreement in Dryden, *Works*, 4:515-25.

39. Except to identify Livius Andronicus rather than Ennius as the first Roman satirist (4:77).

40. For a sample of the lampoons Dryden probably had in mind, see J.H. Wilson's edition of *Court Satires of the Restoration* (1976) rather than the more selective volumes in the Yale *Poems on Affairs of State* series.

41. *Works*, 4:81.

42. He uses the "family" model to describe early Roman satire, which grew "like different Cyens from the same Root" (*Works*, 4:42).

43. The metaphor is Dryden's own, and not found in his sources.

44. Cf. "To the Memory of Mr. Oldham" (1684), in which Oldham's satiric "fruits" are "gather'd ere their prime" (*Works*, 2:175).

45. Boileau's *L'art poetique* has a similar purpose, distinguishing as it does between good and bad models.

46. The distinction is found in Casaubon, and ultimately derives from Aristotle.

47. His editors suggest simply that Dryden wanted to establish satire as a genre and "separate" it from other genres (4:517).

48. Once again, the French were proceeding along a similar path. Dacier's *Essay on Satire* was published with Le Bossu's treatise on epic in 1695.

49. M. Bossu's *Treatise of the Epick Poem* (1695, reprint, 1970), 6.

50. "Casaubon's *Prolegomenon to Persius*," trans. P. Medine, *ELR* 6 (1976): 288, 291. Dryden translates the line at 4:55.

51. Dryden himself argues that Persius is "Inferior" to both Horace and Juvenal (4.73), but elsewhere that though in the main "not equal" to Horace and Juvenal, Persius is "in some things to be preferr'd to both of them" (4.50-51).

52. *Works*, 4:595. In fact, Dryden commends Stoicism as "the most noble, most generous, most beneficial to Humane Kind, amongst all the Sects, who have given us the Rules of Ethiques, thereby to form a severe Virtue in the Soul" (4.55).

53. Dryden accepts the conventional view of Persius's "Crabbed" style (4.51, 73), and remarks on his "defects" of style and temper (4.52).

54. Medine, "Casaubon's *Prolegomenon*," p. 291.

55. Weinbrot, *Alexander Pope* (97-104), brings out that although he borrowed from all three Roman satirists, Boileau chiefly followed Horace.

56. Dryden later identifies "fine raillery" as a French term. See his "Life of Lucian," in *Works*, ed. Scott-Saintsbury, 18:75.

57. Weinbrot remarks that one of Dryden's "polemical purposes" in the "Discourse" is "slowing . . . the popularity of low comic Horatian satire" (*Eighteenth-Century Satire*, 6.

58. For another argument about the limits of Dryden's theory, see Niall Rudd, who notes Dryden's inaccuracies about the misrepresentations of Horace and Juvenal (*Satires of Horace*, pp. 260ff).

59. Dryden, "Life of Lucian," in *Works*, ed. Scott-Saintsbury, 18:74.

60. Peter Schakel concludes (on insufficient evidence) that Dryden treated all satire as bipartite; see "Dryden's *Discourse* and 'Bi-Partite Structure' in the Design of Formal Verse Satire," *ELN* 21, no. 4 (1984): 33-41.

61. Medine, "Casaubon's *Prolegomenon*, p. 291.

62. Ibid., p. 289. Dryden makes the same point (4:56)

63. E.g., Alexander Brome, *The Poems of Horace, Consisting of Odes, Satyres, and Epistles, Rendred in English Verse by Several Persons* (London, 1666); Thomas Creech, *The Odes, Satyres, and Epistles of Horace* (1684); S. Dunster, *The Satires and Epistles of Horace, Done into English, with Notes*, 2d ed. (London, 1712); *The Works of Horace in English Verse, By Several Hands, Collected and Published by Mr. Duncombe, With Notes Historical and Critical*, 2 vols. (London, 1757, 1759).

64. Many classicists have found little unity in the poem. See Anderson, *Essays on Roman Satire*, p. 255.

65. See ibid., 153-55, for the consensus of classicists since Casaubon that there is little relation between the two parts of Persius's *Satire 5*.

66. Juvenal, *Sat.* 1.85-86. Dryden's title page is reprinted in *Works*, 4:2.

67. *Critical Works*, 2:219.

68. Trapp, *Lectures on Poetry*, trans. W. Clarke and W. Bowyer (1742) repr. (Hildesheim: Olms, 1969), p. 232.

69. Bayle, *Dictionary*, 3.426A, 464A, 465A, B; 5.98B, 743-65.

70. Preface to Petronius, *Satyrical Works in Prose and Verse*, trans. Wilson, Burnaby, Blount, et al. (London, 1708), n.p.

71. David Watson and S. Patrick, trans., *The Works of Horace* (1750), quoted in Weinbrot, *Alexander Pope*, p. 22.

72. James Beattie, *Essays* (1776), p. 662.

73. Greene, *The Satires of Juvenal Paraphrastically Imitated* (London, 1763), pp. v, vii.

74. From Francis Bacon, *The Advancement of Learning* (1605), quoted in Morris, *Alexander Pope*, p. 165.

75. "Verses on the Death of Dr. Swift," 313. For a modern argument, see Richard Rodino, "Blasphemy or Blessing? Swift's 'Scatalogical' Poems," in *Essential Articles for the Study of Jonathan Swift's Poetry*, ed. Vieth, pp. 256-58.

76. Pope, "To Fortescue" 105-8.

77. Pope, *Epilogue to the Satires*, 1.212-13, 216-19.

78. Randolph, "Structural Design," in Paulson, *Satire*, pp. 171, 183, 184.

79. Rosenheim, *Swift and the Satirist's Art*, p. 31.

80. Northrop Frye, "The Nature of Satire," *University of Toronto Quarterly* 14 (1944): 75-89. Frye's work was preceded only by Worcester's *Art of Satire* (1940).

81. See Rawson's long essay "The Character of Swift's Satire" in *Focus: Swift* (1971), revised and later republished as *The Character of Swift's Satire* (1983). Though he focuses on Swift, Rawson often cites other satirists, especially Fielding and Johnson.

82. See esp. Weinbrot, *Alexander Pope*.

83. See Weinbrot, *Formal Strain*; Kupersmith, *Roman Satirists*; and Stack, *Pope and Horace*.

84. See Williams, *Tradition and Originality*; Coffey, *Roman Satire*; and esp. Anderson, *Essays on Roman Satire*.

85. See esp. Rudd, *Satires of Horace*.

86. See Courtney, *Satires of Juvenal*.

87. I quote here from Stack, whose *Pope and Horace* is an exemplary reexamination of the "wry scepticism" of Horatian satire (p. 240).

88. Kirk, *Menippean Satire*.

89. Frye, *Anatomy of Criticism*, p. 310.

90. Bakhtin, *Problems of Dostoevsky's Poetics*, esp. pp. 106-37. These ideas are applied to *Gargantua and Pantagruel* in Bakhtin's *Rabelais and His World*.

91. Palmer, *Satire in Narrative*, p. 12.

92. Snyder, *Prospects of Power*, pp. 113, 121, 139.

2. The Rhetoric of Satire: Inquiry and Provocation

1. Bullitt, *Jonathan Swift*, p. 1.

2. Tuveson, "Swift: The View from within the Satire," in *The Satirist's Art*, ed. Jensen and Zirken, p. 67.

3. But they continue to be offered. Satire, says K.J. Berland in 1983, depends on

the reader's recognition of some deviant conduct "and the normative referent against which it is measured and found wanting." The reader's role is "recognition and assent in censure." See his "Satire and the *Via Media*: Anglican Dialogue in *Joseph Andrews*," in Browning, *Satire in the Eighteenth Century*, p. 84. Test, in 1991, insists that "satire cannot succeed by ambiguity or ambivalence (*Satire*, p. 258).

4. Frederick Keener, *English Dialogues of The Dead*, pp. 75-97.

5. Kernan, *Cankered Muse*, p. 118; cf. Rosenheim: "Effective satire can proceed from very minimal commitments to very general values" (*Swift and the Satirist's Art*, p. 184). On moral clichés, see Hume: "Writers of all nations and all ages concur in applauding justice, humanity, magnanimity, prudence, veracity; and in blaming the opposite qualities" ("Of the Standard of Taste," in *Essays Moral, Political, and Literary*, ed. Miller. p. 228).

6. On this point, see Williams on Horace, *Tradition and Originality*, p. 599.

7. Cf. Hume again: "The merit of delivering true general precepts in ethics is indeed very small. Whoever recommends any moral virtues, really does no more than is implied in the terms themselves" (ibid., p. 229).

8. Walter Harte, *Essay on Satire* (1730, reprint 1968), p. 15; Anthony Collins, *Discourse Concerning Ridicule and Irony* (1729), p. 12. Cf. Young's preface to *Love of Fame*: "It is much to be feared, that misconduct will never be chased out of the world by satire" (1728, reprint, 1970), 2:54.

9. Cowper, *The Task*, 2.66-67. Compare Shelley's doubts that satire can "wake the slumbering hounds / Of Conscience" ("Fragment of a Satire on Satire," 1820).

10. Swift, *Battel of the Books*, "The Preface of the Author." See Gruner, *Understanding Laughter*, pp. 170-205.

11. Cf. Worcester: "The author first evolves a criticism of conduct. Then he contrives ways of making his readers comprehend and remember that criticism and adopt it as their own" (*Art of Satire*, p. 13).

12. But as discussed below, the sermon Erasmus writes for Folly and the "bill of Complaint" Pope presents to Arbuthnot open up as many questions as they answer.

13. William Boscawen, preface to *Satires, Epistles, and Art of Poetry of Horace* (London, 1797), p. ix.

14. Preface to *Horace's Satires*, 4th ed. (London, 1750).

15. Cf. the debate between Right and Wrong Reason in Aristophanes' *Clouds*. For a debate in Ennius between Mors and Vita, see Knoche, *Roman Satire*, p. 22.

16. By calling his work "Satyre 2nd," Diderot perhaps acknowledged that it belonged to the long tradition of satire-as-dialogue.

17. *A Modest Confutation of a Slanderous and Scurrilous Libel* (1643), p. 9.

18. See Griffin, *Satires against Man*, pp. 200-206.

19. W.S. Howell, *Logic and Rhetoric in England*, p. 347, and *Eighteenth-Century British Logic and Rhetoric*.

20. Shaftesbury, *Characteristics* (1714), 2.327-28. The passage was drawn to my attention by Stack's fine book *Pope and Horace*, pp. 118-19.

21. Brower, *Poetry of Allusion*, p. 173.

22. I quote from the translation by R.M. Adams, pp. 28-29.

23. Douglas Duncan, *Ben Jonson and the Lucianic Tradition*, p. 69.

24. Howard Erskine-Hill inclines to the latter explanation in "Courtiers out of Horace," in *John Donne: Essays in Celebration*, ed. A.J. Smith (London, 1972). Donne's satires are cited from *Satires, Epigrams, and Verse Letters*, ed. Wingate.

25. Upon reporting that those in attendance for a second time include himself, the poet can only, as it were, shake his head and mumble, "God pardon me."

26. Pope was perhaps troubled by the idea of the satirist's "sin," for in his adaptation of Donne's poem ("The Fourth Satire of Dr. John Dunne Versifyed") he omits three of the four occasions when the satirist refers to his own "sin."

27. But Donne does not simply point to the presence of agents provocateurs, informers, and priest-catchers. He focuses not on the external danger but on the subjective response to guilt.

28. John Donne, *Sermons* 7.408.

29. Thomas V. Moore, "Donne's Use of Uncertainty in Satyre III," *MP* 67 (1969): 41-49.

30. Elkin is a noteworthy exception. Satire, he says, "is valuable for the insights it gives into moral problems, not for providing solutions to them" (*Augustan Defence of Satire*, p. 84).

31. See Ehrenpreis, *Swift: The Man, His Works, and the Age* 3:454; and Michael DePorte, "Swift and the License of Satire," in *Satire in the Eighteenth Century*, ed. Browning, pp. 64, 66.

32. Woodruff, "*Rasselas*," p. 180.

33. See Harry Levin, "The Wages of Satire," in *Literature and Society*, ed. Said, p. 14.

34. For a similar reading of Restoration satire, see Kevin Cope, "The Conquest of Truth: Wycherley, Rochester, Butler, and Dryden, and the Restoration Critique of Satire," *Restoration* 10, no. 1 (1986): 19-40.

35. Swift explicitly makes the application to the "satyrical Poet" in his ironic "Letter of Advice to a Young Poet" (1720), *Prose Words*, 9:342.

36. Cf. Jonson, "Doing, a filthy pleasure is, and short, / And done, we straight repent us of the sport" (untitled trans. from Petronius); Marvell, "Now let us sport us while we may" ("To His Coy Mistress").

37. Cf. Dryden's translation of Horace's *Ode* 3.29 (to Maecenas): "secure from Fortunes blows, / . . . / In my small Pinnace I can sail, / Contemning all the blustring roar; / And running with a merry Gale, / With friendly Stars my safety seek" (*Sylvae* [1685], 97-102).

38. Cf. the angry spider in Swift's *Battel of the Books*, warned by the bee to have patience "or you will spend your Substance" (*A Tale of a Tub*, in *Prose Works*, 1:148).

39. I owe thanks to Christopher Ricks for pointing out the pun.

40. See the chapter on *The Dunciad* in Griffin, *Alexander Pope*.

41. Emrys Jones, "Pope and Dulness," in *Pope: A Collection of Critical Essays*, ed. J.V. Guerinot, pp. 145, 149.

42. Byron, *Letters and Journals*, 10:68; *Don Juan*, 12.39.2.

43. Beaty, *Byron the Satirist*, pp. 142, 126. Beaty continues to see Byron as an untraditional satirist.

44. Paradox was especially popular in England in the 1590s: e.g., Anthony Munday's *Defense of Contraries: Paradoxes against Common Opinions* (1593); Donne's *Paradoxes*, not published until 1633 but written in the 1590s; the *Paradoxes* of Sir William Cornwallis, written c. 1600.

45. Johnson, *Dictionary*, s.v. "paradox." The *Oxford English Dictionary* (OED) gives a related meaning: "a phenomenon that exhibits conflict with preconceived notions of what is possible or reasonable."

46. John Dunton, *Athenian Sport: or, Two Thousand Paradoxes Merrily Argued, to Amuse and Divert*, quoted in Morris, *Alexander Pope*, p. 169.

47. Cf. Rochester's paradoxical praise of "Nothing" in "Upon Nothing."

48. Paulson, *Satire and the Novel*, p. 135; cf. Paulson, *Fictions of Satire*, p. 41.

49. Paulson sees Lucian as the "epitome of the satirist who writes at what he takes to be a time of extreme stodginess and reaction, when values have become standardized and rigid" (*Fictions of Satire*, p. 4).

50. Hughes, preface, to *Fontenelle's Dialogues of the Dead, Translated from the French* (1708), p. xxi.

51. Collins, *Discourse Concerning Ridicule*, p. 11.

52. Fielding's praise. See Rawson, *Order from Confusion Sprung*, p. 312.

53. On Lucian's reputation as a moralist, especially in the seventeenth and eighteenth centuries, see Robinson, *Lucian*.

54. Gilbert Cousin, preface to Lucian's *Opera* (Basel, 1563), quoted in Duncan, *Ben Jonson*.

55. Rapin, *Whole Critical Works*, 2:229.

56. Hughes, *Fontenelle's Dialogues of the Dead*, p. xiv (Hughes uses an alternate spelling of "course").

57. Dryden, "Life of Lucian," in *Works*, ed. Scott-Saintsbury, 18:69. Cf. Robinson: "There is no evidence that Lucian himself subscribes to any particular set of doctrines; nor does he put forward a coherently skeptical or atheistic position" (*Lucian*, p. 54).

58. Duncan, *Ben Jonson*, pp. 2, 49.

59. See, e.g., the prefatory "To the Reader" and the commendatory poems (pp. xv-xvi) in Bishop White Kennett's 1683 translation, *Witt Against Wisdom* (Oxford, 1683).

60. See Arthur Kinney, "Rhetoric as Poetic: Humanist Fiction in the Renaissance," *ELH* 43 (1976): 413-43.

61. Keener, *English Dialogues of the Dead*, p. 22. Robinson says Fontenelle's purpose is "to undermine accepted standards of knowledge, religion, and to a lesser extent social order" (*Lucian*, p. 153).

62. See the translation by Hughes, *Fontenelle's Dialogues of the Dead*; page numbers in the text refer to this edition.

63. Some of Fontenelle's dialogues serve instead to illustrate some conventional moral. As Keener puts it, in describing the weaker dialogues in the tradition (by Prior and Lyttelton), they are "designed to affirm and refine traditional ideas about morals and our famous ancestors" (p. 22).

64. Matthew Prior wrote but did not publish a set of *Dialogues of the Dead*. For a recent account, see Nicholas Nelson, "Dramatic Texture and Philosophical Debate in Prior's *Dialogues of the Dead*," *SEL* 28 (1988): 423-41. In Nelson's view, Prior is more didactic than skeptical.

65. For a survey of its Menippean features, see Eugene Kirk, "Blake's Menippean *Island*," *PQ* 59 (1980): 194-215.

66. See Leslie Tannenbaum, "Blake's News from Hell: *The Marriage of Heaven and Hell* and the Lucianic Tradition," *ELH* 43, no. 1 (1976): 74-99.

67. See Bloom, *Blake's Apocalypse*, p. 71. Later, Bloom decided that the form is not Menippean satire but Blake's own "invention" and "unique in literature" (*Poetry and Prose*, p. 809).

68. Bloom, *Blake's Apocalypse*, p. 85. Bloom examines only the first quarter of Blake's seventy proverbs.

69. Ibid., pp. 85-89. The proverbs, Bloom says elsewhere, have "intellectual shock-value" (p. 72).

70. Lawrence Lipking, *The Life of the Poet* (Chicago: Univ. of Chicago Press, 1981), p. 42.

71. Tannenbaum proposes that Blake's poem works as an answer to Lyttelton's *Dialogues*, presented by their author as the defense of "common sense" morality and described by a friend as "polite" and "grave" ("Blake's News from Hell").

72. Bloom, *Blake's Apocalypse*, p. 70; Blake, Letter to Trusler, Aug. 23, 1799, in *Letters*, ed. Keynes, 3d ed. (Oxford, 1980), 8.

73. See the recent speculation by Michael Seidel that "nostalgia itself may be yet another cynical and suspicious quagmire designed to trap the most gullible of satiric travellers" ("Satire and Metaphorical Collapse," in Browning, *Satire in the Eighteenth Century*, p. 122).

74. Horace, *Epode.* 16.9 (I use the Loeb translation).

75. Cf. Elkin: "A satire is valuable for the insights it gives into moral problems, not for providing solutions to them" (*Augustan Defence of Satire*, p. 84).

76. Traugott, *Discussions of Jonathan Swift.*

77. Elkin, *Augustan Defence of Satire*, p. 84, 201.

78. Even as late as the eighteenth century. See Griffin, *Regaining Paradise.*

79. In Milton's cosmology (as in most others) chaos is the great original; Pope's satiric innovation makes the original state of the mind at creation an image of the universe before creation.

80. Dryden, "Life of Lucian," p. 69.

81. Cf. Rosenheim, who notes that the fiction of the Aeolists "has taken a life of its own" (*Swift and the Satirist's Art*, p. 133).

82. Rawson, *Character of Swift's Satire*, p. 63.

83. Richard Feingold notes that Swift sometimes is more occupied with "the machinery of the joke" than with his ostensible target ("Swift and His Poems: The Range of His Positive Rhetoric," in Rawson, *Character of Swift's Satire*, p. 172).

84. Wayne Booth, *The Rhetoric of Irony* (Chicago: Univ. of Chicago Press, 1974),p. 133; Hegel's *Philosophy of Fine Art*, cited approvingly in Søren Kierkegaard, *The Concept of Irony* (1841), trans. Lee Capel (Bloomington: Indiana Univ. Press, 1965), p. 278.

85. See Erskine-Hill, "The 'New World' of Pope's Dunciad."

86. Booth, *Rhetoric*, pp. 114, 116.

87. See C.J. Rawson, "A Reading of *A Modest Proposal*," in *Augustan Worlds*, ed. J.C. Hilson, M.M.B. Jones, and J.R. Watson (New York: Barnes and Noble, 1978), pp. 29-50.

88. Booth, *Rhetoric*, pp. 248, 49.

89. William Wotton, "Observations upon the *Tale of a Tub*," in *A Defense of the Reflections upon Ancient and Modern Learning* (1705), repr. in *Swift: The Critical Heritage*, ed. Kathleen Williams (New York: Barnes and Noble, 1970), p. 39. Cf. Anthony Collins on the *Tale*: "Religious Matters, and all the various Forms of Christianity have therein a considerable share of *Ridicule*" (*Discourse Concerning Ridicule and Irony* [London, 1729], p. 39).

90. Frye, "The Nature of Satire," p. 83.

91. *Poetical Works of Samuel Butler*, ed. George Gilfillan (New York, 1854), I:vii.

92. Emrys Jones, "Pope and Dulness," in Guerinot, *Pope*, pp. 231-63; *A Chatterton Lecture on An English Poet* (1968), pp. 231-63; rpt. in *Pope: A Collection of Modern Critical Essays*, ed. Guerinot.

93. The satirist's "fascination" with vice has almost become a commonplace. Cf. Kupersmith on Juvenal's "tone of horrified, but fascinated, disgust" (*Roman Satirists*, p. 163).

94. Kierkegaard, *Concept of Irony*, esp. pp. 263-81.

95. Booth, *Rhetoric*, p. 59n.

96. Elliott, *Power of Satire*, p. 274. Cf. Frye on irony as "an automatically expansive and destroying force" ("The Nature of Satire," p. 82).

97. John Marston, *Metamorphosis of Pigmalion's Image*, quoted in Kernan, *Cankered Muse*, p. 136.

98. Hughes, *Fontenelle's Dialogues of the Dead*, p. xxxvi. Dryden says that in *The Hind and the Panther* (1687) he made use of "the Common Places of *Satyr*, whether true or false" (*Works*, 3:122).

99. Gilbert Burnet, *Some Passages of the Life and Death of Rochester*, quoted in *Rochester: The Critical Heritage*, ed. David Farley-Hills. (London: Routledge, 1972), p. 54.

100. Frye, "The Nature of Satire," p. 84.

3. *The Rhetoric of Satire: Display and Play*

1. See also Aristophanes *Frogs*, 389ff.
2. Greene, *Satires of Juvenal Paraphrastically Imitated*, Preface, p.v. Cf. Goldsmith on Young, who "seems fonder of dazzling than pleasing; of raising our admiration for his wit than our dislike of the follies he ridicules," 5:329).
3. Aristotle, *Rhetoric*, trans. Rhys Roberts (New York: Modern Library, 1984), 1358b.
4. Kenneth Burke, *A Rhetoric of Motives* (1950), p. 71. Cf. E.M. Cope, who says epideictic rhetoric was designed to "display the orator's power, and to amuse an audience" (*An Introduction to Aristotle's Rhetoric*, 1867 (repr. Hildesheim: Olms, 1970), p. 121.
5. For an attempt to rehabilitate epideictic rhetoric as a means of appreciation, appropriation, and celebration of some excellence, see Lawrence Rosenfield, "The Practical Celebration of Epideictic," in *Rhetoric in Transition*, ed. Eugene White (University Park, Pa.: Penn State Univ. Press, 1980), 131-56.
6. This is the thesis of Robinson, *Lucian*, esp. pp. 4-45, 61-63.
7. Paulson, *Fictions of Satire*, p. 40. Paulson nonetheless seeks to find in Lucian a set of moral "ideals."
8. "Life of Dryden," in *Lives of the English Poets*, 1:447.
9. Medine, "Casaubon's *Prolegomenon to Persius*," p. 289.
10. Ibid., p. 275. Dryden follows Casaubon here (*Works*, 4:56). Cf. Dryden's remark on *Satire* 6: "He runs himself into his old declamatory way" (4:80).
11. Rigault, Dedication to his 1616 edition of Juvenal, sig. aii, quoted in Dryden, *Works*, 4:562.
12. Rapin, "Reflections of Aristotle's *Poesie*," in *Whole Critical Works*, 2:228.
13. Boileau, *L'art poétique* 2.157-58; trans. by Dryden and Sir William Soames in 1683 as "Juvenal . . . too far did stretch his sharp Hyperbole" (Dryden, *Works*, 2:136) and by John Ozell and Soames in 1712 as "*Juvenal*, with Rhetorician's Rage, / Scourg'd the rank Vices of a wicked Age." Boileau, *Works*, 3 vols. (London, 1711-13).
14. Thomas Shadwell, "The Epistle Dedicatory" to *The Tenth Satyr of Juvenal* (London, 1687), n.p.
15. Gilbert Highet, *Juvenal the Satirist* (Oxford: Clarendon, 1954); E.V. Marmorale, *Giovenale*.
16. H.A. Mason, "Is Juvenal a Classic?" originally appeared in *Arion* 1 (1962): 8-44, and 2 (1962): 39-79. It is reprinted in Sullivan, *Critical Essays on Roman Literature*, pp. 93-176, from which it is cited here.
17. Ibid., pp. 107, 101.
18. In early essays Anderson blurred the distinction between the rhetorical moralist who really feels indignation and the one who merely affects it.
19. William Anderson, "Anger in Juvenal and Seneca" (1964), in his *Essays on Roman Satire*.
20. Anderson, "*Lascivia* vs. *ira*: Martial and Juvenal" (1970), in his *Essays on Roman Satire*, p. 395.
21. Scaliger, *Poetices*, bk. 6, quoted in Dryden, *Works*, 4:563-64.
22. Though Petronius is often admired for his "realism," an eighteenth-century editor noted that the *Satyricon* combines "the Air and Stile of a Declamator" with sententiousness and "Moral Reflections" (preface to *Satyrical Works* [London, 1708], n.p.).
23. Duncan, *Ben Jonson*, p. 31.
24. Erasmus, *Praise of Folly*, pp. 56, 59.
25. Marston, *Scourge of Villanie*, pp. 18, 21.

26. Anthony Caputi overstates the elements of philosophical seriousness, idealism, and moral exhortation in his *John Marston, Satirist* (New York, 1961).

27. See Bernard Harris, "Men Like Satyrs," in *Elizabethan Poetry*, ed. J.R. Brown and B. Harris, p. 193.

28. McCabe, *Joseph Hall.*

29. See Thomas Kranidas, "Style and Rectitude in 17th Century Prose: Hall, Smectymnuus, and Milton," *HLQ* 46 (1983): 46.

30. Harington, *Letters and Epigrams*, p. 66.

31. Donne, *Sermons* 7.408.

32. See P.N. Siegel's comment on Donne's *Paradoxes and Problems*: paradox was a way "to display his mental dexterity in puncturing traditional ideals" (*PQ* 28 [1949]: 510).

33. John Oldham, "Upon a Printer . . .," in *Poems and Translations* (London, 1684), p. 131; bound as bk. 2 of *Works of Oldham, together with His Remains* (London, 1686). Cf. *OED*, s.v. "signalize": "1. to render conspicuous. b. To display in a striking manner."

34. John Wilcox, "Informal Publication of Late 16th Century Verse Satire," *HLQ* 13 (1949-50): 199.

35. Johnson, "Life of Swift," in *Lives of the English Poets*, 3:51.

36. Tuveson, "Swift, p. 56. Traugott and Rawson speak of the same feature: "flamboyant virtuosity" (Traugott, in *Focus: Swift*, p. 77), and "sheer performance," "self-display (Rawson, *Gulliver and the Gentle Reader*, p. 2).

37. Tuveson, "Swift," p. 56.

38. See D.W. Jefferson, "*Tristram Shandy* and the Tradition of Learned Wit," *Essays in Criticism* 1 (1951): 225-48.

39. Cf. Martin Price: "We are as much aware of the ingenuity of the reduction [of a millennium of church history to a tale of three brothers] as we are of its exposure of the church's worldliness" ("Swift in the Interpreter's House," in Browning, *Satire in the Eighteenth Century*, p. 106).

40. See further Griffin, *Alexander Pope.*

41. Rosenblum, "Pope's Illusive Temple," p. 37, one of the best essays on Pope's poem.

42. Twickenham ed., 5:19. Pope quotes from Pliny's *Natural History.*

43. Rosenblum, "Pope's Illusive Temple," pp. 34, 36.

44. Sterne has been treated (unpersuasively) as a late Augustan satirist of Tristram's pride and folly by Melvyn New in *Laurence Sterne as Satirst.*

45. *OED.* "To perform" is a derived sense.

46. Huizinga notes that play can involve display or performance in *Homo Ludens*, p. 13.

47. Kennedy, *The Art of Persuasion in Greece* (1963), p. 152.

48. Geoffrey Hartman, *The Unmediated Vision* (New Haven: Yale Univ. Press, 1954), p. 162.

49. For an early instance, see George Sherburn on the "infinite playfulness" of Swift's mind ("Method in Books about Swift," *SP* 35 [1938]:644).

50. Cf. Price, who says the *Tale* is "a tissue of verbal play" ("Swift in the Interpreter's House," p. 112).

51. Test's chapter "Playing the game of Satire" collects examples of verbal contests, mimicry, wordplay, graffiti, aphorism, and irony *(Satire*, pp. 126-49).

52. Cf. Levin: "When comedy becomes more purposeful than playful, then it is satire" ("The Wages of Satire," p. 3). Auden went on to recognize that "playful anger" is for that reason "intrinsically comic" ("Notes on the Comic," in *The Dyer's Hand* (1963), p. 383).

53. Marston's marginal note to *Scourge of Villanie* (1598), 9.45.

54. But see Van Rooy, *Studies in Classical Satire*, pp. 54-55, who argues that Lucilian satire is derisive rather than innocent.

55. In the manuscript version, Dryden's stallion is even more broadly sketched: he "Heares all, & thinks & loves & helps it with his hands." See W.B. Carnochan, "Some Suppressed Verses in Dryden's Translation of Juvenal VI," *TLS* 21 (Jan. 1972): 73-74.

56. I quote from the translation by Lionel Casson of Lucian's *True History*.

57. Erasmus, *Opus Epistolarum*, ed. P.S. Allen, H.M. Allen, and H.W. Garrod, 12 vols. (Oxford: Clarendon, 1906-1958), 4:16, 118-19.

58. See his commentary on the proverb "Ollas ostentare" in *Adagia*, (*Opera Omnia*, ed. J. LeClerc (Leiden, 1703-1706), 2:460.

59. See Duncan on the tradition of *lusus* (*Ben Jonson*, pp. 26-51).

60. More, *Utopia*, bk. 2 (ed. R.M. Adams), p. 41.

61. Michael Holquist, "How to Play Utopia," in Ehrmann, *Game, Play, Literature*, p. 112.

62. John Traugott, "The Yahoo in the Doll's House: *Gulliver's Travels* the Children's Classic," in Rawson, *English Satire*, pp. 127-50.

63. A.R. Radcliffe-Brown notes the "peculiar combination of friendliness and antagonism" ("On Joking Relationships," in *Structure and Function in Primitive Society* [London: Cohen and West, 1952], p. 95.

64. As Alexander Brome calls them in his 1666 translation (*Poems of Horace*, pp. 215, 223).

65. Pope's words, in the "Epistle to Augustus" (250). See Huizinga, *Homo Ludens*.

66. There is a long tradition of similar slanging matches in English poetry. See Douglas Gray, "Rough Music: Some Early Invectives and Flytings," in Rawson, *English Satire*, pp. 21-43.

67. Cf. the same bilingual pun in Beckett's *Murphy* (New York: Grove, 1957), p. 175. *Cretin* is in fact derived from Christian, *OED*.

68. Gray, "Rough Music," quotes the exchange in Beckett but offers no analysis.

69. Dryden, *Works*, 4:72. In his "Life of Lucian" the pleasure of mere laughter is contrasted to Lucianic irony, a "nobler sort of delight" (p. 76).

70. Congreve's contest also involves sexual tension, as does the full-scale battle of the beaux and belles in Pope's *Rape of the Lock*.

71. For an example, see the unbalanced exchange between an angry friar and a fool in More's *Utopia* (bk. 1), finally halted by Cardinal Morton.

72. See, e.g., Ken Robinson, "The Art of Violence in Rochester's Satire," in Rawson, *English Satire*, pp. 93-108.

73. *Poems of Dunbar*, p. 284.

74. Walter Harte, *An Essay on Satire* (1730), pp. 12, 17. Cf. Mulgrave's *Essay upon Satyr*: "In loyal libels we have often told him / How one has jilted him, the other sold him" (68-69), in Lord, *Poems on Affairs of State*, 1:405.

75. In fact, Buckingham did resent it, complaining of Dryden's tortures and witchcraft. See Lord, *Poems on Affairs of State*, 1:liii.

76. Boileau, *A Discourse of Satires* (1668, trans. 1730); rpt. as part of Harte, *Essay on Satire*, p. [43]. It is said that even the Pope laughed at *Praise of Folly*; see the edition of P.S. Allen (Oxford: Clarendon, 1925), p. xvii.

77. See Ehrmann, "Homo Ludens Revisited," in *Game, Play, Literature*. The point is already implicit in Huizinga himself, who notes how slanging matches can degenerate into real battles (*Homo Ludens*, pp. 67-71).

78. See David Vieth, *Attribution in Restoration Poetry* (1963).

79. See Fiske, *Lucilius and Horace.*

80. Erasmus, *Opus Epistolarum*, 4:21, 254-56; and *Opera Omnia*, ed. J. LeClerc (Leiden, 1703-1706), 1:265-66.

81. Pope, *Correspondence*, 2:484.

82. Cf. Kierkegaard: "If . . . what is said is not my meaning, or the opposite of my meaning, then I am free both in relation to others and in relation to myself" (*Concept of Irony*, p. 265).

83. Traugott, "Yahoo in the Doll's House," in Rawson, *English Satire*, p. 150.

84. A.E. Dyson, "Swift: The Metamorphosis of Irony," in *Discussions of Swift*, ed. Traugott, p. 51.

85. Byron, *Letters and Journals*, 6:208.

4. Satiric Closure

1. Minturno, *L'arte poetica* (1564), facs. ed. (1970), p. 276.

2. Pope, *Epistle to Arbuthnot* 1; *Epistle to Fortescue* 4.

3. Pope, *Epistle to Fortescue*, 51-52.

4. See Mariana Torgovnick, *Closure in the Novel* (Princeton: Princeton Univ. Press, 1981); David Miller, *Narration and Its Discontents* (Princeton: Princeton Univ. Press, 1981); and the special issue of *Nineteenth Century Fiction* (June 1978) titled "Narrative Endings."

5. Johnson, "Life of Butler," in *Lives of the English Poets*, 1:211.

6. Byron, *Letters and Journals*, 8:78.

7. Dryden, "Discourse concerning the Original and Progress of Satire," *Works*, 4:77. Heinsius, *De Satyra Horatiana* (1629).

8. Ralph Rader, "Defoe, Richardson, Joyce, and the Concept of Form in the Novel," in *Autobiography, Biography, and the Novel* (Los Angeles: William Andrews Clark Memorial Library, 1973).

9. Barbara Herrnstein Smith, *Poetic Closure* (Chicago: Univ. Chicago Press, 1968), p. 2.

10. Pope's imitation is more firmly closed than his Horatian original (*Sat.* II.2). Pope concludes his poem not in Ofellus/Bethel's voice but in his own.

11. Cf. the ending of the Pope's "Epistle to Fortescue" (Sat. II.1), discussed earlier.

12. The unsuspected irony is that the "Friend" seems in part to speak for Pope himself, whose "great scheme" in 1740 was a "continuation" of the *Essay on Man* (Twickenham ed. 4:327).

13. Courtney calls the form of the poem a "priamel," in which "the writer leads up to the main point by an examination of related items which contrast with it or by comparison fall short of it" (*Satires of Juvenal*, p. 447).

14. I use the translation by Peter Green. Courtney thinks Juvenal's ironical "lack of respect for the usual method of prayer" is "inopportune," since it "casts doubt on the sincerity of the following advice" (*Satires of Juvenal*, p. 486).

15. Courtney observes that Juvenal delivers not a philosophical treatise but a rhetorical declamation, but nonetheless laments the lack of any "coherent framework of thought" (*Satires of Juvenal*, p. 453).

16. Whether Johnson should be regarded as a "satirist manqué" (as W.J. Bate and others have argued), or a sharply satirical writer (as Donald Greene has rejoined), the point is that he was reproducing a formal feature of his Latin original.

17. Martha emerges as a kind of model, but Pope does not conceal that given the world she had to live in, the life of a spinster must in some sense have been incomplete.

18. To conclude the poem with a series of deathbed vignettes also provides

thematic closure, as does the final line: "'Oh, save my Country, Heav'n!' shall be your last."

19. Quoted in Elliott, *Power of Satire*, p. 39.

20. Rochester, "On the suppos'd Authour of a Late Poem in defence of Satyr," in *Poems*, ed. Walker, p. 115.

21. Rochester, "On Poet Ninny," in *Poems*, p. 116.

22. Rochester, *Poems*, p. 90.

23. For a discussion of the poem along these lines, see Griffin, *Satires*, pp. 133-55.

24. For another analysis of the way the end of satire seems discontinuous with what precedes, see Cope, "Conquest of Truth."

25. Smith, *Poetic Closure*, p. 34.

26. For an acute discussion of the lock's (and the poem's) misinterpreters, see Murray Cohen, "Versions of the Lock: Readers of 'The Rape of the Lock'," *ELH* 43 (1976): 53-73.

27. Twickenham ed. 5:410, 412.

28. Among parody forms, two carry little sense of closure: the session of the poets, and the advice to a painter.

29. See James Norhnberg, "Pynchon's Paraclete," in *Pynchon: A Collection of Critical Essays*, ed. Edward Mendelson (Englewood Cliffs: Prentice Hall, 1978), pp. 157-58, 161.

30. Smith, *Poetic Closure*, p. 172.

31. England, *Energy and Order in the Poems of Swift*, pp. 79-119.

32. Irwin Ehrenpreis, "Swiftian Dilemmas," in Browning, *Satire in the Eighteenth Century*, pp. 224, 231.

33. Levin, "Wages of Satire," p. 14: "The satirist's vocation might be succinctly epitomized in that suspended monosyllable: 'But—.'"

34. Kernan, *Cankered Muse*, p. 31. Later he speaks of "constant movement without change" (p. 33), but by "movement" he means that the satirist simply proceeds to "apply the lash more vigorously."

35. Philip Holland, "Robert Burton's *Anatomy of Melancholy* and Menippean Satire, Humanist and English" (diss., University of London, 1978), quoted in Bakhtin, *Problems in Dostoevsky's Poetics*, pp. 106-7n.

5. Satiric Fictions and Historical Particulars

1. In the 1742 *New Dunciad* they are even more closely allied: Tragedy and Comedy are ready to expire, "But History and Satire held their head" (40).

2. Cf. Pope's remark in a letter that under Augustus "Poets exercised the same jurisdiction over the Follies, as Historians did over the Vices of Men" (*Correspondence*, 3:420); and Fielding's (in *Covent-Garden Journal* No. 2, 1752) that "Historians" join "Satyrists" in reporting on the "Vice and Iniquity" of their own times (*The Covent-Garden Journal*, ed. Bertrand Goldgar [Middletown, Conn.: Wesleyan Univ. Press, 1988], p. 19).

3. Marston "Address to the Reader" in *The Scourge of Villanie*.

4. Henry Higdon, "Preface to the Reader," in A *Modern Essay on the Tenth Satire of Juvenal* (1687), n.p.

5. See Swift's letter (Swift, *Correspondence*, 4:53).

6. Warton, *Essay on Pope*, 1756 ed., 1:333-34.

7. Williams, *Pope's Dunciad*, p. 76.

8. George Lord in *Poems on Affairs of State*, 1.1i. Both Williams and Lord are Yale-trained.

9. Rosenblum, "Pope's Illusive Temple," p. 49.

10. See Michael McKeon, *"Introduction"* to *Politics and Poetry in Restoration England* (Cambridge, Ma.: Harvard Univ. Press, 1975).

11. Fredric Bogel, "'Did you once see Johnson plain?' Reflections on Boswell's *Life* and the State of Eighteenth-Century Studies," in *Boswell's Life of Johnson: New Questions, New Answers,* ed. John Vance (Athens: Univ. of Georgia Press, 1985), pp. 82-83, 80.

12. Rosenheim's *Swift and the Satirist's Art* was not published until 1963, but it was based on his 1953 Chicago dissertation, which seems to have had at least a considerable local influence. Heiserman drew on it for his *Skelton and Satire* (Chicago: Univ. of Chicago Press, 1961).

13. Williams, *Pope's Dunciad,* p. 3. In Johnson's opinion (as reported by Boswell), the "brightest strokes" of Butler's wit "owed their force to the impression of the characters, which was upon men's minds at the time; to their knowing them, at table and in the street" (Boswell, *Life of Johnson,* 2:369).

14. Sacks, *Fiction,* pp. 7, 11. In its original form Sacks's book was also a Chicago dissertation.

15. Rosenblum, "Pope's Illusive Temple," pp. 31-32.

16. Malvin Zirker, in *The Satirist's Art,* ed. Jensen and Zirker, p. 97; and R.B. Gill, "Real People and Persuasion in Personal Satire," *South Atlantic Quarterly* 82 (1983): 171-72. See also Gill's later essay "Dryden, Pope, and the Person in Personal Satire," *Essays in Literature* 13 (1986): 219-30.

17. Woodruff, *"Rasselas,"* p. 163.

18. Harington, *Epigrams,* p. 231.

19. See Johnson's *Dictionary,* s.v. "representation," "representative."

20. Rosenblum, "Pope's Illusive Temple," pp. 30-34.

21. Cf. William Kinsley on the "energetic interaction of fact and fiction . . . that helps distinguish satire from other literary forms" ("The 'Malicious World' and the Meaning of Satire," *Genre* 3 [1970]: 138).

22. See Swift's comment on the use of initials in *Prose Works,* 2:14-15.

23. In some editions "Sibbes Soliloquies" is substituted for "Stillingfleet's Replyes," with virtually no change in satiric effect.

24. Lord Chesterfield, quoted in Vincent Liesenfeld, *The Licensing Act of 1737* (Madison, 1984), p. 146.

25. See James May, "Determining Final Authorial Intention in Revised Satires: The Case of Edward Young," *Studies in Bibliography* 38 (1985): 276-89. May speculates that Young, like Pope, may also have revised because he had a change of heart about some of his victims.

26. The "brothers," statues of "Raving" and "Melancholy Madness" at the gate of Bedlam Hospital, executed by Cibber's sculptor father, were in fact made of stone. See Pope's note at *Dunciad* 2.3.

27. Rosenblum, "Pope's Illusive Temple," p. 32; Sitter, *Literary Loneliness in Mid-Eighteenth-Century England* (Ithaca: Cornell Univ. Press, 1982), p. 82.

28. Hayden White, "Historical Text as Literary Artifact," in *Tropics of Discourse* (Baltimore: Johns Hopkins Univ. Press, 1978), p. 89; Hayden White, "The Burden of History," in *History and Theory* 5, no. 2 (1966): 111-34 (rpt. in *The Tropics of Discourse*); and Dominick LaCapra, who emphasizes that "documents" are themselves texts that "process" reality (*History and Criticism* [Ithaca, 1985], p. 19).

29. Bolingbroke, "Letter 3," in *Letters on the Study and Use of History,* ed. Kramnick, p. 25.

30. Dryden's view of satire may have colored his view of history. Cf. the dedication of his *History of the League* (1684): "All such as are not wilfully blind, may view in it, as in a glass, their own deformities" (*Works,* 18:7).

31. Bolingbroke, "Letter 2," in *Letters*, pp. 18, 25. Kramnick, his editor, cites similar statements from Rapin, Fenelon, and Boulainvilliers (pp. xviii, xxiii).

32. Many of the commonplaces are found in Pierre LeMoine's *Of the Art of History* (1670, trans. 1695). See Herbert Davis, "The Augustan Conception of History," in *Reason and the Imagination*, ed. Mazzeo, pp. 213-29; and Paulson, *Satire and the Novel*, p. 151.

33. Boscawen, *The Progress of Satire*.

34. Bolingbroke, "Letter 3," in *Letters*, p. 28; cf. "Letter 5," p. 71.

35. For example, both Bolingbroke throughout the *Letters* and Pope in the *Dunciad* are hostile to "mere" antiquarianism.

36. Bacon, *The Advancement of Learning* 2.13, 5.

37. Bayle, *Dictionary* 4.142.

38. See White, *Metahistory*, p. 49, on the distinction between "fabulous," "satirical," and "truthful" history in the Enlightenment.

39. Quoted by Kramnick in Bolingbroke, *Letters*, p. xxvi.

40. See Kernan, *Cankered Muse*, pp. 85-86n.

41. Johnson, "Life of Pope," in *Lives of the English Poets*, 3:212. Cf. "Life of Swift," 3:61-62.

42. Swift wanted to be Anne's Historiographer Royal. See his memorial to the Queen, dated April 15, 1714, in which he asks to be appointed to the post in order to tell the "truth" about her reign (*Prose Works*, 8:200).

43. Lock calls it "a mixture of panegyric and satire, disguised as a historical account" (*Swift's Tory Politics*, p. 48).

44. Fielding is in fact quoting from a 1688 sermon by Robert South. See Goldgar, *Covent-Garden Journal*, p. 85.

45. Sitter, *Literary Loneliness*, p. 84. For numerous examples of Pope's stretching of the truth, see the Twickenham (5: passim) notes. Cf. Swift's notoriously untrustworthy notes to his "Verses on the Death of Dr. Swift."

46. See Robert McHenry, "Dryden's History: The Case of Slingsby Bethel," *HLQ* 47 (Autumn 1984): 253-72. McHenry notes that Bethel is "transformed . . . into a comic symbol" (p. 268).

47. Pope, Twickenham ed., 5:205.

48. Rosenblum, "Pope's Illusive Temple," p. 46.

49. for the Johnson example, I am indebted to an unpublished essay by Robert Halsband, who looks from the biographer's angle at satire's power to misrepresent. Lord Hailes corrected Johnson; see Boswell's *Journal of a Tour to the Hebrides* (August 17).

50. Young, preface to *Love of Fame* in *Poetical Works*, 2:55. The remark may be self-serving. Young may here be claiming that, as satirist, he tells no more than a historian would. Bayle, *Dictionary*, 2:160-61.

51. Bayle (*Dictionary*, 4:424) quotes and translates the original Latin of James Bongars.

52. Edward Gibbon, *Decline and Fall of the Roman Empire* (New York: Random House, n.d., 1:69), apparently alluding to Voltaire, whose Ingénu reads history only to discover that "l'histoire n'est que le tableau des crimes et des malheurs" (*L'Ingénu*, chap. 10, in *Oeuvres Complètes* [Paris, 1879], 21:275).

53. Gibbon, *Decline and Fall*, 1:382-83.

54. Bayle, *Dictionary*, 2:160-161.

55. As Hayden White notes, Voltaire assembles facts "to substantiate the proposition that it is 'folly' for a ruler, however powerful and talented, to seek 'glory' through conquest and battle" (*Metahistory*, p. 50). Johnson would have known Voltaire's *History*.

56. But see Hayden White's argument that satire, in its plotlessness and its

focus on degeneration, served as one of the forms of "emplotment" for nineteenth-century historians (*Metahistory*, pp. 7-11, 251-53).

57. See, e.g., James Young, "Interpreting Literary Testimony: A Preface to Re-reading Holocaust Diaries and Memoirs," *NLH* 18 (1986-87): 403-23.

58. As Charles Knight neatly puts it, satire "makes fictive assertions about historical topics" ("Satire, Speech, and Genre," p. 37).

6. The Politics of Satire

1. Snyder, *Prospects of Power*, p. 100. Palmeri suggests that "periods of collision between one cultural paradigm and an alternative . . . seem to favor the writing of narrative satire (*Satire in Narrative*, p. 17).

2. Elliott, "Satire," p. 272. Cf. Rawson: "It flourishes most in an order-minded culture, perhaps at moments when order is felt to be slipping" (*English Satire*, p. viii).

3. Helgerson, *Self-crowned Laureates*, p. 104.

4. Bate, *The Burden of the Past*, p. 123. For the satyr as enemy to love and love poetry, see Helgerson (*Self-crowned Laureates*, p. 126), who cites Weever's *Faunus and Melliflora* (1600).

5. Helgerson—citing Everard Guilpin's *Skialethia* (1598), ed. Carroll (Chapel Hill, 1974), pp. 61-62—silently modernizes Carroll's text and in the process misquotes "concise" for "Concisde" (*Self-crowned Laureates*, p. 107; see also p. 105).

6. Duncan, *Ben Jonson* pp. 27, 44, 82.

7. For an argument that satire is absorbed by the sentimental novel, see Paulson, *Satire and the Novel*, pp. 219-65.

8. Arthur Marotti has recently argued that Donne's satires rest "on the guarantee of intimate communication provided by their coterie circumstances" (*John Donne, Coterie Poet* [Madison, 1986], p. 38).

9. Francis Jeffrey, *Literary Criticism*, ed. D. Nichol Smith, p. 27. Cf. Robert Krapp's Marxist approach in "Class Analysis of a Literary Controversy: Wit and Sense in 17th-Century English Literature," *Science and Society* 10 (1946): 80-92.

10. On the appropriation of the low in high or classic discourse, see Stallybrass and White, *Politics and Poetics of Transgression*.

11. There was a long and well-documented tradition of "Aesopian" satire in the former Soviet Union, sometimes tolerated and sometimes suppressed. If my hypothesis is correct, satire should decline as Eastern Europe becomes more democratic.

12. Under the old ban in the Twelve Tables against *mala carmina*. See Horace *Epist.* 2.1.152-54.

13. Pope, *Epistle to Fortescue* 145-49. Cf. Pope's remark in the *Epistle to Augustus* (257) that poets are "bound" by "wholesom dread of statutes."

14. See Edward Nathan, "The Bench and the Pulpit: Conflicting Elements in the Augustan Apology for Satire," *ELH* 52 (Summer 1985): 375-96.

15. Though one of the few to comment on the conditions that promote satire, Feinberg, *The Satirist*, simply collects opinions.

16. Defoe, *A Review*, 8:7, continues: the wit of Marvell and Rochester "made the Court odious to the People, beyond what had been possible if the Press had been open."

17. Shaftesbury, in *Characteristics*, ed. J.M. Robertson (London, 1900), 1:50-51.

18. Collins, *Discourse*, p. 24.

19. The great example in English is Pope. For his use of innuendo in satiric opposition to Walpole (who did not tolerate open criticism), see esp. Mack, *The Garden and the City*, pp. 128-67.

20. Sigmund Freud, *The Interpretation of Dreams*, trans. James Strachey, in the *Standard Edition of the Complete Psychological Works* (London, 1953), 4:142.

21. Kenneth Burke, *The Philosophy of Literary Form* (Baton Rouge: Louisiana State Univ. Press, 1941), pp. 231-32. Elliott drew attention to Burke's remark, and to Shaftesbury's, in *Power of Satire*, p. 265 (a section first published as "The Satirist and Society," *ELH*, 21 [1954]: 237-48).

22. Marotti, *John Donne*, p. 42.

23. See Satire 4.10, 119, 216, 237, and the notes in Milgate's edition of Donne's *Satires, Epigrams, and Verse Letters* for references to the statutes against treason and the proclamations against Catholics. On the "fear of the law" in Donne's satires, see Erskine-Hill, "Courtiers out of Horace," esp. pp. 278-83.

24. Hodgart finds conditions of perfect freedom in fifth-century Greece and does not note the limitations on general satire (*Satire*, pp. 34-38).

25. Ibid., p. 52.

26. Hodgart would argue that the ancien régime was "inefficient in suppressing its opponents" (ibid., p. 39), but Robert Darnton's work on surveillance of writers by the police would suggest the contrary; see "Policing Writers in Paris circa 1750," *Representations* 5 (Spring 1984): 1-37.

27. See Max Radin, "Freedom of Speech in Ancient Athens," *American Journal of Philology* 48 (1927): 226. I owe the reference to Elliott, *Power of Satire*, pp. 264-65. Elliott is one of the very few critics who have paid attention to the idea that censorship stimulates satire.

28. Daniel Balmuth's 1979 Cornell dissertation, "Censorship in Russia, 1865-1905," pp. 442-58. Annabel Patterson drew my attention to Balmuth in her *Censorship and Interpretation* (1984), pp. 22-23.

29. Ben Jonson, *Works*, ed. Herford and Simpson, 3:423, 449.

30. Marston was a member of the Middle Temple. Donne was at Lincoln's Inn, Guilpin at Gray's Inn, William Goddard at the Inner Temple. Hall remained at Cambridge as a Fellow. In his later career as a dramatist, Marston wrote for the Children of Paul's, in hopes of preferment at court.

31. Marotti, *John Donne*, p. 38; Helgerson, *Self-crowned Laureates*, p. 123. See also Esler, *Aspiring Mind*.

32. Marotti, *John Donne*, p. 39. Marotti later argues that the "thematic center" of Donne's *Metempsychosis* (1601) is "not the bad moral condition of the world or of the Court, but the shared political dissatisfaction of poet and audience" (p. 130).

33. See Helgerson's analysis (*Self-crowned Laureates*).

34. On the few paths open to the wit who lacks wealth—the church, the school, the household—see Oldham's bitter "Satyr. Address'd to a Friend that is about to leave the University, and come abroad in the World," in his *Poems and Translations*, pp. 137-48.

35. Gay's credentials as a satirist—or parodist, or ironist—continue to be debated. See Arthur Sherbo, "John Gay: Lightweight or Heavyweight?" *The Scriblerian* 8, no. 1 (Autumn 1975): 4-8.

36. George Eliot, "Worldliness and Other-Worldliness: The Poet Young," in *Essays* (Boston, n.d.), p. 11.

37. See Mack, *Alexander Pope*, p. 110, on Pope's "aristocratic attitudes towards the writer's profession." Byron, perhaps because he was an aristocrat by birth and had nothing to prove, was not reluctant to write for money and to discuss it openly.

38. In calling the satirist "an economically wise man of humble means," Peter Thorpe ("The Economics of Satire," *Western Humanities Review* 23 [1968]: 187-96) underestimates the significance of his *dependent* status.

39. See esp. Highet, *Juvenal the Satirist*, pp. 5-8. See also Mason, "Is Juvenal a Classic?" pp. 123-24, 165-66.

40. "I am most richly / For service paid" (32-33) means, of course, "I hope you will continue to pay me richly."

41. See Voltaire, "Mémoire sur la Satire" (1739), in *Oeuvres Complètes* (Paris, 1879), 23:53.

42. Ehrenpreis, *Swift*, 3:552-54, 590-93. See also Nokes, *Jonathan Swift*, where the theme of Swift's vain lifelong search for preferment is prominent.

43. Mack, *Alexander Pope*, p. 885.

44. Mack calls Fortescue "[Pope's] and Walpole's long-time intermediary" (*Garden and the City*, p. 177).

45. Persius is the exception. Son of a wealthy equestrian family, educated at Rome but not designed for a profession, independently wealthy and without need of a patron, Persius died at twenty-eight. Cornutus, the Stoic philsopher, was in Dryden's words Persius's "Master and Tutor."

46. Stephen Greenblatt calls it "house arrest" (*Renaissance Self-Fashioning* [Chicago: Univ. of Chicago Press, 1980], p. 132).

47. *OED*, s.v. "time," 7: "prescribed or alloted term."

48. Marotti, *John Donne*, p. 116. Although Wyatt in fact had a remarkably successful career as a courtier and diplomat, his satires were written from the point of view of an outsider—as he temporarily was in 1536.

49. I borrow the term from René Girard, who notes that the "marginal insider is often the victim of persecution" (*The Scapegoat*, p. 18).

50. Mack, *Garden and the City*, p. 234.

51. George Orwell, "Politics vs. Literature: An Examination of *Gulliver's Travels*," in Traugott, *Discussions of Jonathan Swift*, p. 82; see also p. 86.

52. Johnson, "Life of Swift," and "Life of Pope."

53. See Stack, *Pope and Horace*, pp. 9, 120.

54. Cf. the ending of Ariosto's fourth satire ("be gracious to somebody else with such a gift") and Horace's story of Volteius Mena.

55. P.G. Wiggins, *The Satires of Ludovico Ariosto* (Athens: Univ. of Ohio Press 1976), p. 172.

56. In the "Panegyric on the Rev. Dean Swift" (1730), possibly by Swift (according to his latest editor), the Dean is coarsely accused of the same kind of fruitless flattery: to show devotion to his patron he has swallowed "Bob's" [Robert Harley's] spittle mixed with Harry's [Henry St. John's] turd."

57. William Kupersmith finds the poem "half-humorous, half-bitter" ("Swift and 'Harley, the Nation's Great Support,'" *Swift Studies* 1 (1986): 39-45).

58. Elkin, *Augustan Defence of Satire* p. 189. Elliott says the satirist claims to be "a true conservative," the "preserver of tradition" (*Power of Satire*, p. 266).

59. Elliott argues that the ostensibly conservative Molière and Swift are in fact "revolutionary" (*Power of Satire*, pp. 274-75).

60. Paulson, *Fictions of Satire*, p. 18. Later he calls "conservative" satire "defensive" (p. 19).

61. The definition is Sacvan Berkovitch's, in "The Problem of Ideology in American Literary History," *Critical Inquiry* 12 (1986): 635.

62. Ronald J. Corthell, "Joseph Hall and 17th Century Literature," *John Donne Journal* 3 (1984): 253.

63. Fielding, *The Jacobite's Journal*, p. 214.

64. Ibid., p. 215.

65. Schilling, *Dryden and the Conservative Myth*.

66. Pope praised his landed friends, but was himself a renter ("What's Property, dear Swift?") and invested in stocks. For a recent attempt to read the *Dunciad* as a Jacobite allegory, see Douglas Brooks-Davies, *Pope's Dunciad and the Queen of Night*.

67. Mack, *Garden and the City*, pp. 68, 187.

68. See Lock, *Swift's Tory Politics*.

69. See Swift's letter, in French, to the Abbé Desfontaines, in *Correspondence*, 3:226.

70. Orwell, "Politics vs. Literature," pp. 86, 83.

71. Erich Auerbach, *Mimesis*, quoted in Elliott, *Power of Satire*.

72. See Robinson, *Lucian*, chap. 1.

73. See H.L. Stow, "Aristophanes' Influence upon Public Opinion," *Classical Journal* 38 (1942): 87; Stephen Halliwell, "Aristophanic Satire," in Rawson, *English Satire*, p. 8.

74. Dryden knew Shaftesbury would not be indicted and was not in fact seeking to influence the jury. See Philip Harth's "*Legends no Histories:* The Case of *Absalom and Achitophel*," in *Studies in Eighteenth-Century Culture* 4:13-29.

75. Mack, *Garden and the City*, pp. 172, 180.

76. Bertrand Goldgar, *Walpole and the Wits: The Relation of Politics to Literature, 1722-1742* (Lincoln: Univ. of Nebraska Press, 1976), pp. 4, 188, 218.

77. Ibid., p. 22, quoting *An Historical View of the Principles, Characters, Persons, etc. of the Political Writers in Great Britain* (1740), p. 24.

78. R.E. Smith, "The Law of Libel at Rome," *Classical Quarterly*, n.s. 1 (1951): 169-70. As Smith notes (p. 172), Roman law distinguished between the written and the more dangerous spoken word. Even Sulla's *lex majestatis* was not enforced after his time. See Smith, p. 178; and F.R.D. Goodyear's commentary in *Tacitus* (Oxford: Clarendon, 1970), 2:150.

79. See Peter, *Complaint and Satire*, pp. 148-52; McCabe, "Elizabethan Satire" (188-93), argues unpersuasively that the bishops were trying to restrain political criticism.

80. *Daily Gazetteer*, May 7, 1737.

81. Liesenfeld, *Licensing Act*, p. xii.

82. Performance of Gay's *Polly* was banned in 1728, but the play was printed the next year. Liesenfeld cites one progovernment supporter of the act who defends the liberty of the press but not the right to bring "Politicks on the Stage" (ibid., p. 117).

83. Quoted in ibid., p. 147.

84. See the entry "Libel" in Voltaire's *Philosophical Dictionary*, in *Works: A Contemporary Version*, 6:120.

85. Gruner, *Understanding Laughter*, pp. 170-295. Another sociologist, Dorothy Markiewicz, reviews research from 1956 to 1972 and can find no clear evidence that humor influences persuasion ("Effects of Humor on Persuasion," *Sociometry* 37 [1974]: 407-22).

86. *Examiner* 38, in Swift *Prose Works*, 3:141.

87. Lock, *Swift's Tory Politics*, p. 21.

88. But Swift's work had little lasting effect. "The victory was of a strictly limited kind, and made little difference to the general endemic exploitation of Ireland by absentee English authorities" (Nokes, *Jonathan Swift*, p. 295).

89. Goldgar, *Walpole and the Wits*, p. 188.

90. See ibid.; and Gruner, *Understanding Laughter*, p. 201.

91. Anatoly Lunacharsky, "Jonathan Swift and 'A Tale of a Tub,'" in Anatoly Lunacharsky, *On Literature and Art*, comp. A. Lebeder (Moscow, 1965), pp. 308-10.

92. For a fuller discussion, see Chapter 7.

93. Montesquieu, *The Spirit of Laws* (12.13), trans. Thomas Nugent, 2 vols. (New York, 1949), 2:195.

94. For a summary of recent debate about the function and effect of carnival, see Michael Bristol, *Carnival and Theatre: Plebeian Culture and the Structure of Authority in Renaissance England* (New York, 1985).

95. Francis Steuart, "Pasquino and Pasquinades," *Gentleman's Magazine* 300, (1906): 9. Burton tells the story in *Anatomy of Melancholy* 1.2.4.4.

96. I owe the Bacon quotation to Patterson, *Censorship and Interpretation*, pp. 13-14. She notes similar advice in the sixteenth-century *Mirrour for Magistrates*. Cf. also Bacon's *Advice touching the Controversies of the Church of England*: "The punishing of wits enhances their authority" (*Letters and Life*, 1:78).

97. Swift, *Prose Works*, 8:112. Cf. Johnson: punishment may "crush the author" but "promote the book" ("Life of Milton," in *Lives of the English Poets*, 1:108); and Hume, *History of England*, 4:376.

98. From Knightley Chetwode's manuscript "Life of Roscommon," cited in Carl Niemeyer, "The Earl of Roscommon's Academy," *MLN* 49 (1934): 432-37. Addison suggests that the Royal Society was established to turn "the greatest Genius's of that Age to the Disquisitions of natural Knowledge, who, if they had engaged in Politicks with the same Parts and Application, might have set their Country in a Flame" (*Spectator*, 2:519). Remembering Swift's *Tale*, Addison compares tubs thrown out to whales. Cf. Johnson, "Life of Swift," 2:94.

99. Cf. an early letter in which Swift says his mind is like a "conjur'd Spirit" which "would do mischief if I would not give it employment" (*Correspondence*, 1:4), and the *Battel of the Books*, were rival authors (i.e., books) are coupled together, so that "their Malignity might be employ'd among themselves" (*Prose Works*, 1:145).

100. For recent speculations about carnival as a "safety valve," see Stallybrass and White, *Politics and Poetics of Transgression*; and Michael Andre Bernstein, "'O Totiens Servus': Saturnalia and Servitude in Augustan Rome," *Critical Inquiry* 13 (1987): 450-74.

101. See the Countess of Blessington's *Conversations of Lord Byron*, p. 195. Cf. Swift's "In a jest I spend my rage," discussed above.

102. Cited in Liesenfeld, *Licensing Act*, p. 14. George Lord asserts that the Restoration "State Poems" had the effect of eroding "traditional attitudes of awe and respect toward one's betters" and of undermining "confidence" (*Poems on Affairs of State*, pp. xxiii-xxiv).

103. Johnson, "Life of Milton," in *Lives of the English Poets*, 1:108.

104. Lord, *Poems on Affairs of State*, pp. xviii, xxv.

105. My argument here is indebted to Sacvan Berkovitch's discussion of the ways in which American culture assimilated the "radicalism" of the American Renaissance writers. See his "Ideology in American Literary History," *Critical Inquiry* 12 (1986): esp. 642-45.

106. For a discussion of the "subversion-containment debate" in Renaissance studies, see T.B. Leinwand, "Negotiation and New Historicism," *PMLA* 105 (May 1990): 477-90.

107. *Works*, 4:48; Dryden is loosely translating Dacier.

108. See Robert Wolseley's "Preface to *Valentinian*," in Spingarn, *Critical Essays*, 3:12. Wolseley goes on to say that pretenders of all kinds were "cow'd and aw'd under the known force of a sense so superiour to their own."

109. See, e.g., Swift's *Prose Works*, 2:258. Burton also knows the story (*Anatomy of Melancholy*, 1.2.4.4).

110. Montesquieu, *Spirit of Laws*. Cf. Ben Jonson on the traditional political purpose of studying poetry: disposing the reader "to all Civill offices of Society" (*Works*, 8:636).

7. The Pleasure of Satire

1. Oldham, "Upon a Printer that exposed him by Printing a Piece of his grosly Mangled, and Faulty," in *Poems and Translations*, p. 132; See also Oldham, *Poems*, p. 157.

2. Both use the pleasure/displeasure trope: see Marston, *Scourge of Villanie*, Proem to bk. 1; Hall, "Post-script" to *Virgidemiae, in Collected Poems*, p. 97.

3. See Dryden on the "pleasure" of "wit writing" in Preface to *An Evening's Love* (*Works*, 10:207).

4. Frye, "Nature of Satire," p. 78. Rosenheim speaks of our "sheer delight" in Swift's ingenuity" (*Swift and the Satirist's Art*, p. 126).

5. "There is in human nature a vein of malice—a delight in the observation of folly, an inclination to laugh uncharitably at others" (Kinsley and Boulton, *English Satiric Poetry*, [1966] p. 10).

6. Joseph Bentley, "Satire and the Rhetoric of Sadism," *Centennial Review* 11 (1967): 387-404.

7. Alvin Kernan, "Aggression and Satire: Art Considered as a Form of Biological Adaptation," in *Literary Theory and Structure*, ed. Brady, Palmer, Price, pp. 115-29. Cf. W.B. Carnochan, "The Consolations of Satire," in *The Art of Jonathan Swift*, ed. Probyn, pp. 19-42.

8. Freud's work on wit has been both challenged and supported by subsequent research in psychology and sociology. See a brief survey by R.B. Gill, "New Direction in Satire: Some Psychological and Sociological Approaches," *Studies in Contemporary Satire* 9 (1982): 17-28.

9. Originally translated into English in 1916 as *Wit and Its Relation to the Unconscious*. I use the translation in vol. 8 of the *Standard Edition*, cited by page number in the text.

10. "O that a Satyres hand had force to plucke / Some fludgate up, to purge the world from muck" (*Scourge of Villanie*, Proem to bk. 3, p. 79). Marston's original is of course the God of Genesis.

11. Kenneth Burke, *Attitudes toward History*, 2 vols. (New York, 1937), 1:62-69. This is an old idea. Cf. Donne on the satirist's "self-guiltinesse": "We doe but reprehend those things, which we ourselves have done" (*Sermons*, 7.408).

12. He cites a story in Suetonius about Julius Caesar; see *Correspondence of Erasmus*, in *Collected Works* (Toronto: University of Toronto Press, 1976), 3:119.

13. Cf. Freud on humor: "It has something of grandeur and elevation [which] lies in the triumph of narcissism, the victorious assertion of the ego's invulnerability." See his paper on "Humour" (1927), in *Standard Edition*, 21:162.

14. Leavis thought Swift took "a positive delight in his power" ("The Irony of Swift," in Traugott, *Discussions of Jonathan Swift*, p. 39.

15. Dyson, "Swift," p. 51.

16. Quoted in Boswell, *Life of Johnson*, 2:334.

17. Jauss has also discussed what he calls *jouissance esthetique* in *Aesthetische Erfahrung und Literarische Hermeneutik* (1977). Jauss has begun to explore the distinct pleasures offered by different genres; see *Poetique* 10 (1979): 261-74.

18. Francis Hutcheson, *Inquiry Concerning Beauty*, p. 23.

19. See the chapter "Pleasure" in Hagstrum's *Samuel Johnson's Literary Criticism* (1952); W.R. Keast, "Johnson's Criticism of the Metaphysical Poets," *ELH* 17 (1950): 59-70; and Damrosch, *Uses of Johnson's Criticism*, p. 45.

20. Corbyn Morris's *Essay* was reprinted in *ARS*, no. 4 (1947): 37, 42, 44, 51.

21. Dryden, preface to *An Evening's Love*, in *Works*, 10:209. Laughter, he says in the "Life of Lucian," is the pleasure common to satire and comedy." (*Works*, ed. Scott-Saintsbury, 18:76. *Essays*, ed. Watson, 1:152. Laughter, he says in the "Life of Lucian," is the pleasure common to satire and comedy (*Works*, ed. Scott, 18:76).

22. Addison, in *Spectator* 418, in Bond, *The Spectator*, 3:566-67.

23. David Hartley, *Observations on Man* 1:416-17.

24. Freud, *Standard Edition*, 8:121-23.

25. Hutcheson, *Inquiry Concerning Beauty*, p. 113.

26. Hutcheson's notion seems not to have aroused much interest in his own day, perhaps because of the widespread suspicion among his Lockean contemporaries about "innate ideas."

27. Hutcheson's discussion of laughter begin with a denial of Hobbes's "Sudden Glory." Hartley argues that laughter is often based on our love and affection for the friends and children at whom we laugh. (*Observations on Man* 1.440).

28. T.S. Eliot, "John Dryden," in *Selected Essays*, 2d ed. (London: Faber, 1934), pp. 307-11.

29. Recommending the "Commentary" to his *Dunciad*, Pope says, "The reader cannot but derive one pleasure from the very Obscurity of the persons it treats of, that it partakes of the nature of a *Secret*, which most people love to be let into, tho' the Men or the Things be ever so inconsiderable or trivial" (Twickenham ed., 5:8).

30. See *Spectator* 512, in Bond, *The Spectator*, 4:318.

31. James Ralph, *The Touch-Stone* (1728), quoted in Damrosch, *Imaginative World of Alexander Pope*, p. 208. But cf. Swift: "On A's and B's you Malice vent, / While Readers wonder whom you meant" ("On Poetry, A Rhapsody," 159-60).

32. Rawson writes that Pope's analysis of Wharton's ruling passion appeals to the "manifest delights of the controlling intellect" and the "pleasures of conclusive definition" (*Gulliver and the Gentle Reader*, pp. 47, 48).

33. See J.S. Cunningham, "On Earth as It Laughs in Heaven: Mirth and the 'Frigorifick Wisdom,' " in Hilson, Jones, and Watson, *Augustan Worlds*, pp. 131-51; and the application of Cunningham's ideas to satire in Ingram, *Intricate Laughter*.

34. For a contrary view, see Ingram, *Intricate Laughter*.

35. Rabelais, *Gargantua and Pantagruel*, Book 1, chap. 25. Cf. Panurge (4.27), his shirt covered with excrement, laughingly protesting that it is saffron, but providing a dozen synonyms for "shit."

36. Marston, *Scourge of Villanie*, p. 4. Jonson laughs at Marston's neologisms in *Poetaster*, where he has the satirist Crispinus vomit up his fantastic vocabulary. See King, *Language of the Satirized Characters*,

37. Roe, *Sir Thomas Urquhart*, p. 18. Urquhart characteristically elaborates, supplying half again as many epithets and assigning each a derogatory adjective, in his translation of the Rabelais passage just quoted.

38. J. Milton French, "Milton as Satirist," *PMLA* 51 (1936):417.

39. For a good account of the Swiftian list, see Rawson, *Gulliver and the Gentle Reader*, chaps. 4-5, esp. pp. 89-103.

40. For "poignant," Johnson give two additional definitions: severe, piercing, painful; and irritating, satirical, keen.

41. "Concernment" for Dryden is emotional involvement. See Jensen, *Dryden's Critical Terms*, p. 32.

42. Cf. "Methinks some sacred rage warmes all my vaines" (*Scourge of Villanie*, p. 92).

43. *The State of Rome under Nero and Domitian* (London, 1739). Cf. "What honest Spirit can his Spleen contain?" *The First Satire of Juvenal, Imitated* (London, 1740), p. 9.

44. Greene, *Satires of Juvenal Paraphrastically Imitated*, p. xi.

45. Knox, 2:228. Cf. "whose printed lines should glow with manly rage" (*First Satire of Juvenal, Imitated*, p. 12); and Greene, "an animated Glow of Thought" (*Satires of Juvenal Paraphrastically Imitated*, p. xx).

46. Greene, *Satires of Juvenal Paraphrastically Imitated*, p. 7. Cf. Duncombe, who refers to Juvenal's "flaming [i.e., inflaming?] Invectives" (*Works of Horace in English Verse*, 2:iv).

47. Bayle, *Dictionary*, 764-65.

48. Blake, *Marriage of Heaven and Hell*. To "brace" is to "string up or give tone to the nerves" (*OED*).

49. *Letters of T.E. Brown*, ed. S.T. Irwin (Westminster: Constable, 1900), 1:173. Cf. G.S. Street in 1892 on the "quite refreshing power of abuse" in Rochester's lampoons (in *Rochester: The Critical Heritage*, p. 253).

50. Clark, *Studies in Literary Modes* (1946), pp. 31-49.

51. Louis Bredvold, "A Note in Defence of Satire," in *Studies in the Literature of the Augustan Age*, ed. R.C. Boys (1952), p. 13.

52. Thomas Willis, *Two Discourses Concerning the Soul of Brutes*, trans. Samuel Pordage (1683), rpt. Gainesville: Scholars Fascimiles and Reprints, 1971), p. 189.

53. Francis Fuller, *Medicina Gymnastica: or, a Treatise Concerning the Power of Exercise*, 2d ed. (1705), p. 139.

54. Willis, *Two Discourses*, p. 189. There is a suggestive link between Fuller's idea of clearing obstruction of the animal spirits by means of exercise, and Frye's idea that satire clears away anything that "impedes the free movement . . . of society" (*Anatomy of Criticism*, p. 233).

55. Harte, *Essay on Satire*, p. 17.

56. Jean Baptiste Du Bos, *Critical Reflections on Poetry, Painting, and Music*, trans. Thomas Nugent (London, 1748), 1:5, 6, 10.

57. In his essay "Of Tragedy" Hume approvingly reports Du Bos's assertion that the indolent mind "seeks every amusement and pursuit, . . . whatever will rouze the passions, and take its attention from itself." *Essays*, p. 217. Burke adapted Du Bos's ideas to describe the invigorating mental "exercise" induced by terror, in *A Philosophical Enquiry into the Origins of Our Ideas of the Sublime and Beautiful* (1757), pt. 4, sec. 7 ("Exercise necessary for the finer organs").

58. Boswell quotes Du Bos in his essay "On Executions" (*The Hypochondriack*, [No. 68, 1783], ed. Margaret Bailey [1928], 2:278).

59. Matthew Green's well-known *The Spleen* (1737) is based on the idea that satiric mirth drives away melancholy (one of the meanings of "spleen").

60. The definition comes from a 1722 edition of Caelius Aurelianus, *Acutae Passiones* (c. 400 A.D.), quoted in Van Rooy, *Studies in Classical Satire*, p. 180. Johnson includes the word; *OED* gives an example from 1697.

61. Tuveson, "Swift," p. 58.

62. Swift, "Epistle to a Lady" (177-80), in *Poems*, 2:635.

63. Butler, *Hudibras*, 2.2.466. The flogging pedant is a conventional figure. Note that he both punishes and gratifies (claws and curries) his own sin.

64. Swift, *A Tale of a Tub*, "the Preface." Cf. Sir William Temple, Swift's Mentor, who laments that "the vein of ridiculing all that is so serious and good . . . [is] the itch of our age and climate." In *Five Miscellaneous Essays*, ed. S.H. Monk (Ann Arbor: Univ. of Michigan Press, 1963), p. 70. Cf. also Marston on the satirist's "itching fist" (*Scourge of Villanie*, p. 18).

65. In the almost exactly contemporary poem "To his Friend the Author of Juvenalis Redivivus" (1683), an anonymous writer ironically worried that "All will turn wicked to be scourg'd by thee."

66. Johnson, *Lives of the English Poets*, 1:345.

67. Jean De La Bruyère, "Of Polite Learning," in *The Continental Model: Selected French Essays of the 17th Century*, ed. Scott Elledge and Donald Schier (Ithaca: Cornell Univ. Press, 1970), p. 338.

68. Young, Preface to *Love of Fame*, in *Poetical Works*, 2:55.

69. See Rochester's "Fair Chloris in a pigsty lay" (36-37). For the "seat" where Jove "retires for ease," see Pope, *Dunciad* 2:84, in *Poems*, 5:299.

70. Rochester, "Epistolary Essay" (36-42).

71. Marston, *Scourge of Villanie*, p. 65.

72. I have discussed the medical context more fully in Dustin Griffin, "Venting Spleen," *Essays in Criticism* 40 (April 1990): 124-35.

73. Butler, *Prose Observations*, p. 60.

74. Cf. Preface to *Absalom and Achitophel*.

75. Persius, *Sat.* 1.117, in *Works*, 4:275.

76. Pope, *Correspondence*, 1:211.

77. "Tickling also causeth laughter: the cause may be the emission of the spirits, and so of the breath, by a flight from titillation." Francis Bacon, *Sylva Sylvarum*, in *Works*, 16 vols. (London: Pickering, 1825-34), 4:404.

78. Quoted in Hume, *Essays*, p. 218.

79. *OED*, s.v. "tickle," II.7, II.4.

80. On the "uneasiness" that satire can produce, see Patricia Meyer Spacks, "Some Reflections on Satire," *Genre* 1 (1968): 13-20.

81. Pope, *Correspondence*, 2:90. And in his final note to the *Epilogue to the Satires* Pope took the high moral ground, even as he resolved to abandon satire as too dangerous and ineffectual: "He had reason to be satisfied with the approbation of good men, and the testimony of his own conscience."

82. Pope, Twickenham ed., 5:17. Cleland probably would not have written "ought to be" if he had not considered ridicule a pleasure, perhaps of a lower sort.

83. Ibid., 5:19.

84. Hutcheson, *Collected Works*, 1:240, 1:vi.

85. For a range of examples of this commonplace, ancient and modern, see Maynard Mack's notes to Pope's passage in the Twickenham ed., 3-1:157-60.

86. James Beattie speaks of the "powerful emotion" of "moral disapprobation," but he does not go so far as to describe "moral dispprobation" as a source of pleasure ("On Laughter and Ludicrous Composition," in *Essay*, p. 390-96).

87. Samuel Richardson, *Clarissa* (London: Dent, 1932), 2:156.

88. Milton, Preface to *Animadversions*.

89. Knox, 2:148.

90. *Satires of Juvenal Paraphrastically Imitated*, pp. 13-14.

91. *Tatler* 92, in *The Tatler*, 2:74. Cf. *Spectator* 256, and 451, in which Addison, quoting Bayle, worries that we conceive "joy" from the dishonor of another person being defamed.

92. Cf. *Spectator* 23: "Gratification to a barbarous and inhuman Wit."

93. Cf. Horace's *me delectat* (*Sat.* 2.1. 28).

94. Swift in *Intelligencer* No. 3, in *Prose Works*, 12:34.

95. Fielding in *Covent-Garden Journal* No. 52, in Goldgar, *Covent-Garden Journal*, p. 288.

96. Kames, *Elements of Criticism* (1762), 2: 54-55.

97. MacKenzie, *The Man of Feeling* (1771), chap. 40.

98. Knox, *Essays Moral and Literary* 2:227. Cf. his remark later that "the sati ists of our times seem to have little else in view, than to gratify private pique, or party-prejudice" (2:231).

99. Johnson, "Life of Pope," in *Lives of the English Poets*, 3:181. Earlier in the "Life" Johnson asserts that Pope seems to have "contemplated his victory over the Dunces with great exultation" and "rejoiced" in having given them "pain" (3:150).

100. Shenstone, *Works* (1764), 2:14.

101. Cf. his later remark that general satire is "but a *Ball* bandied to and fro, and every Man carries a *Racket* about Him to strike it from himself among the rest of the Company" (*A Tale of a Tub*, "The Preface").

102. MacKenzie, *Man of Feeling*, chap. 40.

103. Addison in *Spectator* 418, in Bond, *The Spectator*, 3:568.

104. Cf. John Morris, "Wishes as Horses: A Word for the Houyhnhnms," *Yale Review* 42 (1973): 360.

105. Nathanael West, *Complete Works* (New York: Farrar, Straus, and Cudahy, 1957), p. 335.

106. Orwell, "Politics vs. Literature." In the same discussion he acknowledged that one feels "a sort of pleasure in seeing that fraud, feminine delicacy, exploded for once [in Swift's dressing-room poems]."

107. Freud, *Jokes and their Relation to the Unconscious*, p. 115.

108. For another speculation, see Tuveson, who imagines that satire "may provide an easy form of vicarious penance for guilt feeling" ("Swift," p. 59).

109. Marston, *Scourge of Villanie*, 2. 21, 9.93.

110. Johnson, "Life of Swift," 3:62. Cf. "such as every other tongue utters with unwillingness and of which every ear shrinks from the mention" ("Life of Pope").

111. Jones, "Pope and Dulness." Cf. Ingram, *Intricate Laughter*, p. 139.

Conclusion: Prospects and Further Investigations

1. See Lewis's essay, "The Greatest Satire Is Nonmoral" (1934), reprinted in Paulson, *Satire*, pp. 66-79.

2. See Wellek, "What Is Literature?" pp. 16-23.

3. "Letter to the Publisher" of the *Dunciad*, signed by "William Cleland" (Twickenham ed. 5:17). Cf. Dryden, for whom the satirist holds a kind of public "Office" (*Works*, 4:60); and Young, *Love of Fame*: "When the law shows her teeth but dares not bite," satire acts as "shining supplement of public laws" (1.12.17-18).

4. According to the *Ars Grammatica* of Diomedes, *satura* is also "some kind of stuffing [*farcimen*] which was crammed full with many ingredients" (e.g., raisins, wine, honey). See Van Rooy, *Studies in Classical Satire*. Charles Knight reflects on Diomedes' suggestive equation of satire and *farcimen* in "Imagination's Cerberus," pp. 141-42.

5. Dryden, "Discourse," in *Works*, 4:65; letter to Caryll in Pope, *Correspondence*, 1:164. Pope hints at another link between cookery and satire through a buried pun on "dress": to prepare for use as food (*OED*), 11a), and to chastise (cf. the more common "dress down"; *OED*, 7). If, he says, the original of Sir Plume should "*Dress* me" (i.e., chastise me), I will see that he is "well heated, and hashed" (cut to pieces) (i.e., *dressed*).

6. In Dryden, the false witnesses to the Popish Plot feed like vipers on their "Mother Plot" and, in a combination of matricide and cannibalism "suck for Nutriment that bloody gore / Which was their Principle of Life before" (*Absalom and Achitophel* 1013-15).

7. Cf. Rochester on "My Lord All-Pride": "His starved Fancy, is compell'd to rake, / Among the Excrements of others Witt, / To make a stinking Meale of what they Shitt" (8-10).

8. David Nokes speaks of "parallels between sexual and alimentary appetites" and says that "food offers a good guide to a person's instinctive reactions to questions of physical gratification and sensual pleasure" (*Rage and Raillery*, pp. 163, 176).

9. Dryden, *Absalom and Achitophel* 621. Cf. Pope on old Cotta: "His kitchen vy'd in coolness with his grot" (*Moral Essays* 3.182).

10. As Nokes says, food can be a metaphor "for need, for kindness and charity, for conviviality and good fellowship, for meanness, for selfishness and self-indulgence, for ostentation and gross display" (*Rage and Raillery*, p. xxx).

11. Cf. Pope's Helluo, "late Dictator of the Feast" (*Moral Essays* 2.79).

12. By contrast, Dryden, in complimenting the "Variety of Entertainment" in

his patron's satires, says that Dorset's "*Coena dubia*" offers "Diversity" and "good Order" (*Works*, 4:25).

13. Eumolpus cites three earlier examples of cannibalism from Roman history (Petronius, *Satyricon*).

14. Bakhtin, *Rabelais and His World*, p. 168.

15. For force-feeding as comic punishment, cf. Pope on Cibber, who "makes poor Pinky eat with vast applause" (Imitation of Horace Epist 2.1.293); Penkethman the actor ate two chickens within three seconds in his role in a Cibber play.

16. See *Memoirs of Mrs. Laetitia Pilkington with Anecdotes of Dean Swift*, vol. 3 (1754), p. 161.

17. Swift, *Correspondence*, 3:107-8. Pope parodies the role of satirist-as-physician in the *Narrative of Dr. Robert Norris* (1713), a satire on John Dennis.

18. Cf. Butler's *Hudibras*, where eating involves violence ("cramm'd 'em till their guts did ache"; 2.2.797) and violence is like cooking (men given a "rib-roasting" and "beaten t'a jelly"; 2.1.244-48).

19. Petronius alludes to Marsyas, who was flayed alive, and to Cassandra, who killed her own children.

20. Cf. the stories of Roman epicures who died from overeating, alluded to in Pope, *Moral Essays* 1.234-37.

21. See Bakhtin, *Rabelais and his World*, pp. 162-63. Bakhtin claims that in Rabelais tripe comes from the lining of the intestine and could contain excrement.

22. Claude, Lévi-Strauss notes the connection in South American Indian myth between laughter and the origin of cooking fire (*The Raw and the Cooked*, tr. John and Doreen Weightman (New York: Harper and Row, 1969), p. 126.

23. Test attempts such an approach. He gathers some pertinent discussions of the social function of "ritual satire" (controlling aggression, enforcing community norms). But although he wants to argue that ritual provides "archetypal antecedents" and analogues for literary satire, Test finally accepts that literary satire and ritual satire (ancient and modern, primitive and civilized) are not "analogous" (*Satire*, p. 66).

24. Frye's three phases are "satire of the low norm," "quixotic phase," and "satire of the high norm" (*Anatomy of Criticism*, pp. 226-36).

25. See Chapter 4, above.

26. White, *Metahistory*, p. 9.

27. See Michael Seidel, "The Satiric Plots of *Gravity's Rainbow*," in Mendelson, *Pynchon*, pp. 198-212; and *Satiric Inheritance*.

Bibliography

Editions cited

Bacon, Francis, Lord. *Letters and Life.* 7 vols. Ed. James Spedding. London: Longman, 1861-74.

Blake, William. *Letters.* 3d ed. Ed. Geoffrey Keynes. London: Hart-Davis, (1956) 1980.

———. *Complete Poetry and Prose of William Blake.* Ed. David Erdman; commentary by Harold Bloom (Berkeley: Univ. of California Press, 1982).

Bolingbroke, Henry St. John, Lord. *Letters on the Study and Use of History.* Ed. Isaac Kramnick. Chicago: Univ. of Chicago Press, 1972.

Boswell, James. *The Life of Johnson.* 6 vols. Ed. G.B. Hill, rev. L.F. Powell. Oxford: Clarendon, 1934-50.

Butler, Samuel. *Prose Observations.* Ed. Hugh De Quehen. Oxford: Clarendon, 1979.

———. *Hudibras.* Ed. John Wilders and Hugh De Quehen. Oxford: Clarendon, 1979.

Byron, George Gordon, Lord. *Byron's Letters and Journals.* 12 vols. Ed. Leslie Marchand. Cambridge: Harvard Univ. Press, 1973-82.

Defoe, Daniel. *The Review.* Ed. A.W. Secord. 22 vols. New York: Facsimile Text Society, 1938.

Donne, John. *Sermons.* 10 vols. Ed. George Potter and Evelyn Simpson. Berkeley: Univ. of California Press, 1953-62.

———. *Satires, Epigrams, and Verse Letters.* Ed. Wesley Milgate. Oxford: Clarendon, 1967.

Dryden, John. *Works of John Dryden.* California ed. Los Angeles: Univ. of California Press, 1961.

———. *Works.* 18 vols. Ed. Sir Walter Scott; rev. and corr. George Saintsbury, Edinburgh: William Paterson, 1882-93.

Dunbar, William. *Poems.* Ed. James Kinsley. Oxford: Clarendon, 1979.

Duncombe, John. *Works of Horace, In English Verse.* 2 vols. London: Dodsley, 1757-59.

Erasmus. *Praise of Folly.* Tr. Betty Radice. Harmondsworth: Penguin, 1971.

Fielding, Henry. *The Covent-Garden Journal.* Ed. Bertrand Goldgar. Middletown: Wesleyan Univ. Press, 1988.

———. *The Jacobite's Journal and Related Writings.* Ed. W.B. Coley. Middletown: Wesleyan Univ. Press, 1975.

Goldsmith, Oliver. *Collected Works*. 5 vols. Ed. Arthur Friedman. Oxford: Clarendon, 1966.

Greene, Edward Burnaby. *The Satires of Juvenal Paraphrastically Imitated*. London, 1763.

Hall, Joseph. *Collected Poems*. Ed. Arnold Davenport. Liverpool: Liverpool Univ. Press, 1949.

Harington, John. *Letters and Epigrams*. Ed. Norman McClure. Philadelphia: Univ. of Pennsylvania Press, 1926.

Jonson, Ben. *Works*. 11 vols. Ed. C.H. Herford and P. Simpson. Oxford: Clarendon, 1954.

Juvenal. *The Sixteen Satires*. Tr. Peter Green. Baltimore: Penguin, 1967.

Lord, George, ed. *Poems on Affairs of State, 1660-1678*. New Haven: Yale Univ. Press, 1963.

———. ed. *Anthology of Poems of Affairs of State*. New Haven: Yale Univ. Press, 1975.

Lucian. *Selected Satires of Lucian*. Ed. and tr. Lionel Casson. New York: Norton, 1962.

Marston, John. *The Scourge of Villanie*. Ed. G.B. Harrison. New York: Barnes and Noble, 1966.

Montesquieu. *The Spirit of Laws*. 2 vols. Tr. Thomas Nugent. New York: Hafner, 1949.

More, Sir Thomas. *Utopia*. Tr. and ed. Robert M. Adams. New York: Norton, 1975.

Oldham, John. *Poems and Translations* (1684). Repr. in *Works* [1686] repr. 1979.

———. *Poems*. Ed. Harold Brooks and Raman Selden. Oxford: Clarendon, 1987.

Pope, Alexander. *Correspondence*. 5 vols. Ed. George Sherburn. Oxford: Clarendon, 1956.

———. *Poems*. Twickenham ed. 11 vols. Ed. John Butt et al. London: Methuen, 1939-68.

Rabelais, Francois. *Gargantua and Pantagruel*. Tr. J.M. Cohen Baltimore: Penguin, 1955.

Rochester, John Wilmot, Earl of. *Poems*. Ed. Keith Walker. Oxford: Blackwell, 1984.

Shaftesbury, Earl of. *Characteristics*. Ed., J.M. Robertson. London: Richards, 1900.

Swift, Jonathan. *Prose Works*. 14 vols. Ed. Herbert Davis. Oxford: Blackwell, 1939-68.

———. *Correspondence*. 5 vols. Ed. Harold Williams. Oxford: Clarendon, 1963.

———. *Swift's Poems*. 2d ed. 3 vols. Ed. Harold Williams. Oxford: Clarendon, 1958.

Voltaire, François-Marie Arouet. *Works: A Contemporary Version*. 22 vols. New York: St. Hubert Guild, 1901.

———. *Oeuvres Complètes*. 52 vols. Paris: Garnier, 1877-85.

Wilson, J. Harold. *Court Satires of the Restoration*. Columbus: Ohio State Univ. Press, 1976.

Young, Edward. *Poetical Works* (1844). 2 vols. Rept., Westport, Ct.: Greenwood, 1970.

Secondary Works

Addison, Joseph. *The Spectator*. 5 vols. Ed. Donald F. Bond, Oxford: Clarendon, 1965.

Anderson, William. *Essays on Roman Satire*. Princeton: Princeton Univ. Press, 1982.

Anselment, Raymond. *"Betwixt Jest and Earnest": Marprelate, Milton, Marvell, Swift, and the Decorum of Religious Ridicule*. Toronto: Univ. of Toronto Press, 1979.

Auden, W.H. "Notes on the Comic." In *The Dyer's Hand*. New York: Random House, 1962.

Bakhtin, Mikhail. *Rabelais and his World*. Tr. Helene Iswolsky. Cambridge: MIT Press, 1968.

———. *Problems of Dostoevsky's Poetics*. Tr. Caryl Emerson. Minneapolis: Univ. of Minnesota Press, 1984.

———. *The Dialogic Imagination: Four Essays*. Ed. Michael Holquist. Tr. Caryl Emerson and M. Holquist. Austin: Univ. of Texas Press, 1981.

Bayle, Pierre. *The Dictionary Historical and Critical*. 2d ed. 5 vols. London, 1734-38. Rept., New York: Garland, 1984.

Beattie, James. *Essays*. 3d ed. London, 1779.

Beaty, Frederick. *Byron the Satirist*. DeKalb: Northern Illinois Univ. Press, 1985.

Bentley, Joseph. "Satire and the Rhetoric of Sadism." *Centennial Review* 11 (1967): 387-404.

Bercovitch, Sacvan. "The Problem of Ideology in American Literary History." *Critical Inquiry* 12 (1986): 631-53.

Bernstein, Michael Andre. "'O Totiens Servus': Saturnalia and Servitude in Augustan Rome." *Critical Inquiry* 13 (1987): 450-74.

Blessington, Marguerite (Power) Farmer Gardiner, Countess of. *Conversations with Lord Byron*. Ed. E. Lovell. Princeton: Princeton Univ. Press, 1969.

Bloom, Harold. *Blake's Apocalypse*. London: Gollancz, 1963.

Bloom, Edward A., and Lilian D. Bloom. *Satire's Persuasive Voice*. Ithaca: Cornell Univ. Press, 1972.

Bogel, Fredric. "'And did you once see Johnson plain?'": Reflections on Boswell's *Life* and the State of Eighteenth-Century Studies." In *Boswell's Life of Johnson: New Questions, New Answers*. Ed. John Vance. Athens: Univ. of Georgia Press, 1985.

Boscawen, William. *The Progress of Satire*. London, 1798.

Boswell, James. *The Hypochondriack*. Ed. Margaret Bailey. Stanford: Stanford Univ. Press, 1928.

Bredvold, Louis. "A Note in Defence of Satire." *Studies in the Literature of the Augustan Age*. Ed. R.C. Boys. Ann Arbor: Wahr, 1952.

Brooks-Davies, Douglas. *Pope's Dunciad and the Queen of Night: A Study in Emotional Jacobitism*. Manchester: Manchester Univ. Press, 1985.

Browning, J.D., ed. *Satire in the Eighteenth Century*. New York: Garland, 1983.

Brower, Reuben. *Alexander Pope: The Poetry of Allusion*. Oxford: Oxford Univ. Press, 1959.

Burke, Edmund. *A Philosophical Enquiry into the Origins of our Ideas of the Sublime and Beautiful* (1757). Ed. James Boulton. London: Routledge, 1958.

Burke, Kenneth. *A Rhetoric of Motives*. New York: Prentice-Hall, 1950.

———. *The Philosophy of Literary Form*. Baton Rouge: Louisiana State Univ. Press, 1941.

———. *Attitudes Toward History*. 2 vols. New York: New Republic, 1937.

Bullitt, John. *Jonathan Swift and the Anatomy of Satire*. Cambridge: Harvard Univ. Press, 1954.

Caputi, Anthony. *John Marston, Satirist*. Ithaca: Cornell Univ. Press, 1961.

Carnochan, W.B. "Some Suppressed Verses in Dryden's Translation of Juvenal VI." (21 January 1972): 73-74.

———. "The Consolations of Satire." In *The Art of Jonathan Swift*, ed. Clive Probyn, 19-42. New York: Barnes and Noble, 1978.

Carretta, Vincent. *The Snarling Muse: Verbal and Visual Political Satire from Pope to Churchill*. Philadelphia: Univ. of Pennsylvania Press, 1983.

Clark, A.M. *Studies in Literary Modes*. Edinburgh: Oliver and Boyd, 1946.

Clark, John. *The Modern Satiric Grotesque and its Traditions*. Lexington: Univ. Press of Kentucky, 1991.

Coffey, Michael. *Roman Satire*. London: Methuen, 1976.

Cohen, Murray. "Versions of the Lock: Readers of 'The Rape of the Lock'." *ELH* 43 (1976): 53-73.

Cope, Kevin. "The Conquest of Truth: Wycherly, Rochester, Butler, and Dryden and the Restoration Critique of Satire." *Restoration* 10 (1986): 19-40.

Corthell, Ronald J. "Joseph Hall and 17th Century Literature." *John Donne Journal* 3 (1984): 249-68.

Courtney, E. *A Commentary on the Satires of Juvenal*. London: Athlone, 1980.

Damrosch, Leo. *The Uses of Johnson's Criticism*. Charlottesville: Univ. of Virginia Press, 1976.

———. *The Imaginative World of Alexander Pope*. Berkeley: Univ. of California Press, 1987.

Darnton, Robert. "Policing Writers in Paris circa 1750." *Representations* 5 (1984): 1-37.

Davis, Herbert. "The Augustan Conception of History." In *Reason and the Imagination*. Ed. J.A. Mazzeo. New York: Columbia Univ. Press, 1962, 213-29.

Dennis, John. *Critical Works*. 2 vols. Ed. E.N. Hooker. Baltimore: Johns Hopkins, 1939-43.

Duncan, Douglas. *Ben Jonson and the Lucianic Tradition*. Cambridge: Cambridge Univ. Press, 1979.

Dyson, A.E. "Swift: The Metamorphosis of Irony." Repr. in *Discussions of Jonathan Swift*. ed. John Traugott.

Ehrenpreis, Irvin. *Swift: The Man, His Works, and the Age*. 3 vols. Cambridge: Harvard Univ. Press, 1962-83.

Ehrmann, Jacques. "Homo Ludens Revisited." In *Game, Play, Literature*, ed. J. Ehrman. New Haven: Yale Univ. Press, 1968.

Eliot, George. "Worldliness and Other-Worldliness: the Poet Young." In *Essays*. Boston, n.d.

Elkin, P.K. *The Augustan Defence of Satire*. Oxford: Oxford Univ. Press, 1973.

Elledge, Scott, and Donald Schier eds. *The Continental Model: Selected French Essays of the 17th Century*. Rev. ed. Ithaca: Cornell Univ. Press, 1970.

Elliott, Robert C. *The Power of Satire: Magic, Ritual, Art*. Princeton: Princeton Univ. Press, 1960.

England, A.B. *Energy and Order in the Poems of Swift*. Lewisburg: Bucknell Univ. Press, 1980.

Erskine-Hill, Howard. "The 'New World' of Pope's *Dunciad*." *Renaissance and Modern Studies* 6 (1962): 47-67.

———. "Courtiers out of Horace." In *John Donne: Essays in Celebration*. Ed. A.J. Smith. London: Methuen, 1972.

Esler, Anthony. *The Aspiring Mind of the Elizabethan Younger Generation*. Durham: Duke Univ. Press, 1966.

Farley-Hills, David. *Rochester: The Critical Heritage*. London: Routledge, 1972.

Feinberg, Leonard. *The Satirist: His Temperament, Motivation, and Influence*. Ames: Iowa State Univ. Press, 1963.

———. *Introduction to Satire*. Ames: Iowa State Univ. Press, 1967.

Fiske, G.C. *Lucilius and Horace: A Study in the Classical Theory of Imitation*. Madison: Univ. of Wisconsin Press, 1920.

Fowler, Alastair. *Kinds of Literature*. Cambridge: Harvard Univ. Press, 1982.

Fraenkel, Eduard. *Horace*. Oxford: Clarendon, 1957.

French, J. Milton. "Milton as Satirist." *PMLA* 51 (1936): 414-29.

Freud, Sigmund. *The Standard Edition of the Complete Psychological Works*. 24 vols. Tr. and ed. James Strachey, et al. London: Hogarth, 1953-66.

Frye, Northrop. *Anatomy of Criticism*. Princeton: Princeton Univ. Press, 1957.

———. "The Nature of Satire." *University of Toronto Quarterly* 14 (1944): 75-89.

Gill, R.B. "Dryden, Pope, and the Person in Personal Satire." *Essays in Literature* 13 (1986): 219-30.

———. "Real People and Persuasion in Personal Satire." *South Atlantic Quarterly* 82 (1983): 165-78.

———. "New Directions in Satire: Some Psychological and Sociological Approaches." *Studies in Contemporary Satire* 9 (1982): 17-28.

Girard, René, *The Scapegoat*. Baltimore: Johns Hopkins Univ. Press, 1986.

Goldgar, Bertrand. *Walpole and the Wits: The Relation of Politics to Literature, 1722-1742*. Lincoln: Univ. of Nebraska Press, 1976.

Griffin, Dustin. *Satires Against Man: The Poems of Rochester*. Berkeley: Univ. of California Press, 1973.

———. *Alexander Pope: The Poet in the Poems*. Princeton: Princeton Univ. Press, 1978.

———. *Regaining Paradise: Milton and the 18th Century*. Cambridge: Cambridge Univ. Press, 1986.

———. "Venting Spleen." *EiC* 40 (1990): 124-35.

Gruner, Charles. *Understanding Laughter: The Workings of Wit and Humor*. Chicago: Nelson-Hall, 1978.

Guerinot, J.V., *Pamphlet Attacks on Alexander Pope, 1711-1744.* New York: New York Univ. Press, 1969.

———. ed. *Pope: A Collection of Critical Essays.* Englewood Cliffs, N.J.: Prentice Hall, 1972.

Guilhamet, Leon. *Satire and the Transformation of Genre.* Philadelphia: Univ. of Pennsylvania Press, 1987.

Hagstrum, Jean. *Samuel Johnson's Literary Criticism.* Chicago: Univ. of Chicago Press, 1952.

Halliwell, Stephen. "Aristophanic Satire." In *English Satire and the Satiric Tradition,* ed. Claude Rawson, pp. 6-20.

Harris, Bernard. "Men Like Satyrs." In *Elizabethan Poetry,* ed. J.A. Brown and B. Harris. London: Arnold, 1960.

Harte, Walter. *Essay on Satire* (1730). Ed. T.B. Gilmore. Los Angeles: W.A. Clark Memorial Library, 1968.

Harth, Philip. "Legends no Histories: The Case of *Absalom and Achitophel.*" *SECC* 4 (1975): 13-29.

Hartley, David. *Observatons on Man* (1749) Facs. repr. 2 vols. Gainesville: Scholars' Facsimiles and Reprints, 1966.

Hartman, Geoffrey. *The Unmediated Vision.* New York: Harcourt-Brace, 1954, 1966.

Helgerson, Richard. *Self-Crowned Laureates: Spenser, Jonson, Milton, and the Literary System.* Berkeley: Univ. of California Press, 1983.

Hester, M.T. *Kind Pitty and Brave Scorn: John Donne's Satyres.* Durham: Duke Univ. Press, 1982.

Highet, Gilbert. *The Anatomy of Satire.* Princeton: Princeton Univ. Press, 1962.

———. *Juvenal the Satirist.* Oxford: Clarendon, 1955.

Hodgart, Matthew. *Satire.* New York: McGraw-Hill, 1969.

Howells, Wilbur. *Logic and Rhetoric in England, 1500-1700.* Princeton: Princeton Univ. Press, 1961.

———. *Eighteenth-Century British Logic and Rhetoric.* Princeton: Princeton Univ. Press, 1971.

Huizinga, Johan. *Homo Ludens.* London: Routledge, 1950.

Hume, David. *Essays Moral, Political, and Literary.* Rev. ed. Ed. Eugene Miller. Indianapolis: Liberty, 1985.

———. *History of England.* 6 vols. New York: Harper, 1979.

Hutcheson, Francis. *Inquiry Concerning Beauty, Order, Harmony, Design* (1725). Ed. Peter Kivy. The Hague: Nijhoff, 1973.

Ingram, Allan. *Intricate Laughter in the Satires of Swift and Pope.* New York: St. Martin's, 1986.

Jack, Ian. *Augustan Satire: Intention and Idiom in English Poetry, 1660-1750.* Oxford: Clarendon, 1952.

Jauss, Hans Robert. *Aesthetische Erfahrung und Literarische Hermeneutik.* Frankfurt: Suhrkamp, 1982.

———. "La jouissance esthetique." *Poetique* 10 (1979): 261-74.

Jefferson, D.W. "*Tristram Shandy* and the Tradition of Learned Wit." *EiC* 1 (1951): 225-48.

Jensen, H. James, and Malvin R. Zirker, Jr., eds. *The Satirist's Art.* Bloomington: Indiana Univ. Press, 1972.

Jensen, H. James. *A Glossary of John Dryden's Critical Terms*. Minneapolis: Univ. of Minnesota Press, 1969.

Johnson, Samuel. *Lives of the English Poets*. 3 vols. Ed. G.B. Hill. Oxford: Clarendon, 1905.

Jones, Emrys. "Pope and Dulness." Chatterton Lecture on an English Poet, repr. in *Pope: A Collection of Modern Critical Essays*, ed. J.V. Guerinot. Englewood Cliffs, N.J.: Prentice-Hall, 1972.

Kames, Henry Home, Lord. *Elements of Criticism*. 3 vols. Edinburgh, 1762.

Kantra, Robert. *All Things Vain: Religious Satirists and their Art*. University Park: Pennsylvania State Univ. Press, 1984.

Keast, William. "Johnson's Criticism of the Metaphysical Poets." *ELH* 17 (1950): 59-70.

Keener, Frederick. *English Dialogues of the Dead*. New York: Columbia Univ. Press, 1973.

Kennedy, George. *The Art of Persuasion in Greece*. Princeton: Princeton Univ. Press, 1963.

Kernan, Alvin. *The Cankered Muse: Satire of the English Renaissance*. New Haven: Yale Univ. Press, 1959.

———. *The Plot of Satire*. New Haven: Yale Univ. Press, 1965.

———. "Aggression and Satire: Art Considered as a Form of Biological Adaptation." In *Literary Theory and Structure*, ed. Frank Brady, John Palmer, and Martin Price, 115-29. New Haven: Yale Univ. Press, 1973.

Kierkegaard, Søren. *The Concept of Irony*. Tr. Lee Capel. Bloomington: Univ. of Indiana Press, 1968.

King, Arthur. *The Language of the Satirized Characters in Poetaster*. Lund Studies in English, vol. 10. Lund, 1941.

Kinney, Arthur. "Rhetoric as Poetic: Humanist Fiction in the Renaissance." *ELH* 43 (1976): 413-43.

Kinsley, James, and James Boulton. *English Satiric Poetry: Dryden to Byron*. London: Edward Arnold, 1966.

Kinsley, William. "The 'Malicious World' and the Meaning of Satire." *Genre* 3 (1970): 137-55.

Kirk, Eugene. *Menippean Satire: An Annotated Catalogue of Texts and Criticism*. New York: Garland, 1983.

———. "Blake's Menippean *Island*." *PQ* 59 (1980): 194-215.

Knight, Charles. "Satire and Conversation: The Logic of Interpretation." *The Eighteenth Century: Theory and Interpretation* 26 (1985): 239-61.

———. "Imagination's Cerberus: Satire and the Metaphor of Genre." *PQ* 69 (1990): 131-51.

———. "Satire, Speech, and Genre." *Comparative Literature* 44 (1992): 22-41.

———. "Listening to Encolpius: Modes of Confusion in the *Satyricon*." *UTQ* 58 (1989): 335-54.

Knoche, Ulrich. *Roman Satire*. Tr. Edwin Ramage. Bloomington: Univ. of Indiana Press, 1975.

Knox, Vicesimus. *Essays Moral and Literary*. 2 vols. London, 1782.

Kranidas, Thomas. "Style and Rectitude in 17th-Century Prose: Hall, Smectymnuus, and Milton." *HLQ* 46 (1983): 237-69.

Krapp, Robert. "Class Analysis of a Literary Controversy: Wit and Sense in

17th-Century English Literature." *Science and Society* 10 (1940): 80-92.

Kupersmith, William. *Roman Satirists in Seventeenth-Century England*. Lincoln: Univ. of Nebraska Press, 1985.

———. "Swift and 'Harley, the Nation's Great Support.'" *Swift Studies* 1 (1986): 39-45.

LaCapra, Dominick. *History and Criticism*. Ithaca: Cornell Univ. Press, 1985.

Leavis, F.R. "The Irony of Swift." Repr. in *Discussions of Jonathan Swift*, ed. John Traugott.

LeBossu, René. *Treatise of the Epick Poem* (1695). Gainesville: Scholars' Facsimiles and Reprints, 1970.

Leinwand, T.B. "Negotiation and New Historicism." *PMLA* 105 (1990): 477-90.

Lévi-Strauss, Claude. *The Raw and the Cooked*. New York: Harper and Row, 1969.

Levin, Harry. "The Wages of Satire." In *Literature and Society*, ed. Edward Said, 1-14. Baltimore: Johns Hopkins Univ. Press, 1980.

Liesenfeld, Vincent. *The Licensing Act of 1737*. Madison: Univ. of Wisconsin Press, 1984.

Lipking, Lawrence. *The Life of the Poet*. Chicago: Univ. of Chicago Press, 1981.

Lock, F.P. *Swift's Tory Politics*. London: Duckworth, 1983.

Lunacharsky, Anatoly. "Jonathan Swift and 'A Tale of a Tub.'" In *On Literature and Art*, ed. A. Lebeder. Moscow, 1965.

Mack, Maynard. "The Muse of Satire." Repr. in *Satire: Modern Essays in Criticism*, ed. Ronald Paulson. Englewood Cliffs: Prentice-Hall, 1971.

———. *Alexander Pope: A Life*. New York: Norton, 1985.

———. *The Garden and the City: Retirement and Politics in the Later Poetry of Pope*. Toronto: Univ. of Toronto Press, 1969.

Marmorale, E.V. *Giovenale*. 2d ed. Bari: Laterza, 1950.

Marotti, Arthur. *John Donne, Coterie Poet*. Madison: Univ. of Wisconsin Press, 1986.

Mason, H.A. "Is Juvenal a Classic?" In *Critical Essays on Roman Literature: Satire*, ed. Sullivan.

Matthews, William, and Ralph Rader. *Autobiography, Biography, and the Novel*. Los Angeles: Clark Library, 1973.

May, James. "Determining Final Authorial Intention in Revised Satires: The Case of Edward Young." *Studies in Bibliography* 38 (1985): 276-89.

McCabe, Richard. *Joseph Hall: A Study in Satire and Meditation*. Oxford: Clarendon, 1982.

———. "Elizabethan Satire and the Bishops' Ban of 1599." *YES* 11 (1981): 188-93.

McHenry, Robert. "Dryden's History: The Case of Slingsby Bethel." *HLQ* 47 (1984): 253-72.

McKeon, Michael. *Politics and Poetry in Restoration England*. Cambridge: Harvard Univ. Press, 1975.

Medine, Peter. "Isaac Casaubon's *Prolegomenon* to the *Satires* of Persius: An Introduction, Text, and Translation." *ELR* 6 (1976): 271-98.

Minturno, Antonio. *L'Arte Poetica* (1564), facs. ed. Munchen: Fink, 1971.

Moore, Thomas V. "Donne's Use of Uncertainty in Satyre III." *MP* 67 (1969): 41-49.

Morris, Corbyn. *Essay Towards Fixing the True Standards of Wit, Humour, Raillery, Satire, and Ridicule* (1744). Repr., *Augustan Reprint Series*, no. 4 (1947).

Morris, David. *Alexander Pope: The Genius of Sense*. Cambridge: Harvard Univ. Press, 1984.

Morris, John. "Wishes as Horses: A Word for the Houyhnhnms." *Yale Review* 62 (1972-73: 355-71.

Nathan, Edward. "The Bench and the Pulpit: Conflicting Elements in the Augustan Apology for Satire." *ELH* 52 (1985): 375-96.

Nelson, Nicholas. "Dramatic Texture and Philosophical Debate in Prior's *Dialogues of the Dead*." *SEL* 28 (1988): 423-41.

New, Melvyn. *Lawrence Sterne as Satirist*. Gainesville: Univ. of Florida Press, 1969.

New Encyclopaedia Brittanica. 15th ed. 32 vols. Chicago: Encyclopaedia Brittanica, 1984.

Niemeyer, Carol. "The Earl of Roscommon's Academy." *MLN* 49 (1934): 432-57.

Norhnberg, James. "Pynchon's Paraclete." In *Pynchon: A Collection of Critical Essays*, ed. Edward Mendelson. Englewood Cliffs, N.J.: Prentice-Hall, 1978.

Nokes, David. *Raillery and Rage: A Study of Eighteenth-Century Satire*. Brighton: Harvester, 1987.

———. *Jonathan Swift: Hypocrite Reversed*. Oxford: Oxford Univ. Press, 1985.

Orwell, George. "Politics vs. Literature: An Examination of *Gulliver's Travels*." Repr. in *Discussions of Jonathan Swift*, ed. Traugott.

Palmeri, Frank. *Satire in Narrative: Petronius, Swift, Gibbon, Melville, and Pynchon*. Austin: Univ. of Texas Press, 1990.

Patterson, Annabel. *Hermogenes and the Renaissance: Seven Ideas of Style*. Princeton: Princeton Univ. Press, 1970.

———. *Censorship and Interpretation*. Madison: Univ. of Wisconsin Press, 1984.

Pilkington, Laetitia. *Memoirs of Mrs. Laetitia Pilkington with Anecdotes of Dean Swift*. 3 vol. London: 1754.

Paulson, Ronald. *The Fictions of Satire*. Baltimore: Johns Hopkins Univ. Press, 1967.

———. *Satire and the Novel in Eighteenth-Century England*. New Haven, Yale Univ. Press, 1967.

———. ed. *Satire: Modern Essays in Criticism*. Englewood Cliffs, N.J.: Prentice-Hall, 1971.

Peter, John. *Complaint and Satire in Early English Literature*. Oxford: Oxford Univ. Press, 1956.

Price, Martin. *Swift's Rhetorical Art*. New Haven: Yale Univ. Press, 1953.

Radin, Max. "Freedom of Speech in Ancient Athens." *American Journal of Philology* 48 (1927): 215-30.

Randolph, Mary Claire. "The Structural Design of Formal Verse Satire." *PQ* 21 (1942): 368-84. Repr. in Paulson, *Satire*.

———. "The Medical Concept in English Renaissance Satire." *SP* 38 (1941): 125-57. Repr. in Paulson, *Satire*.

———. "Thomas Drant's Definition of Satire, 1566." *N & Q* 180 (1941): 416-18.

Rawson, Claude, ed. *Focus: Swift*. London: Sphere, 1970.

———. ed., *The Character of Swift's Satire: A Revised Focus*. Newark: Univ. of Delaware Press, 1983.

———. *Gulliver and the Gentle Reader*. London: Routledge, 1973.

———. ed. *English Satire and the Satiric Tradition*. Oxford: Blackwell, 1984.

———. *Order from Confusion Sprung*. London: Allen and Unwin, 1985.

———. "A Reading of *A Modest Proposal*." In *Augustan Worlds*, ed. J.C. Hilson, M.M.B. Jones, and J.R. Watson, 29-50. New York: Barnes and Noble, 1978.

Robinson, Christopher. *Lucian and his Influence in Europe*. Chapel Hill: Univ. of North Carolina Press, 1979.

Roe, F.C. *Sir Thomas Urquhart and Rabelais*. Oxford: Clarendon, 1957.

Rosenblum, Michael. "Pope's Illusive Temple of Infamy." In *The Satirist's Art*, ed. H. Jensen and M. Zirker. Bloomington: Indiana Univ. Press, 1972.

Rosenfeld, Lawrence. "The Practical Celebration of Epideictic." In *Rhetoric in Transition*, ed. Eugene White. University Park: Pennsylvania State Univ. Press, 1980.

Rosenheim, Edward. *Swift and the Satirist's Art*. Chicago: Univ. of Chicago Press, 1963.

Rudd, Niall. *The Satires of Horace: A Study*. Cambridge: Harvard Univ. Press, 1966.

Sacks, Sheldon. *Fiction and the Shape of Belief*. Berkeley: Univ. of California Press, 1966.

Satire Newsletter. "The Concept of the Persona in Satire." In vol. 3, no. 2, 1966.

Satire Newsletter. "Norms in Satire: A Symposium." In vol. 2, no. 1, 1964.

Schilling, Bernard. *Dryden and the Conservative Myth*. New Haven: Yale Univ. Press, 1961.

Seidel, Michael. *Satiric Inheritance: Rabelais to Sterne*. Princeton: Princeton Univ. Press, 1979.

Selden, Raman. *English Verse Satire, 1590-1765*. London: Allen and Unwin, 1978.

Shenstone, William. *Works*. London, 1764.

Sherbo, Arthur. "John Gay: Lightweight or Heavyweight?" *Scriblerian* 8 (1975): 4-8.

Sherburn, George. "Methods in Books about Swift." *SP* 35 (1938): 635-56.

Siegel, P.N. "Donne's *Paradoxes and Problems*." *PQ* 28 (1949): 507-11.

Smith, A.J., ed. *John Donne: Essays in Celebration*. London: Methuen, 1972.

Smith, Barbara Herrnstein. *Poetic Closure*. Chicago: Univ. of Chicago Press, 1968.

Smith, D. Nichol, ed. *Jeffrey's Literary Criticism*. London: Frowde, 1910.

Smith, G.G., ed. *Elizabethan Critical Essays*. 2 vols. London: Oxford Univ. Press, 1904.

Smith, R.E. "The Law of Libel at Rome." *Classical Quarterly*, n.s., 1 (1951): 169-79.

Snyder, John. *Prospects of Power: Tragedy, Satire, the Essay, and the Theory of Genre*. Lexington: Univ. Press of Kentucky, 1991.

Spacks, Patricia M. "Some Reflections on Satire." *Genre* 1 (1968): 13-20.

Spingarn, Joel, ed. *Critical Essays of the 17th Century.* 3 vols. Oxford: Oxford Univ. Press, 1908-1909.

Stack, Frank. *Pope and Horace: Studies in Imitation.* Cambridge: Cambridge Univ. Press, 1985.

Stallybrass, Peter, and Allon White. *The Politics and Poetics of Transgression.* Ithaca: Cornell Univ. Press, 1986.

Steuart, Francis. "Pasquino and Pasquinades." *Gentleman's Magazine* 300 (1906): 8-12.

Stow, H.L. "Aristophanes' Influence upon Public Opinion." *Classical Journal* 38 (1942): 83-92.

Sullivan, J.P., ed. *Critical Essays on Roman Literature: Satire.* London: Routledge, 1963.

———. *The Satyricon of Petronius: A Literary Study.* Bloomington: Indiana Univ. Press, 1968.

Tannenbaum, Leslie. "Blake's News from Hell: *The Marriage of Heaven and Hell* and the Lucianic Tradition." *ELH* 43 (1976): 74-99.

The Tatler. Ed. Donald F. Bond. 3 vols. Oxford: Clarendon, 1987.

Test, George. *Satire: Spirit and Art.* Tampa: Univ. of South Florida Press, 1991.

Thorpe, Peter. "The Economics of Satire." *Western Humanities Review* 23 (1965): 187-96.

Traugott, John, ed. *Discussions of Jonathan Swift.* Boston: Heath, 1962.

Tuveson, Ernest. "Swift: The View from Within the Satire." In *The Satirist's Art,* ed. H. Jensen and M. Zirker.

Van Rooy, C.A. *Studies in Classical Satire and Related Literary Theory.* Leiden: Brill, 1965.

Vieth, David M. *Attribution in Restoration Poetry.* New Haven: Yale Univ. Press, 1963.

———. ed. *Essential Articles for the Study of Jonathan Swift's Poetry.* Hamden, Ct.: Archon, 1984.

Weinbrot, Howard. *The Formal Strain: Studies in Augustan Imitation and Satire.* Chicago: Univ. of Chicago Press, 1969.

———. *Alexander Pope and the Traditions of Formal Verse Satire.* Princeton: Princeton Univ. Press, 1982.

———. *Eighteenth-Century Satire: Essays on Text and Context from Dryden to Peter Pindar.* Cambridge: Cambridge Univ. Press, 1988.

Wellek, René. "What is Literature?" In *What is Literature?,* ed. Paul Hernadi. Bloomington: Indiana Univ. Press, 1978.

White, Hayden. *Tropics of Discourse.* Baltimore: Johns Hopkins Univ. Press, 1978.

———. *Metahistory: The Historical Imagination in 19th-Century Europe.* Baltimore: Johns Hopkins Univ. Press, 1973.

Wiggins, P.G. *The Satires of Ludovico Ariosto.* Athens: Ohio Univ. Press, 1976.

Wilcox, John. "Informal Publication of Late 16th Century Verse Satire." *HLQ* 13 (1949-50): 191-200.

Williams, Aubrey. *Pope's Dunciad: A Study of its Meaning.* London: Methuen, 1955.

Williams, Gordon. *Tradition and Originality in Roman Poetry*. Oxford: Clarendon, 1968.

Woodruff, James. "*Rasselas* and the Traditions of 'Menippean Satire.'" In *Samuel Johnson: New Critical Essays*, ed. Isobel Grundy. London: Vision, 1984.

Worcester, David. *The Art of Satire*. Cambridge: Harvard Univ. Press, 1940.

Index

238 Index